ASSAULT ON SICILY

ASSAULT ON SICILY
MONTY AND PATTON AT WAR
KEN FORD

SUTTON PUBLISHING

First published in the United Kingdom in 2007 by
Sutton Publishing Limited
Phoenix Mill · Thrupp · Stroud
Gloucestershire · GL5 2BU

British Library Cataloguing in Publication Data
A catalogue record for this book is available from the British Library.

Hardback ISBN 978-0-7509-4301-7
Hardback ISBN 978-0-7509-4302-4

Typeset in Photina MT.

Origination by Sutton Publishing Limited.

Printed and bound in England.

Contents

List of Maps

Acknowledgements

The National Archives at Kew (formerly the Public Record Office) is a great repository of Second World War documents. A student of military history can be overwhelmed by the sheer volume of this resource material from all the theatres over which the conflict was fought, but diligent study and perseverance can eventually track down some remarkable papers. The following categories of records at Kew were found to be the most useful in compiling this book: (PRO) WO214 (Alexander Papers); (PRO) WO169 (Eighth Army War Diaries) and (PRO) CAB 44 and CAB 106 (Historical Section). Thanks are given to The National Archives for the use of this Crown Copyright material and to the Trustees of the Imperial War Museum for permission to reproduce the photographs for which they own the copyright.

List of Illustrations

Introduction

I was born just at the end of the Second World War and therefore have no personal recollections of the conflict. What I do have through my writing, however, is an insight into the experiences of those who lived through it. I have lost count of the number of veterans of the struggle, British, American and German, that I have met and interviewed over the past twenty-five years, each of whom had very definite opinions about a wide range of events, personalities and decisions that shaped the course of the war.

Most veterans have a high estimation of their own country's efforts and more than a little disregard for those of other nations, especially their allies. The same is true of their opinions regarding commanders. Prime amongst these are the differences between the soldiers of the two major western Allies, Great Britain and the USA. In Britain, Field Marshal Bernard Montgomery is recognised as the greatest Allied battlefield commander, while in America the vote goes to the audacious General George Patton Jr. If these nation's veterans are asked to comment on the choice of the other, the results are equally dismissive: in Britain, Patton is seen as a loose cannon, bombastic and arrogant, whose greatest advances were made against sparse enemy forces; in the USA, Montgomery is regarded as being a safe but over-rated general whose victories were achieved only after a slow, ponderous build-up of such strength that defeat was unlikely, if not impossible. Twenty-five years ago my own views similarly ran along nationalistic lines; now they tend to be more pragmatic.

The British people admired Montgomery, for he had given them a great victory at El Alamein in November 1942 when victories were extremely difficult to come by. His success against Rommel in the North African desert coincided with an uplift in British fortunes: Hitler's forces were facing a disaster at Stalingrad in Russia and vast quantities of men and matériel were starting to cross the Atlantic from the USA. Monty's triumph in Egypt marked a turning point in the war which led Churchill later to remark: 'Before Alamein we never had a victory, after Alamein we never had a defeat.' At the time of the invasion of Sicily in July 1943, Montgomery was the most famous and successful of all Allied commanders.

Loved and admired as he was by the whole nation, Montgomery was actually liked by very few who knew him. Of course most of his fellow commanders had a high regard for him as a leader of men and recognised his first-class grasp of tactics and his ability to organise and train great formations, but his prickly personality caused hostility and resentment. Montgomery was arrogant, boastful and conceited. He dismissed personal criticism of him as being uniformed, made by lesser men who lacked his capabilities. He related at every opportunity how he had beaten Rommel and made his army the best in the world, capable of matching any enemy in the field. He was adamant that the decisions he made in battle were correct and later wrote that every one of his campaigns and actions had turned out just as he had planned, even though events had shown other-wise. All these negative aspects were hidden from the public because the publicity surrounding him was all positive

By the end of the war, Patton had achieved a similar reputation as a battlefield commander. He was a hero to many back in the USA and a villain to a few in the war zone, where his blustering manner and sharp tongue put subordinates in fear of his wrath. In action it was a different story: his aggressive tactics and the wide-sweeping movements of the forces under his unique style of command tore apart great swathes of enemy territory during the war in north-west Europe. Patton was able to supply the American people with victory after victory. He grabbed the headlines and loved every minute of the fighting. Much earlier, back in 1943 at the time of the invasion of Sicily, Patton had yet not achieved this public recognition. The cult of 'Patton the hero' was yet to be moulded and he started the campaign as just another, albeit very prominent, senior commander. He went into the Sicilian landings without the legendary status he was to earn later, since up until then his exploits during the invasion of North Africa in November 1942 were against just a few French colonials, and his short tenure of US II Corps during the fighting in Tunisia had earned him only minor headlines. It was the campaign in Sicily that was to shoot him to world prominence.

The Second World War was fought in the first media age, when the combined materials of photographs, film and the radio enabled people at home to follow battlefield events more closely than ever before. By these means both Patton and Montgomery were able to acquire such public acclaim that they eventually became the leading actors in the Allied war effort. Patton deliberately cultivated his image of a swashbuckling military hero. His public persona was of daring general with a fearless, larger-than-life, reputation. He massaged this perception by never missing an opportunity to be photographed close to the action and by having reporters with him wherever he went. Like Patton, Montgomery also courted personal publicity, but his image was more that of a quiet, professional and very competent soldier. He liked to give the impression of being a methodical, all-conquering general who had the complete measure of his enemy.

Almost all of the senior American commanders who came into contact with Montgomery had negative opinions of him. His aloof and condescending attitude caused much resentment. Monty was disdainful of the effectiveness of American troops during their first actions in Tunisia. Like the British back in 1940, it took some time for the American doughboys to hone their battle skills. Their first hostile encounter with German soldiers came as a shock and showed up shortcomings in tactics, command and supply. Then US II Corps' ignominious debacle at Kasserine in February 1943 dented their confidence and their pride. Changes were made and a more ruthless approach to combat followed. The arrival of George Patton at II Corps HQ shook the formation out of its lethargy and set it on the path of recovery. As the campaign in Tunisia wore on, the fighting efficiency of US troops improved considerably.

By the time of the Sicilian invasion in July 1943, there was still an air of superiority about British attitudes to American fighting prowess.

Montgomery in particular had a low opinion of the Allied Supreme Commander in North Africa, Gen Dwight Eisenhower, which for the most part was based on the fact that Eisenhower had never held a combat command. 'He is a nice chap,' he wrote to a colleague a short time after meeting the American general, 'but his knowledge of how to make war, or to fight battles, is definitely NIL.' Montgomery's boss in North Africa, Gen Harold Alexander, also shared the opinion that the Americans in 1943 were not up to the required standard, although he did not agree with Monty's assessment of Eisenhower. In the campaign in Sicily, this mistrust of American capabilities influenced many of Alexander's strategic decisions which in turn led to wasted opportunities. It was not until Patton personally insisted that his troops be given a more active combat role in the campaign to show just what they were capable of, that these entrenched attitudes among the British began to change.

Patton's Anglophobic leanings led him to believe that he had little to learn about fighting the Germans from the British. He had intense pride in his American soldiers and knew that if they were properly led they were more than a match for any enemy. Patton did not think that the British could teach him anything about war and was suspicious of their motives in all that they suggested. His diaries are full of angry outbursts regarding British attitudes and the open desire they displayed to run the war to their advantage. Like many Americans, Patton saw Britain as an imperial power bent on shaping the postwar world to its own needs. Patton was furious with Eisenhower for seeming to be in their pocket, giving way to all British demands even when they went against American interests. Montgomery's uncompromising attitude towards the Americans only exacerbated Patton's paranoia.

At the time of the Sicilian invasion, all of these underlying suspicions led to both parties often shaping their strategies along nationalistic lines. This led to some strange, and sometimes frankly ludicrous, decisions. Fortunately, this was not the whole picture and there were commanders and men of influence in the Allied camp who realised that they were fighting as a coalition with the ultimate aim of destroying Nazi Germany. For the most part sound common sense ruled the day. Differences were set aside sufficiently well to enable the two great Allies in the Mediterranean to concentrate on an overall policy which ultimately led to victory, but it was not an easy ride.

All of the major players in the Sicilian campaign are now dead. Their memoirs were published many years ago and each of them was written to some personal agenda. The truth is always difficult to discover, for the story of how a battle was fought can be re-written after the event. Historians, most of whom have never had to face the ordeal of being under fire, are able to take a more detached view of the war, relying on paper records to interpret the struggle. They can re-assess at leisure the choices made under duress in the heat of the battle. One thing, however, remains unchanged: the signals sent by commanders at the time stay as they were written. I have tried to use these signals, now housed in The National Archives at Kew (formerly the Public Record Office) to construct my own interpretation of how some of the decisions regarding the Sicilian campaign were arrived at. Not everyone will necessarily agree with me, but these records are openly accessible to all and enable individuals themselves to come to their own conclusions.

Ken Ford
Southampton,
October 2006

CHAPTER 1

The Two Generals

In bright spring sunshine on 14 February 1943, Lieutenant General George S. Patton Jr boarded a B-17 bomber aircraft bound for Tripoli. He left the Tunisian battlefield to fly east to hear Britain's most famous general give an address on how he had outwitted Germany's most famous general in the Battle of El Alamein. The next day in Tripoli Patton sat through the two-hour lecture on 'How to Make War', given by General Bernard Law Montgomery.

The talk started with Montgomery announcing that there would be no smoking allowed during his lecture which immediately infuriated the chain-smoking Patton who took out a packet of gum. Unimpressed by the monotonous clipped tones of the British general explaining how he had beaten Generalfeldmarschall Rommel, Patton spent the time chewing and yawning. When the gathering broke for lunch, one of Monty's corps commanders, the amiable Lt-Gen Brian Horrocks, chatted with Patton and asked him what he thought of his master's talk. 'Well,' Patton replied dismissively, 'I may be old, I may be slow, I may be stoopid, but it just doan mean anything to me!'[1] Back in his caravan that night, Montgomery wrote to his boss in London, Gen Alan Brooke, Chief of the Imperial General Staff: 'The party from Tunisia was very disappointing . . . only one American general has come; an old man of about 60.'[2]

George Patton, hero of the Moroccan landings of Operation 'Torch', had met Bernard Montgomery, hero of the desert, and neither of them appeared to be impressed with the other. More than two years later at the war's end, after each of them had further enhanced his reputation as a battlefield commander, their opinions of each other had changed little. Immense self-belief in their own military prowess could only find fault with the performance of the other. Their eccentric natures and love of soldiering allowed neither of them to subscribe to many of the common views held by others as to how battles should be fought.

Montgomery and Patton were made for war. Both were blessed with great ability and blighted by considerable conceit. Both were regular soldiers who had made the military not just a career, but their life's work. They lived to command men and fight battles in their own way, each believing implicitly in his own methods and ideas. Few others ever came up to their own exacting standards; to them virtually all other commanders were to be found wanting in some virtue or other. Both had a sense of history and wished to be seen as being utterly unique. They were insufferable.

The source of the later antagonism between the two generals can be traced back to the invasion of Sicily in July and August 1943 when their armies first fought together as Allies in what should have been a campaign to evict Axis forces from the island. As the battle progressed, there was as much personal quest for glory in their actions as there was determination to annihilate German and Italian formations. While Montgomery and Patton manoeuvred to have their own troops be the first to enter Messina, the enemy slipped away to fight another day.

The campaign in Sicily was the crucible from which developed the future conduct of the war. During this short struggle, just thirty-eight days long, the Allies began to forge an administration that would eventually carry them to victory. It was here that Allied tactics, procedures and support finally came together to formulate the means to carry the fight back to the mainland of Europe. It was also in Sicily that personal relationships would form that would affect the manner and speed of victory.

George Smith Patton Jr was born on 11 November 1885 in the family home near Los Angeles in California. Both of his parents came from well-to-do backgrounds. George's father was a lawyer, the elected district attorney of Los Angeles County. Home life was idyllic on the family's 1,000-acre ranch where his loving father spent a great deal of time teaching the young Patton to ride, swim, shoot, hunt and fish. From a very early age George Patton Junior realised that he wanted to be a soldier and follow in the footsteps of his predecessors. His grandfather and seven of his uncles had served as officers in the Confederate Army.

Patton attended the Virginia Military Institute for a year and then went on to West Point. He was a very bright and intelligent scholar, but suffered from what we now know to be dyslexia. He found it very difficult to read and write in his early years and never fully mastered the arts of spelling and mathematics. His studies at West Point were arduous as he struggled to keep up with fellow pupils. His enthusiasm for all matters military, however, never waned and he was always top for military discipline and deportment.[3]

After graduating in 1909, he was commissioned as a 2nd lieutenant into the 15th Cavalry. His physical condition and his commanding height – he was over six feet tall – led him to excel in sports. He drove himself hard and became accomplished in a range of outdoor activities including swimming, riding, fencing, shooting and polo. He was also good at track events and represented the USA in the military pentathlon at the 1912 Olympic Games in Stockholm. Two years previously he had married Beatrice Dyer, the daughter of a rich industrialist.

Bernard Law Montgomery was born in London in 1887. He was the son of a clergyman who later became the Bishop of Tasmania. Montgomery was the fourth of nine children and spent an unhappy childhood at the hands of a very strict mother. His unruly ways invariably earned some censure; his mother was often heard to remark: 'Go and find out what Bernard is doing and tell him to stop it.'[4] Montgomery attended St Paul's School in London where his performance was below average, but it bucked up somewhat when he learned that he would have to pass a competitive examination to get into the Royal Military College Sandhurst, for he was desperate to become a soldier. By sheer hard work and application he managed to pass the examination to enter the college. After some eighteen months of study he received a commission into the Army in 1908.

The young subaltern entered the Royal Warwickshire Regiment and soon joined his battalion in India. For the next six years he spent a dispiriting time in the colonial outpost surrounded by officers prematurely tired by the climate and the staid conditions of military service. 'As for the officers,' he was later to write, 'it was not fashionable to study war and we were not allowed to talk about our profession in the Officers' Mess.'[5] His battalion returned to England in 1913 shortly before the start of the Great War. When hostilities broke out he was sent to France and arrived just after the British Expeditionary Force began its retreat from Mons. He was seriously wounded after just two months in battle and was awarded the Distinguished Service Order for his actions. Monty was shipped back to England to recover from his wounds, before once again returning to the front in 1916 as Brigade Major of 104th Infantry Brigade. For the remainder of the war he served in various staff positions and by the war's end he had risen to Chief of Staff of 47th Division.

In 1916 the young Patton served with Gen Pershing in the skirmishes along the Mexican border against the followers of Pancho Villa and proved himself to be an expert marksman with the Colt revolvers he always had strapped to his waist. In later years these ivory-handled guns became something of a symbol and Patton liked being photographed with the weapons firmly buckled around him. During the Great War Patton served for a time in Gen Pershing's HQ in France, then moved to the newly formed Tank Corps where he set up a tank training centre. He later commanded the 1st Brigade of the corps as a full colonel during the Meuse-Argonne campaign of 1918 and was awarded America's second-highest award, the Distinguished Service Cross, for bravery on the battlefield. After the war Patton became one of the USA's leading specialists in tank warfare and championed the cause of armoured tactics while the bulk of the US Army was still dominated by the cavalry.

Patton was a great military thinker and a well-read student of history; he spent a good deal of his time studying past wars. From his entire enquiry he came to the conclusion that it was the commander himself that was the greatest influence on how a battle was won or lost. He felt that a commander should influence every encounter on the battlefield by his presence and by gaining the trust of his troops. Patton made it his objective to be seen by his men wherever the action was the greatest and to inspire them to success.

Between the wars, in an ever-shrinking American Army, Patton idled away the time playing polo and pursuing a range of sports during his various tours of duty. During these inter-war years, the USA was gradually turning towards isolationism and had little use for a large tank arm. In the late 1930s, this opinion started to change as European armies began experimenting with the tank as an offensive weapon rather than as just a support for infantry. After the start of the Second World War and the exploits of the German panzers in Poland and France, it became clear that America needed an armoured force of its own. Patton was one of the few experienced officers in that field so he was naturally called to Washington and appointed to command the 2nd Armored Brigade at Fort Benning; he was 55 years of age.

After the Great War, Montgomery served as an instructor at Sandhurst and in 1927 married the widow of an officer killed at Gallipoli in 1915. A son was born in 1928, but the marriage lasted just a short ten years and ended when his wife died of blood poisoning after an insect bite. The loss was a great blow to Montgomery and he now completely devoted himself to his profession. The austere Montgomery had few interests outside the military, neither did he drink or smoke or indulge in any social activities. The Army was his entire life. He was promoted to major-general in 1938 to command British forces quelling an uprising by Arabs in Palestine before returning to England to take over the 3rd Infantry Division three days before the start of the Second World War.

Soon Montgomery found himself in France as part of the British Expeditionary Force (BEF). This time, however, he had the chance to acclimatise with his division before the German blow fell. Montgomery was able to exercise his formation and train it to the peak of efficiency before it was called into action. He rooted out any doubtful subordinate commanders and replaced them with those who were compatible with his way of thinking. When the German *Blitzkrieg* finally broke across the British and French armies in May 1940, Monty's 3rd Division performed with merit, but the Allies were unable to hold the massive enemy onslaught and the their forces fell back to the coast. For a while it looked as though the BEF would be annihilated. As disaster loomed, changes were made in the British high command which resulted in Monty taking over Lt-Gen Alan Brooke's II Corps and helping to organise the British withdrawal via Dunkirk. Lt-Gen Harold Alexander did likewise with British I Corps.

Monty's performance was noted in high places and he was earmarked for future promotion. A corps command in southern England followed and then, in December 1941, Montgomery was appointed to command South-Eastern Army. By this time he had very definite views on the conduct of affairs, insisting that all troops must be physically fit, well trained and their officers competent in all aspects of warfare. He did not tolerate any under-achievement in his officers; all had to pass his meticulous examination of their ability. His prickly personality had by then created many detractors and much criticism, but all units serving under his command made great improvements in efficiency and effectiveness. Churchill met Monty while he was serving as a corps commander and was not impressed enough to single him out as being destined for high command. Alan Brooke, by then Chief of the Imperial General Staff, thought differently.

During this same period Patton rose to command 2nd Armored Division and then, in April 1942, I Armored Corps. He trained and exercised these formations with a fanatical zeal which tried hard to simulate the actual conditions of war and in so doing created a great personal reputation as an aggressive and forceful commander and gained the nickname 'old blood and guts'. Patton was fortunate to have friends in high places, for both the retired but still influential Gen Pershing and the Chief of Staff of the US Army, Gen George Marshall, both admired his ability.

In the third year of the war, Montgomery's career surged forward through a stroke of extremely bad luck for a fellow general. The campaign in North Africa, against Axis forces including Gen Erwin Rommel's *Afrika Korps*, had gone from bad to worse for the British with defeat following defeat. Prime Minister Churchill had decided that there needed to be a shake-up in command in the Middle East, and in particular a new leader for Eighth Army. Gen Claude Auchinleck was to be replaced as Commander-in-Chief, Middle East, by Gen Alexander and Churchill's suggested that Lt-Gen William Gott, already serving in North Africa as a corps commander, should take over as head of Eighth Army, although Brooke favoured Montgomery for the role. Churchill got his own way and Gott was given the post. Misfortune then befell Gott when his plane was shot down en route and he was killed. In stepped Montgomery at what was a crucial time in the progress of the war.

Britain was at low ebb and desperately needed a victory. Montgomery gave the country one in the Battle of El Alamein in October/November 1942 when he defeated Rommel's army and put it to flight. His arrival at the head of Eighth Army transformed the morale of the troops and weeded out the dead wood among its commanders. He refused to attack the enemy until his army was numerically stronger than Rommel's, despite constant urging and great criticism from Churchill. He was the master of the big build-up and set-piece attack and displayed this admirably in the desert at Alamein. With this one triumph Montgomery was catapulted to national and international fame. It was, for Britain, a turning point in the war and was the last great victory achieved solely by British Empire forces before American troops entered the conflict in Europe and North Africa.

When America declared war in December 1941, its politicians and military quickly looked for a theatre in which to commit their as yet untried forces. An attack across the English Channel was deemed to be too hazardous at that time and so, for a variety of reasons, it was decided that an Anglo-American force would be landed in north-west Africa in November 1942 to engage Axis forces.

Operation 'Torch', as the invasion was called, began with three landings – at Casablanca, Oran and Algiers – followed by a drive into Tunisia to seize all of French North Africa. Gen Dwight D. Eisenhower was appointed Supreme Commander for the invasion and his forces were grouped under the British Gen Kenneth Anderson in First Army. Patton led the Western Task Force with his I Armored Corps HQ and formed a successful beachhead in Morocco. Little real resistance was met at any of the landings, but when Allied forces moved into Tunisia they found that Axis troops had taken over the country. From then on a desperate struggle developed which lasted until May of the following year.

After Montgomery had routed Axis forces at El Alamein, Rommel led his troops back across North Africa with the British snapping at his heels. Monty never managed to overtake the elusive German field marshal, nor pin him down in another decisive battle, even though British forces outnumbered the enemy by a large margin. At places of Rommel's choosing, he would turn on Eighth Army and make a stand. Montgomery then waited, built up his strength and attacked. Rommel stood for a while, inflicted a bloody nose on Monty's army, and then pulled out to continue his retreat towards a link-up with German forces in Tunisia.

The battle for Tunisia took place during a cold wet winter over broken terrain and high mountains. The country was vast and barren and it required a good number of men to try to hold down the elusive enemy. First Army performed adequately, but at no time did it have enough men to do what was expected of it; nowhere did it hold more than isolated positions surrounded by wide open spaces and never was it able to take command of the enemy. The result was a gradually grinding down of men, equipment and morale. The Americans had a cruel baptism into action and took a great deal of time to hone their offensive capabilities. When Rommel arrived in the north of the country, with British Eighth Army in close pursuit, he failed to be intimidated by the fact that the Allies were both in front and behind him. Aggressive as ever, instead of remaining on the defensive, he resorted to the attack and turned on the American sector of the line. Rommel launched a brilliantly executed drive through the mountains and inflicted a very costly defeat on Eisenhower's forces at Kasserine. American troops of Lt Gen Lloyd Fredendall's US II Corps broke and ran and it took some time for order to be restored. British troops were called in to help stop the rot, most notably 6th Armoured Division, in an action which helped to reinforce the idea that the Americans were still short of what was needed to counter the Germans. The failure at Kasserine influenced British opinion into thinking that the US troops and their commanders were inferior.

Eisenhower decided that II Corps needed a new leader with drive to instil some order and pride into the formation and sent George Patton into Tunisia to do the job. Patton's arrival at II Corps HQ was like a whirlwind; every man in the formation was in no doubt that the top management had been changed. He drove up in a cavalcade of cars, sirens howling, flags streaming, in a cloud of billowing dust. Patton, as ever, was immaculately dressed, helmet highly polished and armed with his ivory-handled revolvers strapped around his waist. He breezed into the headquarters and immediately began to impose his will on all inside. Strict discipline, full Army protocol, smart dress and everything by the book was the order of the new regime. Patton gave an intimidating exhibition of personal leadership to the officers and men of II Corps. He required everyone, officers and enlisted men, to salute smartly, to button buttons, to shave daily and to wear neckties in action. Steel helmets were to be worn at all times by everyone in the corps area, even the nurses in field hospitals. Fines would be imposed on anyone, regardless of rank, who was caught flouting these orders. No one was in doubt that Patton had arrived and everyone hated him.

In contrast to the strict code imposed by the American martinet, Montgomery had a very relaxed attitude to dress. Unique in the British Army, the officers and men of Eighth Army could dress how they pleased. It was common to see a variety of attire on display from silk scarves to bush hats. Montgomery was intent on producing an impression within Eighth Army that labelled it as being special. He made sure that every man in his army had sight of him and felt that they knew him. Fired up by their great victory at Alamein, morale among the officers and men was high. Monty used the press and newsreels to foster a belief that Eighth Army had the measure of the enemy and victory would surely follow victory until the end of the war. Monty was of a like mind; his doctrine was never to attack unless he was sure of success. Once he had built this aura around him as the greatest battlefield commander the British had, he was never about to let it slip. Monty and his army were famous and his men loved him for it.

Patton's performance in Tunisia with US II Corps started slow and success was hard to come by. It took time before significant accomplishments followed. On 15 April 1943, after five weeks of battle and a restoration of American pride, Patton handed the corps over to Maj Gen Omar Bradley and left to concentrate on a new task that had been placed before him. Eisenhower had given him command of American forces earmarked to land in Sicily once North Africa had been cleared of the enemy. Patton was now to help plan the attack and train the formations allocated to carry it out. He left behind a corps of troops who knew his name, but were unimpressed by his blustering manner and over-the-top theatricals. The officers and men who had served under him basically hated his guts. The cult of Patton the great general had yet to be born. In the meantime, Montgomery continued with the increasingly difficult task of pushing the enemy into the final trap that was to be sprung about them by Anderson's Anglo-American First Army in Tunisia, while at the same time considering how he might land alongside Patton in Sicily with the British contingent of the invasion.

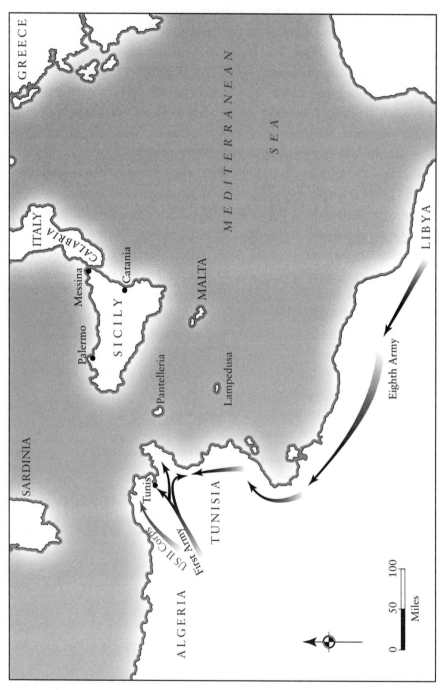

The Mediterranean Theatre, 1943

CHAPTER 2

Planning the Invasion

Early in 1943, with events in Tunisia moving towards a victory, it was necessary for Britain and the USA to establish future strategy. After the conquest of North Africa, and the elimination of all Axis forces, what was to be their next move? The Americans, most notably their Chief of Staff Gen George Marshall, favoured a cross-Channel invasion in 1943 to strike at Germany along the shortest route: maximum force aimed at the principal enemy. Any other venture, they considered, would be just a diversion that would weaken the main event. Churchill and his Chief of the Imperial General Staff, Gen Brooke, saw things differently for they were convinced that such an undertaking at that stage in the war would be premature and liable to end in disaster. Allied strength in the UK was insufficient to ensure that the assault would be successful. Nor was the infrastructure in place at that time to transport, deliver and protect an Allied army on the shores of France. Germany's shorter supply lines and greater number of divisions on the continent would enable superior forces to be brought up to counter the landings quicker than the lodgement could be reinforced.

While many of these objections were quite sound militarily, the Americans were suspicious of Churchill's motives. Britain had more to gain by continuing with a Mediterranean strategy, for by eliminating French and Italian influence in the region Britain's position postwar would be strengthened. Many of President Roosevelt's advisors felt that Britain's

intentions were more those of a colonial power than of an equal ally.
Marshal Josef Stalin was also suspicious of British motives. While the
British and Americans tied down a few German divisions around the
periphery of the Axis Empire, Russia was bleeding to death trying to resist
the advance of over 150 Nazi divisions. Stalin had been waiting a long
time for the opening of the Allied second front, only to be met with
promises and side shows. Progress on an agreement for any future strategy
was exceedingly slow, as nothing could be formally decided through
diplomatic channels. It was now thought that the time had arrived for
President Roosevelt and Prime Minister Churchill to meet face to face to
sort out just what the western Allies planned to do next.

Churchill and Roosevelt agreed on a top-level conference to be held in
Casablanca, in French Morocco, timed to begin on 14 January 1943.
Marshal Stalin was invited to attend, for Roosevelt was keen to sit down at
the table with the Russians, but he was too busy to leave his country for
the long battle for Stalingrad, which had begun in November, was
reaching its climax. Also summoned to attend the summit were the British
and American Combined Chiefs of Staff so that all the main commanders
and their leaders could meet around the table to decide what to do next.

For the American head of state the journey to Africa was long and
tortuous. It marked the first time an American president had flown and
the first time that such a leader had left the country in time of war. The
journey began on 9 January with a train ride from Washington to Florida.
In Miami the President and his party boarded a Pan American flying boat
bound for Trinidad. The slow-flying amphibious aircraft took ten hours to
complete the 1,400-mile trek. The next stage endured by the Americans
was a nine-hour flight to Belém in Brazil. Then came the long crossing of
the southern Atlantic: nineteen hours of cramped tedium, droning across
seemingly endless miles of ocean at 4,000 feet, until they at last arrived at
Bathurst in British Gambia. A short rest, then another eight hours of
flying took the party northwards over the Atlas Mountains to their final
destination at Casablanca. For the partially disabled 61-year-old Roosevelt,
the journey seemed interminable.[1]

The conference was housed in a comfortable forty-room hotel set amid a
group of luxurious villas. As the local commander, Gen Patton was given
the responsibility of arranging the security and domestic needs of the VIP
visitors, but took no part in the formal discussions. He did, however, meet

with all of the major players during their stay and dined with most of them after each day's formal discussions were over.

The question of the next Allied moves was the topic of often heated debate. The British and American staffs had prepared papers for discussion well beforehand and met in conference without the two leaders to try to reach mutually acceptable recommendations. Both principals were kept constantly informed as to any agreements that were reached. When any such settlements were impossible, Roosevelt and Churchill were called into conference to mediate. During the course of the summit, the Combined Chiefs of Staff met in formal session fifteen times without the two leaders and three times with them.

Three main items dominated the discussions: first, something had to be done to engage German forces to help relieve at least a portion of the enemy strength being aimed at Russia; second, the British wished to carry on with operations in the Mediterranean rather than implement a cross-Channel attack before they were completely ready, and third, the Americans' inclination to switch more resources, especially naval, to the Pacific theatre if the attack on north-west Europe could not be implemented in 1943. As with all conferences between allies, some compromise had to be reached before a final decision on any point could be made.

During the course of the long meetings both sides made concessions. The Americans accepted that a cross-Channel invasion could not go ahead that year and the British acknowledged that more needed to be done in the Pacific theatre, including aid to China. Marshall and his American colleagues eventually agreed that activities in the Mediterranean could continue in a limited way to bring some relief to Russia, secure Allied sea lanes through the Mediterranean and possibly knock Italy out of the war. This green light enabled a final decision to be made on what to do next: after the completion of the campaign in North Africa and the elimination of Axis forces there, Sicily was to be invaded as soon as possible by forces under the supreme command of Gen Eisenhower. Reporting to him would be three British commanders: Gen Harold Alexander, at that time in command of 18th Army Group which contained both First and Eighth Armies, was nominated as commander land forces, Admiral Andrew Cunningham was to be the naval commander and Air Chief Marshal Arthur Tedder the air commander.

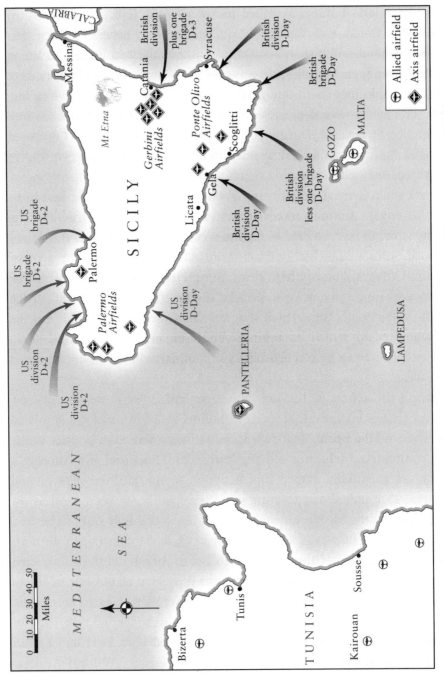

Operation 'Husky': the original Combined Chiefs of Staff plan, January 1943

Other major military decisions were made regarding such items as raising the priority given to the U-boat war, stepping up supplies to Russia, intensifying the bomber war against Germany and the build-up of American strength in Britain as a forerunner to an invasion of France. The Casablanca Conference also gave rise to a major policy decision, one which was to have far-reaching effect on the conduct of the war. Roosevelt made a statement indicating that nothing short of unconditional surrender by the three Axis powers would be accepted by the Allies. Such a declaration was not universally welcome, as many observers felt that the policy left no room for a negotiated settlement of the war and might prolong Axis resistance.

Gen Eisenhower, as Supreme Commander Allied Forces, lost no time in acting upon the political decision to invade Sicily. The Joint Planning Committee in London had already presented an outline plan for the invasion to the conference and this had been approved by the Combined Chiefs of Staff as the basis for the operation. At that time both Eisenhower and Gen Alexander were tied up running the campaign in Tunisia, so an Anglo-American planning team under the British Maj-Gen Charles Gairdner was organised to begin the preliminary work associated with the invasion which had by now been given the title Operation 'Husky'. Gairdner was to have the support of Brig Gen Arthur Nevins on his team to put forward the American perspective. The planners had their initial meeting in the St George Hotel in Algiers. As a security measure they decided to name their group after the number of the room where this meeting was being held, and from then on Gairdner's team became Force 141. For their headquarters they selected the *école normale* in Bouzarea just outside the capital.

Force 141 began work on the provisional outline plan on 12 February. It had been decided that the invasion of Sicily would require two task forces, one American (Force 343) and one British (Force 545). Early in February the commanders of these forces had been agreed. Gen Sir Bernard Montgomery would lead the British assault force; Lt Gen George Patton Jr would command the American formation. Patton's force would be assembled and leave from French North African ports while Montgomery's task force would be mounted from Middle East Command, mainly from ports in Libya and Egypt.

The major problems facing the planners were, what would be the size of the assaulting forces and where were the landings to be made on the island? It was estimated that ten divisions would be needed to take the island, but only enough shipping for six divisions in the assault was available. There were other difficulties, for both of the force commanders allocated to the operation were at that moment fully engaged in the fighting in Tunisia, both trying to eliminate the Axis presence from North Africa. Some of the divisions that it was hoped would take part in 'Husky' were also still fighting the enemy. As to where the landings would be made, there were a number of beaches suitable, but all had problems associated with them.

Sicily lies at the toe of Italy and is separated from the mainland by a very narrow strip of water, the Strait of Messina, barely 2 miles wide at its narrowest point. Guarding the restricted waterway was the city of Messina itself, the principal port of the island and the point through which virtually all Axis movement to and from the Italian mainland was routed. Messina would be the gateway for enemy reinforcement and the exit for any withdrawal. There were two other major ports on Sicily and several other minor harbours. Palermo on the north-western coast was the island's second port with Catania on the eastern coast only slightly smaller.

Maj-Gen Gairdner's initial tasks were twofold: first, to find suitable beaches close enough to Allied airfields in Malta and Tunisia for the landings to be given fighter protection, and, second, to ensure that these beaches were close enough to major ports which could be captured within a very short time of the initial landings. It was imperative that a port be captured immediately so that sufficient supplies could be landed to support operations inland.

Messina was immediately ruled out as a usable port; it was located too far to the north, outside the range of air cover, and the Italian minefields and fortifications defending the city would inevitably prove to be too costly to breach. This left Palermo and Catania. Palermo was large enough to cope with the requirement of handling the 500 tons of supplies per division per day needed to keep formations in the line, providing the port was captured more or less intact. However, an assault directed solely in the north-west area around Palermo would leave the enemy free to reinforce through the eastern ports. Catania was not large enough to cope as the sole supply port, so the decision was made to direct the landings against both of the ports with the Americans concentrating against Palermo and the British against Catania.

There was also a third major factor in deciding on the location of the landing beaches. It was necessary that the airfields on the island be seized as soon as possible to deny their use to enemy aircraft. The mountainous nature of Sicily meant that all of these airfields were located on the coastal plains which ringed the rocky interior of the island. The airfields were sited in three main groupings all within 15 miles of the sea. The most prominent of these clusters was a collection of six landing grounds located in the Catania–Gerbini area, just a short flight away from the Messina Strait. The next group consisted of the three airfields north of Gela along the south-east coast at Comiso, Biscari and Ponte Olivo. The third grouping consisted of six air bases around the north-western tip of the island protecting Palermo. It therefore became a requirement of the landings to be within striking distance of the Gela and the Palermo airfields in the south-east and north-west of the island. Early capture of these airfields would eliminate a great deal of enemy airborne interference and allow them, once captured, to be used to extend the air cover required for the seizure of the ports.

All these factors were taken into consideration when the outline plan for the invasion of Sicily was produced. The plan proposed simultaneous assaults by Eastern and Western Task Forces. The British force would land three divisions on D-Day on the south-eastern coast to secure the airfields at Comiso, Biscari and Ponte Olivo and the small ports of Syracuse and Augusta. Three days later a fourth infantry division would be landed in the Catania area, supported by a brigade group and an airborne division, to seize the eastern group of airfields and that port. The Americans would also land an infantry division on the south-western coast at Sciacca on D-Day to secure the western airfields. Two days after these had been captured for Allied use, a further two divisions would be landed near Palermo and the large port captured. Both of these forces would each be reinforced by the landing of a further division some time later through Catania and Palermo. By D+7 the Allies would have nine divisions ashore.

Throughout February, the planners at Task Force 141 worked on the detail and presented a plan to Gen Eisenhower and his senior commanders for preliminary discussion at their headquarters on 13 March. Not unnaturally, all found fault with the proposal. As commander of ground forces, Alexander thought that there was not enough punch in the proposed landing at Avola in the south-east, stating that the one division landing there was inadequate to take Syracuse and Augusta soon after its assault. Another division would be needed to ensure success. He proposed switching the division that was to land at Gela over to Avola to strengthen the push for the ports. Such a move would, however, leave the south-eastern group of airfields at Comiso, Biscari and Ponte Olivo untaken. This, of course, was unacceptable to Air Chief Marshal Tedder who needed the air bases for his own aircraft to support the advance on the ports. Admiral Cunningham was likewise unimpressed. He was not willing to accept the risk of leaving these airfields available for Axis use against his warships which would be anchored just a few miles away.

When Montgomery had sight of the plan he felt that it had no hope of success, claiming that it broke every common sense rule of battle and was completely theoretical. Certainly it was a plan that needed refinement, but Monty's criticism went much further. He was rattled that his own Eighth Army's planners were not involved in producing it and thought that Gairdner was not the man for the job.

Montgomery had selected and scrutinised every senior man in his Eighth Army and was suspicious of all others. He was beginning to gain an inflated sense of his own ability since beating Rommel, for the victory had brought him world renown and given him a position unsurpassed in the minds of the British people and the British establishment. It is therefore not surprising that criticism of others and their abilities was starting to come quite naturally to him. He now saw himself as the great oracle on all matters relating to fighting the Germans; in his opinion his methods were the only way.

The 45-year-old Maj-Gen Charles Gairdner was on paper an Eighth Army man. He had commanded 6th Armoured Division in training in England for ten months before being transferred to Egypt in August 1942 to take over 8th Armoured Division. The division had arrived in the Middle East the previous month to join Eighth Army, which was at that time under the command of Gen Auchinleck. Gairdner's arrival coincided with Auchinleck's replacement by Montgomery and Alexander. Gairdner was therefore not a Montgomery choice to command an armoured division.

The 8th Armoured Division did not have an illustrious war; it never saw action as a complete formation. Immediately on arrival in the theatre it was forced to provide replacements for casualties in other formations. During the battle of El Alamein its HQ Royal Artillery formed the base for an *ad hoc* formation called 'Hammerforce' and its two armoured brigades saw action as independent brigades. Gairdner never fought his division as a division in any of Montgomery's battles, nor did 8th Armoured Division take part in the pursuit of Rommel. On 1 January 1943 the divisional headquarters was disbanded in Egypt and 8th Armoured Division ceased to exist. The next month Gairdner was appointed Chief of the General Staff North Africa and given the task of planning 'Husky'.

It was clear that Montgomery had a poor opinion of Gairdner and never ceased to report this fact to his superior in London, Gen Brooke. Over the next few weeks he sent many signals and letters belittling Gairdner and his planners. On 3 April in a letter to Alexander Montgomery wrote: 'There is some pretty woolly thinking going on – tactically and administratively. I have no intention of doing the things they suggest.'[2] On 12 May he wrote to his Chief of Staff, Maj-Gen Francis de Guingand, 'I have persuaded Alex to remove Charles Gairdner; he is useless.'[3] In his notes for a discussion with Gen Brooke in June he suggested that the planning staff at Force 141 were a menace. 'Gairdner of no use & does not know what is wanted.'[4]

Part of the distrust of Force 141's planners stemmed from Monty's opinion that Eighth Army should run the invasion. He saw it as a continuation of his victorious advance from Alamein. He wrote to Brooke on 16 February that full use must be made of the Eighth Army name and morale. 'We must use all that experience to ensure success.'[5] He also did not like the British contingent being labelled Force 545 by the planners, or even the land component of Eastern Task Force: it was Eighth Army as far as he was concerned. What Montgomery failed to take on board was that 'Husky' was very much an Anglo-American operation and one which also involved the other services of both nations. Admiral Bertram Ramsay, Commander of the Eastern Task Force, put him right on this matter when he wrote to Montgomery on 7 April: 'I appreciate your desire to retain the name Eighth Army, and I do not suppose there has ever been any intention to call it by any other title, but the Eastern Task Force is the whole British Force, Naval, Military and Air, while it is on the sea, and it can only be known as such.' Ramsay went on to point out that as Naval Commander Eastern Task Force his directive stated that he had executive control of the whole force until Eighth Army was firmly established ashore.[6]

Alexander discussed the first outline plan with representatives of both army commanders at Bouzarea on 18 March. At that time Monty was organising his attack on the Mareth Line and Patton was involved in the fighting east of Gafsa with US II Corps. Montgomery had sent the news that he wanted another division in on his assault. This seemed a simple request in itself but it was one that created a major problem, for all sea transport and landing craft available in the Mediterranean for the invasion had already been allocated. The only way to accommodate Monty's wishes was to redistribute forces within 'Husky''s existing resources.

Alexander considered Monty's request and suggested that the American division intended for the assault at Sciacca be moved eastwards to land at Gela. He then put this proposal to Eisenhower on 20 March. Surprisingly the Supreme Commander agreed, although with some reservations. The move would put the American division under British command and also mean that the western group of airfields near Palermo would have to be neutralised solely by long-range fighters and bombers from bases in North Africa and, perhaps, from the airfields captured by the British assault. This change of plan would also mean that the landings against Palermo would have to be put on hold until fighter cover for the attack could be guaranteed. It might well involve Patton's forces having to wait at sea until it was clear for them to carry out the landings, most likely not until D+5 at the earliest.

Three days later Eisenhower was having even more doubts and wrote to Alexander: 'In agreeing to Montgomery's demand for an additional division . . . we are adopting a plan which we consider the least objectionable of any we can devise. I am not too happy about this matter.'[7] When news of these proposals reached London and Washington, both sets of Chiefs of Staff were disturbed. Montgomery, however, had no qualms regarding the subordination of the American attack to his own needs.

With the shifting of an American division eastwards from the Sciacca being unacceptable to the highest authorities, Gairdner and his planners set to work on a new plan. Progress was made on this and Alexander invited Monty to come over to 18th Army Group's HQ to discuss the matter. Montgomery, however, felt that it was quite impossible for him to leave his headquarters at that time – it was the night before his attack on Wadi Akarit – and suggested that Alexander and Gairdner fly over to see him, which they duly did on 5 April.

An extra division had been made available from North Africa for Montgomery to use in the assault and, by cancelling the planned landings against Catania on D+3, shipping would be made available to it for the invasion. The division that had been earmarked for the Catania landing would be held in immediate reserve at Malta ready to be shipped across to Sicily in the vessels that had been used in the assault. Added to this plan was the proposal to use airborne troops to attack defences just prior to the landings and to help open up the subsequent move inland against vital objectives. It was also proposed that the timings of the actual assaults be staggered in an attempt to draw off enemy reserves from other parts of the island. It was a plan to which Montgomery felt he could give his approval and Alexander flew back to Tunisia feeling that he had a suitable suggestion that he could put to the Supreme Commander.

Meanwhile, Montgomery was having second thoughts. He was now unhappy at using two of his experienced Eighth Army divisions securing mere airfields. He suggested that they be switched to the landings closer to Syracuse and signalled Alexander accordingly. The planners signalled back that if plans were once again to be changed, the landings would have to be delayed, possibly by up to a month. It had been agreed at the highest level that 'Husky' had to be undertaken by July. Monty realised that such a move would have powerful repercussions and withdrew his proposed changes on 9 April. That same day he wrote to Gen Brooke: 'I have now managed to get the 'Husky' affair put on a proper basis and a good layout agreed to.'[8] On 11 April Eisenhower approved the new proposals and notified the Combined Chiefs of Staff in Washington of the changes. It seemed that Alexander had a plan for the invasion agreed at last.

On 16 April Alexander put forward a new draft plan as the solution to the previous problem. The first part of the invasion would start in the east with Eighth Army landing four divisions by D+1. Enemy reaction would therefore be focussed in the south-east corner of the island. The Americans would then land their division at Sciacca on the south-western part of Sicily on D+2, to be followed by landings against Palermo on D+5. Each of these landings would be supported by overwhelming naval and fighter cover to ensure they became firmly established. The Germans and Italians would then have to split their forces to contend with them. The plan would put a large port in American hands for the build-up of forces and supplies, eliminate all hostile airfields in the south of the island and convert them for Allied use, put Eighth Army on the direct and shortest road to Messina and have seven infantry divisions and two airborne divisions ashore in the first week, with the possibility of two more being landed at any time later. It all sounded like a pretty good plan.

The date for the invasion of Sicily was set for 10 July. On 21 April Monty sent a copy of the draft plan to Lt-Gen Oliver Leese, commander British XXX Corps, and asked him to go through it with Monty's Chief of Staff, Freddie de Guingand, in Cairo. The army commander wanted to have the views of two of his most trusted subordinates before the whole matter was discussed more openly at a three-day conference that was due to take place with Force 545 planners on 23 April.

When Montgomery arrived in Cairo he was met with a host of negative comments about the plan from Leese and de Guingand which once again reinforced his own misgivings about the operation. One thing that he picked up on was that too much attention was being given to the logistical side of the landings – the capture of the ports – rather than to tactical considerations – dealing with the enemy. Montgomery also thought that to operate with dispersed forces would invite disaster. Concentration was his watchword; Eighth Army's forces must not be dispersed. He felt that his assault force was being dissipated over two separate landings, each of which had independent objectives. On studying the proposals further, he had decided that he had insufficient troops to capture both the vital ports and the south-eastern airfields. Once again he felt he must propose changes to the master plan for the prospect of defeat in detail loomed before him. Montgomery of Alamein, hero of the desert, was not going to move until he was sure that he had such overwhelming strength that failure was out of the question.

He also felt that a lot of assumptions were being made about the quality of the enemy troops that would be opposing his landings. It was being inferred that there would only be slight resistance from the static Italian coastal troops and that the Germans would not reinforce the island too quickly. Monty took exception to this and insisted that the Italians were fighting desperately in Tunisia and would continue to do so when the Allies invaded the Italian homeland.

Montgomery was quite wrong in his assertion that Force 141 had evolved its plan in the belief that opposition would be slight. All earlier appreciations had suggested that the invasion was likely to meet strong German and Italian resistance. The British official history of the campaign takes Monty to task over this matter and notes that the Combined Chiefs of

Staff outline plan had stated: 'It would be wise to expect Italian troops to fight hard in the defence of Italian soil,' and that Monty's assumptions were not in accord with contemporary appreciations.[9]

The question of what kind of reception the invasion would get from Axis forces and what was to be the size and composition of the defenders was one which bothered not only the planners but Eisenhower as well. In the initial planning paper it was pointed out that, if substantial German ground troops were placed on the island prior to the assault, the chances of success were slim. On 7 April, after Eisenhower had consulted with his commanders in Algiers, he reported to the Combined Chiefs of Staff that the operation would offer scant prospect of success if the six or seven Italian divisions in the region were back by substantial German forces – that is more than two divisions. He reminded them that, in that eventuality, the Allies would be launching an operation without tactical or strategic surprise against an enemy force of eight or nine divisions. If there were German formations present, there would also be a German command with the German units kept free to counter-attack. In such a case the project should be abandoned.

When Churchill got to hear of this dispatch he exploded. He at once fired off a minute to his Chiefs of Staff in Whitehall, one which the British official history of the campaign regards as being among the most memorable of the war. In it the Prime Minister questions whether the war can be carried on if:

> . . . the presence of two German divisions is held to be decisive against any operation of an offensive or amphibious character open to the million men now in North Africa. Months of preparation, sea power and air power in abundance, and yet two German divisions are sufficient to knock it all on the head . . . 'Husky' is to be abandoned if there are two German divisions (strength unspecified) in the neighbourhood. What Stalin would think of this, when he has 185 German divisions on his front I cannot imagine.[10]

The next day the Chiefs of Staff met and, chastised by the belligerent tone of Churchill's minute, found Eisenhower's views to be unacceptable and they informed the Combined Chiefs of Staff in Washington of their strong dissent from these opinions. It was unthinkable that 'Husky' should be abandoned solely because the number of Germans in Sicily had reached 'a small predetermined fraction of our own strength'. Nor did they agree that the operation would be launched without either tactical or strategic surprise. The enemy hardly knew the selected day and the exact time and location of the beaches at which the landings would take place. Moreover, by his attitude Eisenhower was expecting the cover and deception plans then under way to be failures. Understandably, Washington agreed with London's sentiments and informed Eisenhower accordingly. No more was to be said on the matter.

On 24 April Montgomery fired off a signal to Alexander demanding changes to the draft plan which allowed a concentration of the whole of Eighth Army's forces closer to Syracuse to the north of the Pachino Peninsula, and completely disregarded the requirement to capture the south-eastern group of airfields. He also wished to keep his winning team from the desert together and said it was also essential that Eighth Army had close and intimate air support and that he must therefore have the Desert Air Force working with him. He now demanded that Air Vice-Marshal Harry Broadhurst, his staff and his experienced squadrons be assigned to the operation. He further stated that he had given orders that, as far as Eighth Army was concerned, all planning work would now proceed along the lines of his new proposals. He was, in fact, unilaterally recasting the 'Husky' plan and presenting Alexander with what looked like a *fait accompli*.

When the commanders-in-chief of the other services read the signal they were incensed. It had earlier been considered and agreed that the capture of the south-eastern group of airfields was essential to the landings. Montgomery was now dismissing their requirements, allowing the landing grounds be left in enemy hands while the biggest seaborne invasion yet seen in the war was coming ashore just 30 miles away. It is not clear how Gen Alexander personally greeted Monty's new proposals, but he must have been greatly disheartened that his subordinate commander took little notice of the difficulties he was creating among his superiors and among his fellow commanders. Montgomery appeared to be looking at the invasion of Sicily solely in terms of what was best for Eighth Army.

Tedder and Cunningham were particularly annoyed with Montgomery. Admiral Cunningham made sure that his criticism of Eighth Army's commander was heard in higher places. On 28 April the admiral sent off a signal to the First Sea Lord in London: 'I am afraid that Montgomery is a bit of a nuisance; he seems to think that all he has to do is to say what is to be done and everyone will dance to the tune of his piping. Alexander appears quite unable to keep him in order.'[11] Air Marshal Tedder was equally upset at the high-handed way that Montgomery imagined he was the only commander with any tactical or strategic vision and that he could complete ignore the requirements of the Allied air forces with impunity and annoy their American ally. He also took exception to Monty's demand that Air Vice-Marshal Broadhurst should command the whole air-support operation, rather than the more senior RAF commander in Malta, Air Marshal Sir Keith Park. Tedder signalled the Commander-in-Chief Air Forces in Cairo that under no circumstances would he accept Broadhurst's promotion to command air operations over the invasion.

When word got back to Montgomery that Cunningham and Tedder disagreed with his proposals, he once again cabled Alexander expressing even more forcibly his view that the existing plan would result in failure, but the plan put forward by him would succeed.

Alexander called a conference in Algiers on 28 April to present Montgomery's latest proposed change of plan. The army group commander found himself in an awkward position. The best course of action would have been to tell Montgomery that no further change of plan could be accommodated, but Monty had the ear of both the Prime Minister and the Chief of the Imperial General Staff and his views carried a lot of weight throughout the British Army. He also had a great deal of experience in fighting the Germans and was a successful battlefield commander. Alexander did not have the strength of character to ignore these new proposals nor to dismiss them out of hand; indeed, as army group commander, he could see some sense in them. He was more or less forced to have them considered by the other commanders-in-chief and the American land commander, Gen George Patton.

Alexander's 'Husky' conference at Algiers was not a straightforward affair. It was dogged by ill luck, controversy, arguments and delays. There was one notable absentee, the commander of Eighth Army himself. Montgomery was taken ill on the 27th with tonsillitis and remained in bed for two days. In his place he sent his Chief of Staff, Brig de Guingand, to read a paper that he had prepared for the conference outlining his changes to the agreed plan of 5 April.

De Guingand was also plagued with bad luck on his way to Algiers when the aircraft he was travelling in crash-landed just after taking off from a refuelling stop outside Tobruk. The brigadier was injured, fortunately not seriously, and taken back to Cairo for hospital treatment. Montgomery then ordered XXX Corps' commander, Oliver Leese, to fly immediately to Algiers to take his place at the conference. Patton was also delayed in trying to get to Algiers, this time by the weather, and did not arrive until the afternoon of the 28th. Alexander decided that the meeting should be postponed until the next day. When Leese finally arrived at Maison Blanche airfield at Algiers there was nobody to meet him and his ADC, Ion Calvocoressi. Both men had to hop onto a lorry and make their own way to Alexander's HQ.

The conference began at 1000 hrs on 29 April. Present were Alexander, Leese, Cunningham, Tedder, Ramsay, Air Marshal Coningham (Commander North African Tactical Air Force), Alexander's RAF advisor Air Marshal Wigglesworth (Commander RAF Middle East Command), Maj-Gen Browning (Airborne Forces), Gairdner, and Monty's liaison brigadier at Alexander's HQ, Charles Richardson. All of these senior officers were British. The American contingent comprised Gen Patton and Brig Gen Nevins, the American representative at Force 141.

Patton knew that he was walking into a British gentlemen's club and he was very much the outsider. Leese was also very conscious of his surroundings as he arrived hot foot from his thumbed lift from the airport. He later recalled walking into the meeting filled with top brass: 'I went into the Conference Room to find a table surrounded with flags of the Allied Nations, and a group of senior officers, all very well and correctly dressed. I had on my usual shirt and shorts and no medal ribbons.'[12]

Alexander began by explaining that he had called the meeting to consider the changes to the draft plan proposed by Montgomery. Cunningham interrupted to enquire whether it was too late to change. 'We will hear what the Eighth Army wants,' replied Alex.

Leese then took the floor and read out the paper provided by Montgomery, outlining the need for the plan to be altered to suit the requirements of Eighth Army. The army commander now thought that his formation should not be split around the south-eastern part of the island, but kept concentrated to land in the area of Syracuse. The proposed attack near Licata by the two divisions of XXX Corps was too weak to carry out the assault and capture the Comiso group of airfields. Montgomery was concerned that during the initial build-up phase the Germans could move four divisions to the island and make his landings untenable unless his plan was adopted.

Patton listened to the address and remained unimpressed. He saw the change of plan as Montgomery's way of making the invasion a 'sure thing attack for Eighth Army and its ever victorious general'.[13]

Tedder immediately protested that such moves set the air aspect aside and thirteen landing grounds would be left in enemy hands. It would be impossible to neutralise them all by air action alone. Without these airfields the Allied air forces based in Malta could not hope to complete the tasks expected of them. In addition, the American landings on the western part of the island needed to be covered from these airfields. Without them, the Western Task force could not be protected even for a few days. 'I am definitely opposed to this new plan,' insisted Tedder.

Admiral Cunningham then weighed in with his views. He said that Montgomery's new plan seemed to concentrate the effort against the most strongly defended part of the coast. This would result in a large number of ships operating close offshore with little or no air protection. It was essential that airfields be captured and used by Allied aircraft if ships were to stay off the beaches at anchor for a long period.

Alexander was being put under great pressure. As overall commander of ground forces he accepted Monty's new proposals, but could see that they viewed the invasion as being a land operation only. He explained that, from his viewpoint, that of the army, the new plan was necessary and that he must do it. Tedder reminded him that all three arms were in it and that 'Husky' was not just 'an army show'. 'Besides,' remarked the air marshal, 'we can't support Patton unless we get the airfields.' Patton now chipped in with his view: 'I would like to stress that point because I am sure that without the airfields, while I may get ashore, I won't live long.'[14]

Alexander thought for while and then asked Leese if he could do his part if he got an extra division and Cunningham found sufficient transport to carry it over. Leese replied that Monty would never consent to splitting his army. Patton thought that this response was a small-minded attitude and very selfish. He turned to Tedder and whispered, 'My force is split by more than 45 miles.' Tedder told Patton to say it out loud which he did. Alexander was a little embarrassed by the remark and could only respond,

'The man on the ground must decide.' Patton replied immediately: 'In view of General Alexander's remark, I withdraw mine. But,' he went on, 'I feel sure that if I refused to attack because my force was split, I would be relieved.'[15]

The room felt silent; the thought held by almost everyone present was now out in the open. What could Alexander say? There was no way that Montgomery could be relieved of the command of Eighth Army; the country would not stand for it.

Alexander said that he would wire the Prime Minister. 'Why not ask Eisenhower?' suggested Cunningham, reminding Alexander that he and the air commander were subordinate and responsible to Eisenhower and not to Churchill. 'After all, he is the Supreme Commander.'

Eisenhower had already given guidance on this matter, for he had earlier decreed that any officer who endangered the spirit of cooperation that he had taken great pains to build up should be removed. The cause of Allied unity was paramount. Here Montgomery was risking a breach with the American Army as well as the US and Royal Navies and the USAAF and the Royal Air Force. Alexander did nothing.[16]

The meeting carried on in this vein for almost three hours without any compromise being reached. Cunningham suggested in exasperation: 'If the army can't agree, let them do the show alone. I wish to God they would.' Alexander, now beginning to tire, eventually asked Cunningham and Tedder straight out if they would accept the plan. Both replied that they would not. Alexander then asked them if they would go with him to Monty and argue with him. The admiral, now very angry, replied: 'I shan't go. I have something to do.'

The conference had arrived at an impasse. As the official history of the campaign was to explain many years later: 'The deadlock was British and complete.'[17] Patton could only look on at the proceedings with total bemusement. It was a peculiar way to plan an operation. It was certainly not how the Americans worked. He later confided his thoughts regarding the lack of force on the part of Alexander in his diary and wrote that the British general cut a sorry figure at all times: 'He is a fence walker.'

When the conference broke up Patton asked Cunningham if he had been too frank. The admiral assured him he had not and complemented him on his tactful retraction. It had, he thought, had a profound effect. Tedder remarked that he was on Patton's side and had a few harsh words to say of Montgomery: 'He is a little fellow of average ability who has had such a build-up that he thinks himself as Napoleon – he is not.'[18]

Eisenhower was placed in a very difficult position by this lack of consensus. Above him he had his boss in Washington, Gen Marshall and his great ally in London, Prime Minister Churchill, both applying pressure to get 'Husky' implemented in June even though there was no possibility of the operation getting under way before July. Below him, he had squabbling subordinate commanders who were unable to come to an acceptable decision as to how the invasion should be launched. He was profoundly irritated that Alexander and the others could not arrive at a solution that they could all agree to, without his intervention.

Alexander was equally embarrassed and went to see Monty at his tactical headquarters the next day. He found his army commander completely intransigent. Montgomery was unmoved by the crisis he had caused. He seemed unconcerned at having forced Cunningham and Tedder to a point where the matter was now one of personal prestige. He further resisted Alexander's attempts at a compromise and even suggested that Alexander now send a signal to Eisenhower recommending the abandonment of Patton's proposed landings and that the Americans should join in a single thrust on the south-eastern corner of Sicily.

The planning for 'Husky' had arrived at a stand-off. Montgomery had engineered a crisis so that he would get his own way. If no agreement could be reached then the operation would not take place even in July. This would unleash all manner of criticism from political leaders in London and Washington and could well lead to changes in command. None of this fazed Montgomery, for he really believed that he was too great a battlefield commander to be relieved of his leadership of Eighth Army. To him the fault lay elsewhere, with the planners at Force 141, or with Eisenhower for not giving strong direction, or with Alexander for not having a firm grip on the requirements of 'Husky'. There was no easy way to break this stalemate other than all parties getting together to thrash it out around a table. A summit was therefore arranged in Algiers for 2 May in which Eisenhower, Alexander, Cunningham, Tedder, Patton and Montgomery would meet and, it was hoped, resolve the situation.

Two days before the Algiers meeting Montgomery sent a letter to Gen Brooke in London. This was nothing new, for ever since he had taken command of Eighth Army in August 1942, he had corresponded over the head of his boss Alexander, directly with the chief of the British Army on details and criticism of the most pointed kind. The letter once again started with a list of all that was wrong with the present fighting in Tunisia: '. . . the plan of First Army had no hope of a quick success . . . I suggested to Alexander where to put in the big blow for Tunis . . . I fear it was never done . . . I told Alex it was just madness to go on as we are doing . . . we have lost a great opportunity.' All this negative comment now seems to be very strange, for the end of the successful Tunisian campaign and the total destruction of all Axis forces in North Africa, with 240,000 enemy troops being taken into captivity and removed from the Mediterranean theatre, was just thirteen days away.

Then Montgomery got around to the planning for 'Husky': 'It is in a fearful state . . . the proposed plan would involve us in a first-class disaster . . . we cannot go on this way.' And so his carping went on, implying that the whole show was in a hopeless mess and would fail. 'Unless we get a good and firm plan <u>at once</u>,' he explained, '<u>there will be no 'Husky' in July</u>. I hope that is realized at your end,' he commented to the Chief of the Imperial General Staff, ensuring that Churchill would get to hear of the possible delay.[19] Then, having elevated the problem to a political level, he offered to resolve matters with a solution of his own. 'The proper answer is to bring two USA divisions in to land at Cent [the beaches at Scoglitti] and Dime [the beach at Gela], on the south coast, and get the aerodromes. And chuck the Palermo landing for the present.' That was it; Montgomery now intended to get his own way by forcing the abandonment of the planned landings by the Western Task Force, disregarding the need to capture Sicily's second largest port, leaving the western airfields in enemy hands and then getting the Americans to shift across to his sector to do part of the unglamorous job that had originally been assigned to his Eighth Army. Once again, everyone would have to dance to his tune. But, first, he would need Eisenhower to back the plan for he knew that Alexander would acquiesce without resistance.

Montgomery flew into Maison Blanche airfield on 2 May in his personal Flying Fortress that had been given to him by Eisenhower as the result of a wager. He arrived at AFHQ Algiers to find that Alexander and Patton were not able to attend that day as their aircraft were grounded by bad weather. All the other players were there, but Cunningham and Tedder refused to sit in conference without Alexander. Without them at the table, Monty was unable to present his new plan and the Supreme Commander was powerless to resolve the impasse. He could not, after all, arrive at a decision without his land force commander. It looked as though the stalemate would continue.

Montgomery, however, was anxious that his latest idea should be at least put to the Supreme Commander. He resorted to guile. In his diary he claims to have met, by chance, Eisenhower's Chief of Staff, Brig Gen Walter Bedell Smith in the lavatory.[20] Monty said that he found Bedell Smith was rather upset by the impasse and worried that by not finding a military solution to the problem a political crisis might arise. It was absolutely essential to reach a firm decision as soon as possible. Monty now stepped in with his latest plan, implying that he had the solution to the whole problem. Bedell Smith invited him to go ahead.

The situation was perfect; Monty now could put his new plan directly to Eisenhower, for Bedell Smith was sure to report the conversation immediately to his boss. Monty explained that, if the American landings at Palermo were scrapped and the whole Western Task Force's effort put in on the south coast around Gela, the controversial airfields so dear to Cunningham and Tedder could be secured as originally planned. Montgomery was offering a way out of the crisis for Eisenhower, and getting his own way in return.

Bedell Smith could see at once that the idea had merit. It would at least involve American troops in the main attack and resolve the thorny problem of the airfields. It did throw up logistical problems, but it was a possible way out of the stalemate for it offered a solution to the stand-off that had ground matters to a halt. Bedell Smith told Monty that he would put it to his boss.

Eisenhower was consulted and was prepared to go with the plan, strictly on the understanding that a formal decision could not be made until it was approved by Alexander. In the meantime, he permitted a provisional planning meeting to take place with senior staff officers representing Cunningham and Tedder. Not surprisingly the naval side protested at the logistical problems the new plan would create. How would the Americans be supplied without the use of a major port? What would Patton say about the new role assigned to the Western Task Force? No problem there; unlike Montgomery, Patton would follow orders. As Cunningham was later to recall, 'Alexander was aware, from the Tunisian campaign, of General

Patton's punctilious and scrupulous sense of duty, and knew that his orders would not be questioned.'[21]

It soon became clear to Cunningham and Tedder that this latest plan of Montgomery's was one that could in fact be made to work. It was also a plan of last resort, for time was running out for Eisenhower who had to cable his boss in Washington that a final plan had been reached to stave off a political crisis. Little could be gained by further objection. Cunningham did think that the Allies had surrendered one of their greatest assets, the capability of being able to assault the island in numerous places at once at will,[22] and he was certainly not pleased that all of his shipping would now be concentrated in one area at the mercy of Axis aircraft should the aerial battle not be won. Nor did he think that the American ground forces could be supplied over open beaches for a long period. But there it was; Monty had got his own way at last.

Gen Patton heard of the new plan late in the day. He had been delayed in arriving by the same bad weather that had stopped Alexander attending the meeting. Patton's journey by road to Algiers was tiring – he had been forced to drive hundreds of miles through heavy rain and around numerous detours of flooded areas. He arrived exhausted early in the evening, long after the meeting was finished, to learn of the new role which had been assigned to his army. Brig Gen Nevins had prepared a short summary of the changes in 'Husky' for him.

Nevins was mad at the changes and suggested that they were likely to have a negative effect on American morale. Months of planning would now have to be discarded. The Western Task Force had been put back to square one and they would all have to start again. American participation had been subordinated to the views of Gen Montgomery. Everyone was hailing the new plan as a way out of the deadlock, but few were considering its disadvantages. The western airfields were to be left untaken, presumably to be used by the enemy to harass the landings. The small ports of Syracuse, Augusta and Catania would not be able to support the two armies and re-supply would have to be made over open beaches, a concept that did not please either the US Army or the Navy. A port the size of Palermo was what was needed. Monty did pledge that Patton could share Syracuse to bring in his supplies, but the ever-suspicious American general had doubts that this would happen. To cap it all, after all that Monty had said about concentration of effort, the two landings would not be mutually supporting; they would be split by a gap of over 40 miles.

At a meeting with Eisenhower, Patton learned that Monty's new plan was most definitely the final one. 'Husky' must now be made to work. Later that night, as Patton pondered the plan, he realised that the campaign that was to follow the invasion had not been mapped out. What was to happen after a bridgehead had been gained? Patton's forces would no longer be grouped around Palermo with a direct road along the north coast to the key city and the main objective in Sicily, Messina. His divisions would be gathered on the south coast with just mountains in front of them. Montgomery, on the other hand, would have a short drive up the eastern coast through Catania to Messina, with, presumably, Patton protecting his flank and rear. It was clear that once Messina had fallen, the battle for Sicily would be over. It looked like the campaign had been mapped out for Eighth Army and its general to win a great victory, while the Americans played a subsidiary role. It now became much clearer as to why Monty was so insistent upon grouping his landings south of Syracuse ready for a drive northwards, rather than struggling around the hills in the south clearing airfields. The Americans, and Patton in particular, had been outfoxed and out-manoeuvred by a very cunning British general. But there was more to come.

Later that day, Montgomery signalled Alexander about his coup even before the new plan had been put to the army group commander by Eisenhower. In the message was the line: 'Suggest you go all out for this plan.' Flushed with the success of having been able to manoeuvre the Supreme Commander to his way of thinking, and having Alexander agreeing to his every move, Montgomery decided to go one step further. He now wished to make the whole of 'Husky' his own. He finished his signal with an outrageous suggestion: 'Consider proper answer would be to put US Corps under me.'[23]

Montgomery had moved on to the next stage of his plan; British Eighth Army was to run the operation with a single US corps under command. After all, in his eyes his victorious army had the beating of the enemy, while the Americans were still in the process of gaining experience. Only a month before, he had made his view clear in a letter to Maj-Gen Frank Simpson, Director of Military Operations at the War Office in London. On 5 April he wrote: 'The real trouble with the Americans is that the soldiers won't fight; they have not got the light of battle in their eyes. They have no confidence in their generals.' He also included faint praise of Eisenhower: '. . . a nice chap and probably quite good in the political line'. But, and here was the crux of the American problem, 'His knowledge of how to make war, or to fight battles, is definitely NIL.'[24]

Monty confided in his diary that, with US II Corps landing close to Eighth Army, it would make good sense for one army HQ (his) to command the whole of 'Husky'. He also felt that he did not want anyone to interfere with his running of the invasion and was of the opinion that 18th Army Group should not be involved in the actual operation. He was now angling to be the only ground commander in Sicily. If such moves were implemented, both Patton and Alexander would be frozen out and he would deal directly with Allied Force HQ. He would report immediately to Eisenhower. This latest move was the last straw; he had given up all pretence of being an Allied commander, he was simply a British commander seeking a great victory for himself and his Eighth Army.

Unsurprisingly, in view of Alexander's previous actions following Monty's dictates, Alexander did not knock this latest piece of nonsense on the head but actually put the proposition forward to Eisenhower on 4 May, although he omitted to name Monty as the proposed single commander of 'Husky'. Alexander reasoned that now British and American landings had virtually become one operation, each dependent on the other, it made some sense for the invasion to be undertaken by one commander and a joint staff.[25] In putting forward Montgomery's proposal, Alexander seems to have forgotten that 'Husky' already had an overall land commander, himself.

On 7 May Gen Montgomery travelled to Algiers to meet with Bedell Smith to press his claim to 'control the whole operation', believing that Eisenhower's Chief of Staff was a firm ally of his. He had earlier sent a message to Brooke claiming that if he did not get agreement 'we shall be sunk.'[26] Bedell Smith would have none of it. Such a move would raise hell back in the USA. Imagine what public opinion would say if, after six months' fighting in North Africa, the only Americans in action against Axis forces were in one US corps as part of a British army. Sanity had to prevail; Montgomery was left under no illusions that the Americans had their pride too, and that the war with Italy and Germany was being waged by Allied forces.

It seemed clear to all observers that Alexander could not control Montgomery. It was also apparent that Eighth Army's commander had to be spoken to about his attitude and conduct towards other commanders. He needed a stern reminder that he was now involved in coalition warfare. Gone were the days when he was master of the desert and in command of all land forces in the area. He was now a commander who was subordinate to others and only a part of a great international crusade. Alexander could not do it, Eisenhower, paying due respect to Monty's national status, would not do it, and so it was left to the Chief of the Imperial General Staff to do it.

Brooke visited Algiers in early June along with Churchill and the King. During this visit it appears that Brooke must have given a few home truths to Monty about his conduct. He must have been hard on the army commander, for when he got back to England he sent Monty a note, almost apologetic in tone, hoping that Monty bore 'no ill will'. Brooke stressed that he was anxious that Monty should not do things that would lay him open to criticism and that he should realise the importance of good relations both with Allies and other services. He finished in a very friendly tone, called him 'old Monty' and hoped that the letter would be taken in the spirit it was meant.[27] The tenor of letter is almost that of a father realising that he has scolded his son too hard and trying to ameliorate the distress he has caused. Did the dressing-down have an effect? Not at all; Monty remained a law unto himself until the end of the war, inspiring the nation and the men who served under him while all the while infuriating those above him and equal to him in the other services.

In accepting Montgomery's revised plan for 'Husky' and totally discarding the draft plan produced after Casablanca, Alexander had made Maj-Gen Gairdner's position untenable. Monty's continual chipping away at the original intentions of the overall plan, and his criticism levelled at the ability of Gairdner and his staff, had thoroughly discredited Force 141. Monty wanted Gairdner removed and removed he was, although the actual process was achieved by Gairdner offering his resignation. Alexander accepted it and softened the ignominy of the act by blaming himself. The British official history of the campaign hints at where the failures in Force 141 lay, and they were not with its Chief of Staff: 'Gairdner had shown loyalty, energy, tact, firmness, persuasion and initiative in trying to make work the plan given to him. He had not had a commander, free from

commitment to other active operations, to serve.'[28] Gairdner could have no
further future in the war in Europe; Montgomery's grip on all things
military would see to that. He was shipped out to India along with many
other senior commanders who had been found to be lacking in ability. He
spent the remainder of the conflict as Commander Armoured Fighting
Vehicles India. It did not, however, prove to be a graveyard, for Gairdner
was twice more promoted and eventually ended his career as a full general.

On 15 May Force 141 was absorbed into Alexander's army group
headquarters and at the same time Alexander's command was changed
from 18th Army Group and renamed 15th Army Group. Force 545 had
become what Monty insisted it should have been from the start, Eighth
Army, and George Patton's command was elevated to army status. Force
343 was to be reborn as US Seventh Army, although this was not made
public until the day of the invasion. Patton was now equal in the
hierarchy to Montgomery.

CHAPTER 3

Final Plans

The roll-out of preparations for 'Husky' was given an enormous boost on 12 May when all Axis resistance ended in Tunisia and the enemy surrendered totally. Although the ports of Sicily were only a hundred miles away across the Mediterranean there was to be no 'Dunkirk' for the Germans and Italians. Evacuation would have meant the Italian fleet taking to the open sea to protect the disembarkation. This it was not prepared to do and so remained at anchor in the Italian ports where it had spent most of the war hiding from the Royal Navy. On 8 May Admiral Cunningham sent a message to all his ships initiating Operation 'Retribution': 'Sink, burn and destroy,' he ordered. 'Let nothing pass.' The result was not a naval victory, for few of the enemy were prepared to run the gauntlet. The total catch was two merchant ships, three small tramp steamers, a barge, a fishing boat and an assortment of rowing boats and rubber dinghies. Just over 700 escapees were pulled from the sea. On land, over a quarter of a million of the enemy went into captivity in a victory that rivalled Stalingrad. Italian colonialism had been wiped from North Africa and the continent cleaned of Nazi occupation.

Whist all the manoeuvrings and machinations were going on between Montgomery and the planners during the first few months of 1943, Patton was waiting to see how the plan for 'Husky' would eventually play out. From the start to the finish of these planning stages, he never knew exactly where, when, how and with what he was supposed to invade Sicily.

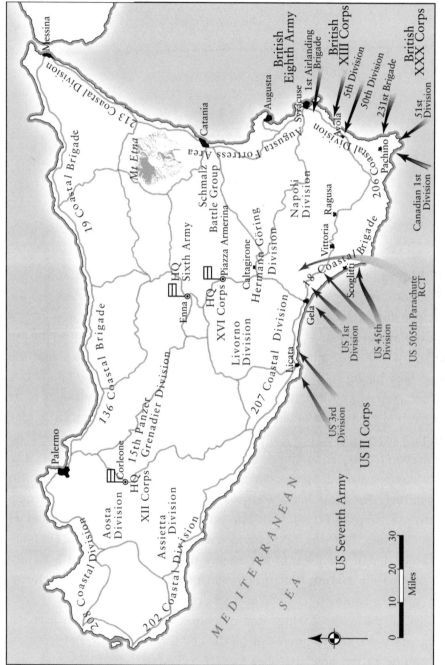

Operation 'Husky': The Final Plan and Positions of Axis Forces on Sicily

When, in May, a scheme for the invasion had at last been agreed at all levels up to the Combined Chiefs of Staff in Washington, everything was set for the preparations for 'Husky' to begin in earnest. The date of the assault was just two months away.

Many of the formations earmarked for the Sicilian campaign had been involved in the battle for Tunisia. Before the end of the fighting in North Africa, these units had been gradually removed from the front line and sent to the rear areas for a period of rest and replenishment, followed by weeks of training for the tasks which lay ahead. It was Montgomery's intention that his part in the forthcoming battle would be conducted by the veterans of Eighth Army. The same was true for Patton and his new army; he wanted veterans to carry out the assault. It was natural that both commanders should wish to use tried and tested units with experienced officers and men. However, war dictates that all new formations must be introduced to battle at some point, and so it was with the invasion of Sicily. Both armies were told to use divisions in the assault that had up until then not seen action.

Early in the planning it was found that the damaged ports of the Middle East limited the numbers of ships that could be handled at the same time. It soon became clear that it would be necessary for both Britain and the USA to draw some formations and shipping direct from their home ports. For the Americans, the 45th Infantry Division was to be combat-loaded in the USA and carried directly over to Sicily to be landed at H-Hour on D-Day. Its baptism into the war in the Mediterranean theatre would be as assault troops in the invasion.

The Canadian 1st Division was also to be transported by sea straight into action, although the British commanders had not selected it as their first choice new division for the campaign. The Canadians had been in England since 1940, carrying out training and guard duties along the south coast and the morale of the division was beginning to suffer. Canadians were getting a bad reputation locally for being unruly. The citizens and government of Canada, and the long-suffering civilians in England, were anxious to see the division in action with the enemy. Canadian public opinion was questioning the wisdom of sending an all-volunteer army overseas just to have its men guarding the borders of the mother country. Enforced inactivity was beginning to have a bad effect on everyone concerned. Pressure was put on Churchill by the Canadian government to find employment for the Canadian Army in whatever way was deemed appropriate. Participation in the forthcoming invasion of Sicily seemed to offer the ideal solution.

There was, however, a problem, for British 3rd Division had already been selected for the operation and had been rehearsing a programme of training for the assault for some time. Nonetheless, in the cause of Commonwealth harmony, Churchill decided that the 3rd Division's role in 'Husky' should be taken over by the Canadian 1st Division and the Canadian 1st Army Tank Brigade, even though there was now less than two months available for training and planning.

The 15th Army Group's plan for the campaign in Sicily was laid out by Alexander in five phases: Phase One, naval and air operations to neutralise enemy activities at sea and to gain air superiority; Phase Two, seaborne and airborne assaults to capture certain airfields and the ports of Syracuse and Licata; Phase Three, establish a firm base from which to conduct operations to capture the ports of Augusta and Catania, and the group of airfields at Gerbini; Phase Four, the capture of these ports and airfields; Phase Five, the reduction of the island.

In the assault, British Eighth Army would use two of its three corps. XIII Corps (Lt-Gen Miles Dempsey) would land 5th Division (Maj-Gen Horatio Berney-Ficklin) 15 miles south of Syracuse near Cassibile with 50th Division (Maj-Gen Sidney Kirkman) coming ashore 5 miles further south at Avola. Dempsey's task was to capture Syracuse and then Augusta. XXX Corps (Lt-Gen Oliver Leese) was to assault the Pachino Peninsula with 231st Brigade (Brig Roy Urquhart) attacking the beaches north of Pachino itself, 51st (Highland) Division (Maj-Gen Douglas Wimberley) assaulting the southern end of the peninsula and Canadian 1st Division (Maj-Gen Guy Simonds) landing on the south-western side of the feature. Leese's role was to capture the Pachino airfield, relieve XIII Corps at Avola, secure the centre of the lodgement and to make contact with US Seventh Army. Eighth Army would also use the airborne support of 1st Airborne Division (Maj-Gen George 'Hoppy' Hopkinson) to speed up the move from XIII Corps' beaches to Syracuse. The 46th Division (Maj-Gen John Hawkesworth) and the 78th Division (Maj-Gen Vivian Evelegh) were the reserve formations to be introduced into the campaign at a later date if required. Monty's third corps, X Corps, commanded by Lt-Gen Brian Horrocks, was to remain in North Africa ready be used in later operations in the Mediterranean.

The Eastern Task Force carrying Eighth Army to its beaches was commanded by Admiral Bertram Ramsay. It comprised three assault forces and a support force. Assault Force A was to carry XIII Corps from Middle Eastern ports to its beaches around Avola; Assault Force B was to land 51st Highland Division and 231st Infantry Brigade on the south-eastern end of the Pachino Peninsula and Assault Force V was to bring the 1st Canadian Division all the way from the Clyde in Scotland to its landing point on the western side of the Pachino Peninsula. Support Force K was to provide the seaborne security screen on the last stages of the voyage with its four cruisers and six destroyers, before reverting to a bombardment role in support of the landings.

On the left flank of the invasion, Patton's US Seventh Army would use US II Corps (Lt Gen Omar Bradley) for the actual assault in the Bay of Gela on the south coast. Its objectives were to capture the port of Licata, seize and occupy the airfields at Ponte Olivo, Comiso and Biscari and to make contact with, and to protect the flank of, British Eighth Army. Seventh Army would put three divisions into the attack: 45th Division (Maj Gen Troy Middleton) either side of Scoglitti, 1st Division (commanded by Maj Gen Terry de la Mesa Allen and known, from its insignia, as the Big Red One) at Gela and 3rd Division (Maj Gen Lucian Truscott) east of Licata. It would also have the use of its 82nd Airborne Division (Maj Gen Matthew Ridgway) to help open up the routes inland from the beaches. The army reserve formations comprised 2nd Armored Division (Maj Gen Hugh Gaffey) and 9th Infantry Division (Maj Gen Manton Eddy).

Vice-Admiral Kent Hewitt's Western Task Force supporting Seventh Army comprised three attack forces, each of which was to support one of the assault division landings. In addition, Hewitt had under command a control force which was to protect the final approach to Sicily. Admiral Cunningham's main covering force for both Eastern and Western Task Forces was British and consisted of six battleships and two fleet carriers, with an attendant number of cruisers, destroyers and submarines. The great fleet would cover the whole of the western Mediterranean, seeking to interdict any movement of Axis surface ships and submarines that might attempt to interfere with the invasion convoys.

Air Chief Marshal Tedder's air plan was split into three stages. The first of these was implemented just after Axis forces had been cleared from Tunisia when all bomber aircraft were switched to systematic attacks on

Axis airfields and on Italian industry and morale. The attacks were distributed across the whole of the mid-Mediterranean area, so as to give no indication of where the next Allied blow might fall. During this period, these raids were increased to include strategic bombing of Italian, Sicilian and Sardinian ports and airfields. The second stage started at D-7 (3 July) until D-Day (10 July) when the Allied air forces were concentrated against those enemy aircraft likely to be encountered during the landings and against communications targets on and around the island of Sicily. The final stage was to interdict enemy air activity in the region of the landings themselves on the day of the assault.

Patton had laid out his plan on 5 May at a meeting with his deputy commander, Maj-Gen Geoffrey Keyes, and the rest of his staff. He told them which formations he wished to use in the assault. Keyes suggested at the meeting that they hold back one combat team of each of the assaulting divisions as a reserve. Patton agreed and there were no objections from the remainder of the staff even though the move would result in some administrative changes. Patton was happy to leave the tactical details of the landings to his individual divisional commanders. The plan was accepted and the meeting was over. Patton later mused in his diary that historians would ponder how they came to these decisions and credit him and his team with profound thought. His role in the meeting was leadership and to make the concept clear. It was all over in an hour; decisions made, Patton now left his team to get on with the meticulous organisation required to make it happen.[1]

As Patton's deputy, Keyes was able to relieve his commander of many of the day-to-day activities connected with 'Husky'. Patton also delegated much of the responsibility for detailed planning to Keyes, leaving himself more time to monitor the readiness of his troops and to evaluate the abilities of their commanders. Patton only intervened directly in the major decisions associated with the landings, leaving Keyes to deal with routine business with II Corps and the Navy.

A meeting was called for 7 May in Algiers at which Montgomery and Patton and their staff could work out a few mutual particulars of the new plan. At the meeting Patton felt that Monty appeared to have very definite ideas, but avoided being pinned down on any of them. The American general tried to get him to agree to fix a boundary line between the British and American forces and to decide on a phase line showing initial objectives. Monty refused to be precise. Exasperated, Patton decided to send a message to ask Alexander to set boundaries and a general plan of the campaign.

While in Algiers, Patton went to see Vice-Admiral Hewitt. He found the admiral in a pessimistic mood, objecting to everything that was suggested. Patton countered by saying that all objections were pointless. They had been ordered to attack in the Bay of Gela and that was just what they were going to do. He found the same attitude among the American staff at Alexander's headquarters. Everyone seemed confused and each had a myriad reasons why things could not be done. Patton claimed that he straightened them out by showing a great deal of confidence in the plan, which he confessed to himself that he did not have. He told them that this was the kind of challenge which Americans ought to love. It was a chance to show their flair for overcoming the most stubborn physical problems. American organisation and American ingenuity, coupled with their natural mechanical skills, would get them ashore, keep them ashore and be triumphant. The new plan, he believed, was actually easier to execute than the old. At the other end of the North African coast there was no such gloom. Monty's staff were storming ahead with their preparations, everyone behind their commander and his sound plan. The doubts that the Royal Navy and the RAF had about the arrangements were set aside.

The victory by the Allies in Tunisia had left Italy and Germany a little shaken, with the Italians especially beginning to lose their resolve. This was a perfect time to chase the fleeing enemy across the Mediterranean and hit them in Sicily before their armies could be re-established. Gen Marshall and his Chiefs of Staff in Washington urged Eisenhower seriously to consider this course of action.[2] Unfortunately, the one thing the Allies were never able to do in the war was to react quickly. Every operation required planning down to the last detail. For the Allies it was their industrial strength that was to be the deciding factor in beating the enemy. Such strength was slow to assemble but devastating in effect. The invasion of Sicily would have to wait until everything and everybody was prepared to go.

There were, however, intermediate objectives to occupy Eisenhower's planners. Between North Africa and Sicily are two small islands, Pantelleria and Lampedusa, each bounded by steep sheer cliffs and with craggy volcanic interiors. Both had been fortified by the Italians and the larger of the two, Pantelleria, had been turned into a complete fortress. Significantly, the island had an airfield which could be of great use to the Allies during the invasion.

The fortress-island idea had been conceived by Mussolini in 1937 as a counter to Britain's naval base on Malta. Although much smaller in size than the British possession, its strategic location did bar the sea passage through the straits between Sicily and Tunisia, or at least it would have done if the fighter force based there had been effective. The fortress was built with underground hangars large enough to protect eighty aircraft and was garrisoned by the 12,000 men of the Brigata Mista Pantelleria from Gen Guzzoni's Italian Sixth Army, a collection of second-rate troops with a fortress mentality.

After the victory in North Africa the Allies had little to fear from the two islands, although there was a radar outpost located on each of them, but possession of Pantelleria's airfield would be most useful. To leave the islands unmolested would be a mistake for their position would risk enemy detection of the Sicilian convoys and the Allies would lose the element of surprise. Eisenhower decided that they would have to be taken.

The main problem with the capture of Pantelleria was its rocky coastline. There were few landing beaches and just one landing stage to serve the island. For a landing there to have any chance of getting ashore, the defences and the defenders would have to be softened up by aerial bombardment. This task was given to Lt Gen Carl Spaatz and the USAAF, while a landing by British 1st Division was planned for Pantelleria, supported by warships.

Carl Spaatz was an airman with a mission. He was convinced that the war could be won by air power alone, providing that all resources and all commitments were diverted to that task. Such a policy was, of course, politically unacceptable and so he was always alert to opportunities to prove that a tactical operation could be won by bombing alone. The attack on Pantelleria was a perfect opportunity to see if the island could be bombed into submission without the need for land troops.

His experiment began on 18 May with attacks by medium bombers on the underground hangars. Two weeks later, on 6 June, the heavy bombers joined in on the main target area spread over 8 square miles. From 7 June onwards the bombing became continuous, but with no word of surrender from the Italian garrison. The date for the seaborne attack was set for

11 June and the bombing went on. Between 6 and 11 June, 5,324 tons of bombs were dropped on the island from 3,712 bomber and fighter-bomber sorties. Since mid-May a total of 6,400 tons of bombs and 5,218 missions had been flown over Pantelleria.[3] On 11 June it was the turn of cruisers and destroyers to bombard the Italian fortress. Off shore an assault convoy stood ready to attack the island. The garrison was invited to surrender but nothing was heard. Under another terrific barrage, the landing ships turned towards the island and picked up speed. Soon the leading troops of Maj-Gen Walter Clutterbuck's 1st Division were touching down on the narrow beaches, but the end was at hand, for the island's commander, Admiral Pavesi, had had enough. He gave the signal for the white flag to be raised and surrendered his fortress and the dazed garrison inside without firing a shot.

The capture of Pantelleria was followed the next day by the surrender of Lampedusa and two other tiny Italian islands nearby. On a map, they could readily be seen as the stepping stones from Tunisia to Sicily. It was important that the Italian/German Axis be kept guessing as to where the next Allied blow might fall, but many enemy commanders had already guessed it would be Sicily. Mussolini was shocked at the loss of his Italian 'Gibraltar'. The head of the Italian High Command, Marshal Ambrosio, however, pessimistically accepted the loss of the island as another inevitable setback, concerned that the aerial might that had demolished the fighting ability of its garrison would soon be turned on Italian cities and harbours. To the Germans, the loss of Pantelleria had little significance, save to reinforce their low opinions of the Italians' fighting prowess.

CHAPTER 4

Preparations

Major-General 'Hoppy' Hopkinson, commander of 1st Airborne Division, was in Maj-Gen Frederick 'Boy' Browning's bad books and had gone to ground somewhere in Tunisia. Hopkinson had approached Eighth Army's commander with a proposition direct, rather than going through the normal channels. It was Browning's task to coordinate all airborne operations and Hopkinson had gone over his head. Worse still, Hopkinson had sold the idea to Montgomery of using the glider arm of the Airborne Division as an attack force in the forthcoming invasion. He suggested that Monty could use it to help capture the route between the landing beaches and Syracuse, thereby ensuring the port's capture on the first day. This idea went against Browning's earlier suggestion that the glider force should be used to bring in follow-up waves after the seaborne landings.

The allocation of all aircraft and gliders for airborne operations rested with Allied Force Headquarters Mediterranean Air Command and 18th/15th Army Group. Any suggestions for new operations should have been channelled via Browning. Montgomery, who had no experience of airborne operations, had accepted Hopkinson's suggestion at face value and had told the airborne division's commander to go ahead with the plan. This decision created a myriad problems. One of the most serious of these was that, other than Lt-Col George Chatterton's advance party of glidermen who had recently arrived in Tunisia, there were no glider pilots in

North Africa. Even these few pilots had had very little training because of the shortage of tug aircraft in Britain. It was true that there were aircraft available in Algeria and Tunisia, but they were nearly all troop-carrying aircraft belonging to the United States forces. In view of this, all allocations were subject to severe scrutiny.[1]

It would seem that Hopkinson had acted a little prematurely but, having raised Montgomery's expectations, there was to be no turning back. Montgomery's wishes were invariably accommodated without too much confrontation. Both Alexander and Eisenhower were reluctant to oppose any suggestion coming from Montgomery that might improve the Allies' chances of gaining an important objective, and the early capture of the port of Syracuse was one of the most important objectives of all. Hopkinson's suggestion now developed a momentum of its own and the green light was given for glider forces to be used in the assault. It is no wonder that Browning was rather put out, and certainly no wonder that Hopkinson was staying out of his way and refusing to travel to Algiers to see him to discuss the operation.

'Hoppy' Hopkinson was a small man of boundless energy. His nickname 'Hoppy' was thought to have derived from his gait; he walked as though he had springs in his heels.[2] He was certainly not a desk-bound individual and always contrived to have himself in the thick of the action. Unfortunately, his close involvement in the activities of his division would end in tragedy, for just five months later in Italy he was injured by shell fire when up with his leading troops. He died of his wounds on 12 September 1943, the only airborne general to be killed in action during the war.

Lt-Col Chatterton was summoned to Hopkinson's HQ to be greeted by a very cheerful general brim-full with what he thought was good news. 'Well George,' he began, 'It's nice to see you. I have a very interesting operation for you to study.' Hopkinson informed him that Gen Montgomery had agreed to use Chatterton's gliders on a night assault on the island of Sicily. The general explained that he had persuaded Monty that the 1st Airlanding Brigade could be landed to the south of Syracuse on the night before the seaborne landings to seize strategic targets to help facilitate the advance of ground troops to Syracuse. The date of the landings had not yet been fixed, but it was hoped they would take place in June, although it was more likely that, because of the fighting still under way in Tunisia, they would not happen until early July.

Chatterton quickly realised that he now had only three months to prepare for the operation – and most of his pilots were not even in North Africa. There were also no airstrips on which to train, no tugs available to pull the gliders and, most important of all, no gliders. Even were the whole of his fledgling battalion present in Algeria, they would still be woefully short of experience. Most of their training had been on simulators and they had had very little actual flying time under their belts – four and half hours was the average. There had been almost none at all in the preceding three months because of the lack of available aircraft. They certainly had not had any experience at night flying.

That was not the worst of it, for Hopkinson had more bad news. 'The Americans are going to provide the tugs and gliders,' he said. 'American gliders?' Chatterton replied in amazement. 'Yes,' snapped the general, 'What difference will that make?' The colonel explained that they hardly knew British gliders, so short had been their training. Changing over to American aircraft would cause all kinds of problems. The general remained unmoved and told Chatterton that he would have to put up with it.

Then the glider chief was shown a map and some aerial photographs of the landing places. Chatterton became even more alarmed. The landing zones were alongside the jagged coast, lined with cliffs and strewn with rocks; the fields beyond were edged by stone walls. The gliders would have to come at these obstacles in the dark, from over water, a tall order even for accomplished pilots. Hopkinson could see that Chatterton was very apprehensive about the whole operation and completely failed to share the enthusiasm that he had for the enterprise. He now became irritated and told the colonel that he would leave him for half an hour to study the photographs. When he came back, he explained, if Chatterton still felt that the operation was too difficult, he could consider himself relieved of his command. Hopkinson then walked to the door, turned round and looked at the hapless colonel and said: 'Half an hour. You see? I shall return.'[3]

The colonel pondered long and hard on the problems he faced. He was being ordered to commit his pilots to an unsound operation. They were going to be asked to fly in aircraft of which they had no previous experience, at night, even though they had had no night training, to land from the sea on sloping landing zones covered with boulders and interlaced with stone walls. The Glider Pilot Regiment was in its infancy and this, its first operation, was to be a task hazardous in the extreme.

Chatterton knew that the attack would go ahead whatever decision he made. He decided that his only choice was to stand by his men; he would have to go through with the 'mad' operation, even though it might prove to be suicidal.[4]

From this inauspicious start, the final decisions relating to the 1st Airborne Division's part in the invasion were worked out. The division would be committed in three phases, the first of which saw the 1st Airlanding Brigade, commanded by Brig Philip Hicks, a veteran of the First World War, being carried in gliders the night before the seaborne landings to capture the important bridge across the River Anapo south of Syracuse. The operation was planned to speed up the advance of 5th Division from its landing beaches, 8 miles to the south, to Syracuse. The next night, 2nd Parachute Brigade (Brig Eric Down) would land north of Syracuse to help the ground troops advance further up the coast to Augusta. A third operation would involve 1st Parachute Brigade (Brig Gerald Lathbury) landing north of Augusta to capture the bridge over the River Simeto at Primosole to ease the progress of the land troops towards Catania, the date of the operation to be set later by the army commander.

Gen Patton's US Seventh Army had also been provided with airborne troops when Maj Gen Matthew Ridgway's 82nd Airborne Division was placed under his command. Patton decided that he would use the division to help capture the airfields and to ease the passage inland of his seaborne troops. The shortage of aircraft, however, made it impossible to deliver all the airborne troops in one lift. It was therefore decided that only the two parachute regimental combat teams would take part and that they would be dropped on consecutive nights. On the night preceding the landings, Colonel Jim Gavin's 505th Parachute Infantry Regiment would make the first drop, with Colonel Reuben Tucker's 504th Regiment flying in during the evening of the seaborne landings or the day after as decided by Patton. Ridgway's air-landing troops, Colonel Harry Lewis's 325th Glider Infantry, and the remainder of the division would have to be transported over to Sicily by sea as follow-up troops because there were no gliders available; they had all gone to the British.

Ridgway was not pleased with the way that Hopkinson had gained approval for his plan to use his airlanding brigade. The American general was sore with the British airborne commander for going behind Browning's back rather than through proper channels where Ridgway could put forward his own views and objections. The decision, sanctioned by Eisenhower, for the British to use American gliders meant that his own airborne operation had to curtailed to fit in with it. That was not all, for these gliders had to be towed by American tugs, which resulted in even fewer aircraft being available for the 82nd Division. It was this shortage of aircraft that made it impossible for more than just one combat team of regimental size to be included in the assault phase. Ridgway had to plan for the invasion, the first active deployment of his division, with only a third of his force available to use. And it was all the fault of the British.

The problems associated with the availability of these aircraft were complex. The British had little air transport of their own and relied heavily on the Americans. Two formations of troop-carrying aircraft were allocated for the operation. One of them, US 51st Troop Carrier Wing, was already in North Africa; the other, 52nd Troop Carrier Wing, was due to arrive in May. It was decided that the 51st Wing would carry the 82nd Airborne Division and the 52nd Wing would fly the British airborne division. In mid-May Allied North African Air Forces decided to reverse this decision. At first this seemed logical, for 51st Wing had already worked with the British in North Africa and the 52nd Wing had carried out three months of training with the American 82nd Airborne in the States prior to its move across the Atlantic. Then came Hopkinson's back-door manoeuvring and Montgomery's decision to use glider-borne forces. It altered everything. The 52nd Wing had been trained in glider operations in the USA, but it had now been committed to paratroop operations. The 51st Troop Carrier Wing's aircraft had by then been modified to suit British needs, for the dropping techniques of British and American paratroopers were different. It was too late to switch the missions back and start training all over again.[5]

The gliders to be used in the assault were American Waco CG-4As. Five hundred of these were being shipped from the USA in crates ready for assembly on the training airfields in North Africa. The CG-4A was a smaller glider than the Horsa type used in Britain, capable of carrying a payload of 3,200 pounds (a section of 14 men or one jeep) as opposed to the Horsa's ability to carry 6,900 pounds (up to 32 men or a combination of loads). Planners soon decided that the Waco gliders were not capable of carrying the loads required by 1st Airborne Division and they would have to be supplemented by a number of Horsas. This was a decision that was easier to make than to implement for there were no Horsa gliders in North Africa; they were all back in the UK.

In the time available, it would prove impossible for the gliders to be shipped out to Africa by sea. Shipping space was not readily available and the time taken to dismantle, crate, transport and reassemble the aircraft would be too long. The only way they could be got out to Chatterton's pilots was by air; they would have to be towed out all the way from England across airspace patrolled by German fighters.

The operation to bring the gliders out to Africa was a task of endurance. The RAF's 295 Squadron was assigned the problem. It was ordered, over a period of six weeks, to ferry 36 Horsas in non-stop flights from Portreath in Cornwall to Salé in French Morocco, a distance of 1,400 miles. The Horsas all had to be in North Africa by the end of June. Certain Halifax crews had to be specially trained for the assignment and experienced navigators provided by Coastal Command. Extra fuel had to be taken on board by the bombers and none of it was jettisonable – all was carried within the bomb bay – which meant that a forced landing was liable to result in the plane exploding into a giant fireball. The tow would be made at a speed of 130–135mph, which did not leave much of a margin of error above stalling speed. The flights had to be made in daylight and in good weather, avoiding clouds.

Much time was wasted waiting for the right weather and the operation took all of the time allocated to it. The journey did not end after the long tow to Morocco, for there was another thousand miles to travel to the airstrips near Kairouan in Tunisia from where the invasion would be launched. Part of the route involved climbing over the 7,000-foot peaks of the Atlas Mountains. Inevitably there were some mishaps along the way. Of the 30 gliders that left Cornwall, 3 had to be released and landed in the sea en route, 3 force-landed in inaccessible parts of North Africa and 4 crashed on landing near Salé. The first Horsa arrived in Kairouan on 28 June, just eleven days before the invasion.

The bulk of the 1st Airborne Division reached North Africa in two main convoys on 26 May. Training was then carried out on a number of airfields scattered over Algeria and Tunisia. Towards the end of June the whole of the division moved to the operational base for the airborne invasion located at Kairouan, along with the US 82nd Airborne. Six airstrips were constructed for the British and a number of others for the

Americans. The towing of the Horsa gliders was to be undertaken by a detachment from 38 Wing RAF – Nos 296 and 297 Squadrons – with 28 Albemarle and 7 Halifax aircraft. The Waco gliders were towed by C-47 Dakota aircraft from Colonel Ray Dunn's 51st Troop Carrier Wing USAAF. The glider training shared the airstrips with the aircraft carrying the paratroopers. A programme of practice loadings, take-offs, landings and jumps went on throughout the final weeks of preparation, although few of those participating felt that they had enough time or enough training.

Those feeling the pressure most were the men of the Glider Pilot Regiment. They had not done any real training for three months and now had to convert to the CG-4A gliders. The main difficulty appeared to be with the tug aircraft. Few of the American pilots had any experience at towing so everyone was on a steep learning curve.

Conditions at Kairouan were appalling. The men were housed in temporary camps in stifling heat. All day long a stiff wind blew across the sandy airstrips, coating everything in dust and sending the temperature soaring. Water had to be strictly rationed, food supplies were erratic, flies were everywhere and in everything, dysentery was rampant. Morale started to plummet, boredom set in and the men began to get annoyed. The days were counted down monotonously until the point came when men could not wait for the operation to start. They had become fighting mad.

The task of the British 1st Airlanding Brigade was to land by glider to capture the Ponte Grande, a bridge over the River Anapo just south of Syracuse, and to hold the crossing place until the troops of 5th Division had landed near Cassibile and advanced to relieve it. The bridge itself was to be seized in a *coup de main* by the troops carried in six Horsa gliders who were to land close by on either side of the river. The remainder of the brigade was to land on two other landing zones. The first was between 2 and 3 miles south of the bridge close to the sea, the other 1 mile west of the objective. The proximity of the bridge to Syracuse would mean that the anti-aircraft batteries protecting the port were ominously near to the landing zones.

Col Jim Gavin's 505th Parachute Infantry Regiment was to spearhead US Seventh Army's invasion. Jumping at just before midnight, its drop zones were located to the east of Gela, grouped between the sea and the town of Niscemi near the Ponte Olivo airfield, roughly in the centre of the

American seaborne landings. Gavin's main tasks were to hold the enemy back from the beaches, capture the airfield and disrupt enemy communications.

Gen Patton knew that, once his army was ashore, the pace of the build-up during the first few days would be governed by a number of things beyond his control, all of which could leave his assault troops vulnerable. He decided that the quickest way to reinforce his army ashore was by air. For the assault 82nd Airborne Division could only fly in one of its formations, Col Gavin's 505th Regiment. The second regiment, Col Reuben Tucker's 504th, would therefore become the Seventh Army's first reserve and be flown in soon after the landings, at a time of Patton's choosing, to reinforce the lodgement. Col Tucker's men would be dropped by parachute, with supporting artillery landed by glider, to reinforce Gavin's regiment. The remainder of the 82nd Division would land later by sea.

Maj Gen Matthew Ridgway, commander of the 82nd, was already sore that his whole division was not being employed in an airborne role as a result of British demands on American air transport and was also extremely unhappy about the second part of the plan which would involve his men flying over Allied ships offshore post D-Day. He asked Lt-Gen Browning, Alexander's airborne advisor, for assurances from the naval authorities that they would respect a cleared corridor for the air transports and prevent their anti-aircraft guns opening fire. He loathed the idea of his men being caught by a barrage of friendly fire as they flew over the anchorage area. Browning approached Admiral Cunningham's staff and expressed Ridgway's anxiety, but such assurances were not forthcoming. They agreed that as far as possible fire from warships would be withheld, but they could not guarantee that gun crews on merchant vessels and smaller craft would all react in the same way. Every precaution would be taken, but no guarantee could be given. They explained that anti-aircraft gunners had to react quickly to any aircraft flying over their ships, particularly those flying at low altitudes.

Ridgway was not pacified by this evasive reply and approached Eisenhower on 22 June and repeated his request for an assurance. Once again Cunningham's command replied that it could not promise that friendly fire would not happen. Ridgway stuck to his guns and approached Patton with what amounted to an ultimatum. He would not risk a night-time parachute drop without a guarantee from the Navy. Unless given this assurance he would protest against using his 504th Regiment in a follow-up drop.

Patton now became involved and pressured the naval commanders to give the assurance that the airborne commander required. Reluctantly, they agreed on the proviso that the air transports followed a designated route with the last leg of the fly-in being over land. Ridgway then cooperated with Tedder's staff to work out a route that was acceptable to Cunningham. Then he waited for the course to be cleared with Alexander's staff. Finally confirmation was given on 6 July and passed on to Seventh Army.

Ridgway and Patton discussed the route on board the army commander's headquarters ship *Monrovia* moored in Algiers harbour. Present with the two generals was Maj Gen Joseph Swing, the commander of the newly formed 11th Airborne Division. who was on a tour of the North African theatre. Also visiting Patton that day was Eisenhower's Deputy Commander, Maj Gen John Lucas. The discussion centred on how the instructions relating to the follow-up parachute drop could be briefed to those troops already embarked for the invasion fleet. All their anti-aircraft gunners as well as those on board ships would also have to refrain from opening fire. Lucas asked why such important instructions had not been disseminated before this late date. Patton explained that he had been trying to get agreement from the air forces and from Alexander's head-quarters since 3 July.[6]

With confirmation of the route, Patton now personally made sure that all of his corps and divisional commanders received a message outlining the details. He explained that each of them would warn their commands to expect these flights sometime post D-Day, even up to six days after the invasion, for he was still not sure on what date he would commit his airborne reserve. Patton outlined the type of transport, the likely time of the fly-in – between 2230 hrs and 2400 hrs – and the duration of the flight. He then ordered his generals to advise their respective naval commanders, even though they should have received these instructions through their normal channels.

So concerned was Patton that this message had got through to everyone in his command that he arranged for Maj Gen Swing to go ashore after the landings and reinforce his instructions with all Seventh Army's major headquarters. Swing was to request that all commanders especially notify their anti-aircraft units. Patton could now turn to Ridgway and give the assurances the airborne commander so desperately needed for the safe conduct of his parachute troops.

There were other tasks to be completed before the assault troops stormed ashore from their landing craft, for several of the landing beaches were covered by long-range coast artillery sites. One such position at Cassibile covered the most northerly of the seaborne landings to be made by British 5th Division; another was at Capo Murro di Porco. It was important that these guns were eliminated before the assault troops landed, but such actions could not be guaranteed by naval bombardment alone. Lt-Gen Dempsey decided that he would need to land special forces prior to the seaborne attack to take out the batteries in his corps' sector. Fortunately, he had call on 3 Commando, which was newly arrived in Egypt, and the elite troops of Lt-Col Blair 'Paddy' Mayne's 1st Special Air Service Regiment, which had been causing mayhem behind German lines in North Africa for some time.

Paddy Mayne and his SAS were old hands at attacking enemy positions by night and had built up a considerable reputation in Egypt and Libya. They were given the task of eliminating the guns on Capo Murro di Porco. No. 3 Commando was likewise experienced in raiding the enemy. Its commander, Lt-Col John Durnford-Slater, was probably the most experienced commando officer in the Army. Durnford-Slater was in fact the first commando soldier of the war, having been ordered to raise and command 3 Commando in June 1940 when, as a captain, he had volunteered for 'special service of a hazardous nature' in response to Winston Churchill's call for the Army to develop a reign of terror down the enemy coasts. At that time 1 and 2 Commandos did not exist for it had been originally intended that they should be airborne units. Over the next two years Durnford-Slater led his men on a number of attacks on German-occupied territories, taking part in raids on the Channel Islands, Lofoten Islands, Vaagso and the ill-fated landings at Dieppe in August 1942.

Dempsey met Durnford-Slater and outlined the proposed operation to silence the guns at Cassibile. He asked Durnford-Slater how long he thought it would take to land, overpower the enemy defences and advance 3 miles inland to knock out the battery. Unable to make a decision there and then, the colonel retired to make a plan. He would attack the objective with half of his commando, leaving Maj Peter Young and the remainder to deal with the pillboxes and beach defences. This type of attack was one that had been practised countless times in England on the defences of Plymouth and Weymouth, Durnford-Slater knew to the minute what his men were capable of doing. He later told Gen Dempsey that it would take 90 minutes from the moment he landed to eliminate the battery and 45 minutes to clear the enemy out of their positions on the beach.[7]

With the Sicilian campaign now agreed and given over to the planners, thoughts among the Allied high command were being trained elsewhere. It might seem obvious to us now that the elimination of Axis forces from Sicily would be quickly followed up by an invasion of Italy, but at the time this was far from being the next clear step. There were people in high places who most definitely did not want to get involved in conquering Italy and clearing it of German troops. They believed that Italy was a blind alley that led nowhere and could have little bearing on the declared aim of bringing Hitler and his regime to their knees.

The problem of what to do next was mainly political rather than military. Certainly Axis forces had to be engaged somewhere by the Western Allies in order to give support and encouragement to Stalin in his struggle with the bulk of the German Army in the east. The British and the Americans could not sit and wait until a favourable moment arrived for them to launch what was always intended to be their main effort, the assault across the English Channel and an invasion of Germany along the shortest and most easily supplied route.

In May, Churchill travelled across to Washington for another conference with President Roosevelt. On the agenda were many significant problems concerning the conduct of the war that needed agreement at the highest level. Most pressing among them was the question of what next to do in the Mediterranean. Before the start of the conference it seemed that everyone had a particular view on the matter and had produced papers for discussion.

Gen Marshall was convinced that even limited operations in the Mediterranean would be very detrimental to the war against Germany and told his Joint Chiefs of Staff that, if a full-scale cross-Channel invasion could not be launched by the spring of 1944, then troops and landing craft should be transferred to the Pacific to aid in the war against the Japanese. American public opinion supported Marshall's view for there was a sense in the country that American manpower and manufacturing might were being used in a subsidiary role, rather than being gathered together for a mighty punch which would knock Germany out of the war. Of course a shift in American political will away from the stated aim of President Roosevelt to 'finish Germany first' was the worst thing that could happen to the British.

The Washington Conference was a meeting both of the political heads of government and the leaders of the Allied military high command. Gen Marshall and Gen Brooke began the meeting poles apart on the question of what to do next in the Mediterranean theatre, each pointing out the weaknesses in the other's case. Brooke noted that American strategy failed to make any provision of what to do in the case of a sudden Italian collapse. Such a situation would have to be dealt with, even if only to keep Germany from taking over the country. Marshall replied by reminding Brooke just how quickly the Germans were able to react to any situation and how, in North Africa, a relatively small number of German troops had been able to inflict serious delays to Allied operations.

It was not just a case of what to do with regard to Italy; the British leaders also had an eye on operations in Yugoslavia, Greece, Sardinia and so on. Marshall went on to point out that once armies became involved in operations, every commander invariably asked for more troops and more supplies than were originally estimated as being necessary. Further actions in the Mediterranean would act as a siphon, sucking in more men and matériel and lengthening the course of the war.

As with all successful conferences, some compromise had to be reached. It came by each side giving a little ground. Marshall and the American contingent agreed to further limited engagement against Italy, provided that such operations were an exploitation of the invasion of Sicily and that these operations were framed to eliminate Italy from the war and tie down the maximum number of German troops. So Brooke and the British could continue with at least some part of their own proposed strategy, albeit severely limited. Any such operations would have to have the approval of the Combined Chiefs of Staff. The Allied Commander-in-Chief North Africa could use those forces he already had in the theatre, providing he withdrew four American and three British divisions to Britain by 1 November to take part in actions to secure a lodgement on the Continent. This was proposed to take place by 1 May 1944. All air power temporary supplied for Operation 'Husky' would be withdrawn after the successful completion of the Sicilian campaign and there would be rigorous restrictions on the use of landing craft.

So there it was: Eisenhower and the British could continue in a limited way with operations against Italy, but they were to take no part in other adventures elsewhere. Operations would also have to be firmly controlled so that the required number of divisions could be shipped back to Britain in time for the cross-Channel invasion. If the British wanted to get involved in the Balkans, then they would have to do so alone without American participation and, more importantly, without American supplies or landing craft.

While these discussions were going on, and for the next few weeks, preparations for the 'Husky' invasion continued gathering pace all along the coast of North Africa, in the USA and in Britain. Divisions in both armies earmarked for the assault trained and exercised in all aspects of seaborne and airborne landings. Naval and air plans were slowly honed into shape and coordinated with the requirements of the ground forces, using the experience gained in the 'Torch' invasion of North Africa eight months previously. Then, on 9 July, Eisenhower signalled he was ready to launch the greatest seaborne invasion the world had ever seen.

CHAPTER 5

The Defenders

Long before the defeat of Axis forces in North Africa the Italian people were becoming tired of the war. The glory days of the fascist regime had long faded and the reality of the misery that war brings was striking home among all layers of society from princes to peasants.

Mussolini, the great Italian dictator and father of the fascist movement, was in decline. His power was on the wane, with criticism of him now being openly voiced. His health was worsening, subjecting him to great mood swings. Around him, high-ranking politicians and military officers were giving vent to their long-standing dislike of their German ally. Even the head of Commando Supremo, Gen Vittorio Ambrosio, Chief of the Army General Staff, had little time for his German opposite numbers. Indeed he was sometimes even hostile towards them, always looking for ways to get Italy out of the war. Political intrigue was everywhere, with an anti-Mussolini faction growing in size daily. Overtures were being made to King Victor Emmanuel for him to take power and remove the dictator with a view possibly to replacing him with Marshal Pietro Badoglio, the old Chief of the General Staff who had resigned in 1940 when Mussolini had led the country into the war.

This lessening in the Italian resolve to continue the fight was not lost on Hitler. He was very suspicious of all moves made by his ally and by Ambrosio in particular. Hitler felt that his future strategy should not only be directed against Allied plans in the Mediterranean, but also towards ensuring German control of Italy, should its government collapse. He wished to keep the war as far from Germany's borders as possible by defending all of his conquered and satellite territories.

Hitler saw the danger to Sicily after the defeat in Tunisia, but equally feared that the Allied blow might fall elsewhere. He believed that Sardinia was the most threatened of the Italian islands and expected further attacks at the same time in the Aegean. His apprehension of landings in the eastern Mediterranean – not the most suitable area in which to wage war – was triggered by the threat they would pose to the sources of vital raw materials in the Balkans, and, more especially, to supplies of Romanian oil. Once the Allies had got ashore in that region they would be very difficult to evict.

To feed on these fears, which were obvious to both the Allies and to the Germans, a deception plan was organised by British Intelligence. Known as Operation 'Mincemeat', the ruse involved placing a body in the sea off Cadiz in Spain carrying certain letters. It was hoped that enemy spies would be alerted by the sympathetic Spanish that the corpse of a British officer had been washed ashore, seemingly from a crashed aircraft. In his briefcase were a number of letters from the Chief of the Imperial General Staff's office to Alexander, Cunningham and Eisenhower. Within their texts were subtle comments which pointed to Allied intentions to invade Greece, but with a diversionary attack at the same time to be made against Sardinia. True to form, the Spanish allowed German access to these letters and the contents were sent to Berlin. After long discussions and detailed appreciations of their possible validity, it was decided that they were genuine and the results were briefed up to Hitler.

The letters served to increase Hitler's fears about both an Allied invasion of the Balkans and a capitulation of the Italian forces defending the region. As a precaution he did in fact move more troops into the area, including one whole panzer division. None of these, however, came from Italy or Sicily and so the moves did not weaken the Axis forces defending the island.

Earlier that spring, Hitler had offered Mussolini German reinforcements but these were initially refused. Those German units that were already in the country had been on their way to North Africa before the collapse. In June pressure from Generalfeldmarschall Kesselring, German Commander-in-Chief in the Mediterranean, on Marshal Ambrosio concerning the readiness of the Italians to resist an invasion led to more German troops beings sent south and accepted into the Italian defence plan. Mussolini then decided that he would more fully accept Hitler's earlier offer and so presented the Germans with a shopping list of requirements which included 2,000 aircraft, equipment for 18 tank battalions and 70 field, Flak and artillery batteries. It was a wish list that the Germans found impossible to satisfy. Hitler's Chief of Staff, Generalfeldmarschall Keitel, saw the request as a ruse to provoke a refusal which could then be used as a pretext for Italy to leave the war.[1] The equipment could not be delivered but agreement was reached whereby six Germans divisions would be in the south of Italy and on the Italian islands by the end of May or early June.

In the meantime, Hitler put his planners to work on schemes to stabilise the Mediterranean should Italy collapse. They came up with Operations 'Alarich' and 'Konstantin'. The first was an arrangement to take military control of Italy should the Italians pull out of the war; the second was to remove Italian garrisons in the Balkans. In 'Alarich', seven divisions from Russia and six from France would be transferred to northern Italy under the command of GenFM Rommel. These would be in addition to the six divisions already in southern Italy under the control and command of Kesselring.

On paper, the Axis chain of command in the central Mediterranean, and most especially in Italy, was headed by Mussolini. Reporting to him was the Commando Supremo, the headquarters of the Italian armed forces, under Ambrosio. Hitler and the German Armed Forces High Command (OKW) could, in theory, only make their views and considered opinions known on any matter via GenFM Kesselring who was Commander-in-Chief (South) of German forces. In reality, Hitler's wishes were dictated directly to the Italians. German Army formations in Italy were nominally placed under the tactical command of Italians, but effectively remained under Kesselring's control.[2]

The field marshal also had ideas as to what the Allies would do next. Kesselring originally expected an attack against Sardinia and Corsica after which the islands could be used as a base for further operations against Italy, more especially Rome, and even against southern France. However, such moves would leave the Allied flank open to air attacks from Sicily. He therefore decided that it was more likely for the blow to fall on Sicily.[3]

Albrecht Kesselring was a Luftwaffe officer who had assumed command of German operations in the central Mediterranean in October 1941. He

had fought in the First World War with the 2nd Bavarian Foot Artillery
Regiment and transferred to the newly raised Luftwaffe in 1932 with the
rank of Generalmajor. He later led Luftflotte 1 throughout the Polish
campaign in 1939, then Luftflotte 2 during the Battle of Britain in 1940
and then participated in the invasion of Russia in 1941 before being sent
to the Mediterranean theatre.

Kesselring was a confirmed optimist, always ready to believe that
matters could be made to get better rather than to assume the worst. He
felt that way about his Italian allies, choosing to believe that they would
keep their word and remain in the Axis alliance. Indeed, Hitler once
remarked of him: 'We must be very cautious. Kesselring is a great optimist
and we have to make sure that because of his optimism he doesn't miss
the hour when optimism is no longer called for and drastic measures are
required.'[4]

At the time of the Sicily invasion, Gen Alfredo Guzzoni, Commander
Italian Sixth Army, was responsible for the defence of the island. The 66-
year-old general was a career soldier and veteran of the Great War. Despite
his years he was still an active individual and a professionally competent
soldier. Under the Mussolini regime he had commanded a corps in Albania.
He was then transferred to the General Headquarters of the Italian Army
in Rome where he served as Under-Secretary of State for War. Dissatisfied
with life in Rome, he retired from the service, only to be recalled after two
years to be given the task of defending Sicily, even though he had never set
foot on the island.

Guzzoni had ten Italian divisions based in Sicily with which to defend
the island against Allied attack. These were organised into the Italian XII
and XVI Corps. He also had tactical command over German Army
formations on the island. Six of the Italian divisions were static coast-
defence formations; the other four were standard divisions. The coast-
defence divisions were regarded as being of low calibre. They had little
transport; they were poorly armed; most of their weapons were obsolete;
their fixed defences were mainly field works; and their morale was low.
Many of their men lived locally and wished for nothing more than to
return home. The other divisions had a slightly better reputation, although
none of them were equal to Allied or German formations. The pick of
these divisions were the *Livorno* and the *Napoli* Divisions, which were
probably the best then available in the whole of the Italian Army. The

other two, the *Aosta* and *Assietta* Divisions, were less well thought of. None of these four had seen action, but the *Livorno* Division had been trained as an assault landing division, albeit back in 1940.

In addition to these divisions, Guzzoni had eight 'mobile groups' and eight 'tactical groups'. The mobile groups had little equipment to justify their transportable description. They usually consisted of two companies of obsolescent tanks – Italian CV3 or captured French R-35 types – or sometimes self-propelled 47mm guns, a troop of light artillery and a battery of anti-tank weapons. The tactical groups were often just a battalion of *Bersaglieri* or Blackshirt Militia, supported by a machine-gun platoon and a motorcyclist company.[5]

The two German divisions on the island were the 15th Panzergrenadier Division (Generalleutnant [GenLt] Eberhard Rodt) and the 1st Parachute Panzer Division *Hermann Göring* (GenLt Paul Conrath). Both of these formations were what could be termed elite divisions, especially when compared to the Italian formations. The 15th Panzergrenadiers had been formed in Sicily from remnants of the 15th Panzer Division that had escaped destruction in North Africa. To these were added survivors from the 22nd Panzer Division from the Russian Front. The division was going through the process of training and re-equipping when the Allies landed. While not up to the full complement of a standard panzergrenadier division, it could still muster 60 Panzer III and IV tanks and a deadly *Nebelwerfer* unit fielding 36 rocket projectors. When the Allies invaded, the 15th Panzergrenadier Division was located in the western part of the island, positioned to counter any possible landings around Palermo.

The 1st Parachute Panzer Division *Hermann Göring* was a 'parachute' division in name only. The title was purely honorary and related to the division being an all-volunteer unit made up of Luftwaffe personnel. The more usual title for the formation was the *Hermann Göring* Panzer Division. It had been raised in France in 1941 as a single regiment and was expanded to full divisional status in Belgium in January 1943. A short time later, units from the division were hurriedly sent to Tunisia to help stem the collapse, but shared the same fate as all of the Axis forces who surrendered in May. Although now short of infantry, its two tank battalions could assemble 99 serviceable tanks (Panzer IIIs and Panzer IVs) and 13 Panzer VI Tigers. The third tank battalion was equipped with self-propelled assault guns. Guzzoni had positioned the *Göring* Division in the central area of the south of the island, able to act against possible landings in the Bay of Gela. Part of this division, together with elements of the 15th Panzergrenadier Division, were grouped together under Oberst Wilhelm Schmalz into a formation known as the *Schmalz* Battlegroup and located south of Catania. The group formed a powerful mobile unit able to stiffen the defences of the three eastern ports of Syracuse, Augusta and Catania.

With Hitler now very suspicious of Italian motives, he wished to have greater operational control of the German divisions serving under Italian command. He therefore decided to send an experienced general to Guzzoni's headquarters to act as a 'liaison' officer. While this officer was not authorised to direct the operations of German troops he did have authority over their administration.[6] An important part of this officer's brief was to report daily to Kesselring on all matters affecting the defence of the island. Hitler chose GenLt Fridolin von Senger und Etterlin for the task and summoned him to the daily situation conference at Führer headquarters at Obersalzberg on 22 June.

Fridolin von Senger und Etterlin was a general of great ability. He had been a Rhodes Scholar at Oxford before the First World War and was commissioned into the German Army in 1917. He was a brilliant international horseman who joined the cavalry school in 1919. At the outbreak of the Second World War he commanded the 3rd Cavalry Regiment and saw service in Poland, France and Russia where he led 17th Panzer Division. As a cavalry officer of the old school, he never did subscribe to the Nazi ideals and was often fairly open in his criticism of Hitler. Nonetheless, he was a well-respected, exemplary officer and commander who won great admiration during the war for his handling of defensive positions, most notably at Cassino in 1944.

With Hitler at the conference to greet von Senger was his Chief of Staff, GenFM Keitel, and General der Artillerie Walter Warlimont, Deputy Chief of the Armed Forces Operational Staff. The field marshal outlined von Senger's new duties as liaison officer to the Italian Sixth Army command and his responsibilities regarding the defence of Sicily. Hitler then went into a great discourse on how the island might have to be defended by the two German divisions already stationed there, without having to rely on Italian forces. His increasing suspicions of Italian intent led him to expect a possible weakening of Axis resolve. Was it possible, he wondered, for the 30,000 German support personnel stationed on the island to be used on active defence? It became clear to von Senger that Hitler intended that Sicily should be vigorously defended should the Allies invade, with a view to holding on to the island at all costs. The Führer then went into a long commentary on Allied strategy and explained that, by failing to leap across to Sicily after their landings in North Africa, they had already lost the struggle in the Mediterranean.

After the meeting, both Keitel and Warlimont spoke to von Senger separately. Unlike their leader, each of them felt that, if the Allies invaded Sicily, it would be best to withdraw all troops back across the Strait of Messina to the mainland. Warlimont thought that all of their equipment would most likely have to be abandoned. Keitel had been briefed by Gen Hube, who was already stationed in Italy, regarding the situation on the island and believed that the topography of Sicily would prevent the two German divisions being used in their original role as a mobile reserve to the Italian forces. The mountainous roads and probable Allied air superiority over the island would make all movement in daylight impossible.[7]

Three days later von Senger met Kesselring in Rome and received a different appraisal of the situation, more in line with Hitler's views regarding the defence of the island. Should the Allies land in Sicily, Kesselring thought the chances of holding the island to be quite favourable. The ever-cheerful Kesselring, 'smiling Albert' as he was known, believed that events at Dieppe the previous year had shown that a seaborne landing could be stopped on the waterfront and defeated. The field marshal's views of the unified Italian/German command were also positive. He well understood that the Germans could not fight two opponents on the island, the Allies and defecting Italians, so the alliance must be made to work by cooperation with their ally in the defence of what was part of their homeland.

Von Senger was never impressed by Kesselring's over-optimistic nature. Such an approach to events often overwhelmed those who urged caution. Von Senger believed that many of those who had fought in North Africa held similar views, claiming that Rommel's opinions were often over-ruled by Kesselring in favour of an impossibly optimistic assessment of what was possible. 'During the entire Italian campaign,' von Senger was to write, 'the field marshal never changed his optimistic outlook; at least that is how he chose to present his views to a senior officer such as myself.'[8] In the later stages of the war, this was just the attitude that Hitler wanted from his commanders.

After meeting Kesselring, von Senger had a discussion with GenFM Wolfram von Richthofen, Commander-in-Chief Luftflotte 2, which he found to be less positive. Speaking alone with von Richthofen, he learned that the Luftwaffe was going its own way as it had so often done before, believing that the Allies would choose Sardinia rather than Sicily to invade. He had therefore moved the main concentration of air defences to Sardinia. Von Senger was appalled: 'All this revealed a regrettable divergence of views between the two C-in-C's.'9

The charismatic 47-year-old von Richthofen was a fighter ace from the First World War, who had flown in the same squadron as his more celebrated cousin Manfred, the legendary Red Baron. Between the wars he was Chief of Staff of the Condor Legion which fought for Franco in the Spanish Civil War. In that struggle he helped to develop dive-bomber tactics with his Ju 87 Stukas, which he put to good use in the Polish campaign of 1939, the capture of France and Belgium in 1940 and at Crete in 1941. He won further acclaim from the use of his Luftflotte 4 in Russia and was elevated to field marshal early in 1943. Sadly he did not have long to live, for soon after the battle for Sicily he was diagnosed with an inoperable brain tumour.

Von Richthofen was officially subordinate to Kesselring but in practice, as von Senger had seen, he often acted independently, dealing directly to Luftwaffe HQ in Berlin and its chief Reichsmarschall Hermann Göring. Relations between von Richthofen and Kesselring were not always as harmonious as they could be. The problem of the tactical command of Luftwaffe personnel on the island was always a thorny one. The German Air Force had many important ground forces stationed on Sicily during the battle, the most important of which were the *Hermann Göring* Division and, later, the 1st Parachute Division. Technically they came under General der Flieger Kurt Student's Fliegerkorps XI, along with Luftwaffe ground forces in Italy, and were thus subordinate to von Richthofen's Luftflotte 2, yet they took orders from Kesselring. Friction between the two C-in-Cs was often just under the surface.

Axis air forces had around 1,750 aircraft, excluding transports and coastal craft, based in Sardinia, Sicily and Italy. Of these about 960 were German. All of the bombers were based in Italy, but only half of them were within flying distance of Sicily; the remainder were dispersed within effective range of Sardinia, Corsica and southern France. By the time of the invasion, the Germans had 775 operational aircraft within range of Sicily, 289 of which were based on the island. The Italians could muster 145 aircraft on Sicily, 75 per cent of which were fighters and fighter-bombers. But as each day drew nearer to the invasion, Allied air forces whittled down this number considerably.

By the beginning of July, Kesselring had established a general defence plan for Sicily, southern Italy, Sardinia and Corsica. In addition to the Italian garrisons he had the two German divisions in Sicily, one in south Calabria and another in Sardinia, with just a weak brigade supporting the local troops in Corsica. To guard against air attack he concentrated the bulk of his Flak formations on the main threatened areas of Sicily, western Calabria and Sardinia, with a particularly strong concentration centred on Messina covering the strait between Sicily and the mainland of Italy.[10]

The stretch of water between Sicily and the mainland was the one weak link in the defence plan for Sicily. It was the main crossing place for virtually all of the supplies and reinforcements bound for the island. It was true that the large port of Palermo and several smaller ports were still open, but Allied air interdiction and bombardment meant that any ships using them had to run a terrible risk of being destroyed by enemy action. The same was true for the sea lanes off the island. The Royal Navy patrolled them with great vigour, intercepting at will any traffic that strayed into the path of its ships. So it was that most anti-aircraft guns were stationed in the Messina area, protecting the great port and trying to keep it open to waterborne traffic.

The German ferry service across the Strait of Messina, throughout the battle and in the subsequent retreat, was ably organised by Admiral Wilhelm Meendsen-Bohlken with naval barges, supplemented by engineer assault boats and Siebel ferry boats. The Italians ran and controlled a ferry service of their own. Kesselring recognised this weak point in the island's defences and was given assurances by the Italians that they would keep all of the ferries open, as he was later to recall:

> Our ferries were numerically inferior and handicapped by the narrowness of the area in which they could operate. I had lost all faith that the Italian Navy would carry out any of the plans prepared for

different eventualities. There were often times when I reflected that it
would be far easier to fight alone with inadequate forces than to have
to accept so bewildering a responsibility for the Italian people's aversion
to the war and our ally's lack of fighting qualities and dubious loyalty.[11]

When the Allies did not immediately follow up their victory in Tunisia
with landings on any of the Italian islands, a programme was quickly
implemented by the Germans to help strengthen the defences. German
construction groups moved to Sicily with troops and building materials to
instruct the Italians in the latest methods of static defence. Further
attempts were made to improve their fighting efficiency with more plentiful
quantities of arms and ammunition. Supply dumps were located in areas
that were likely to be free from Allied air attack so that resistance could
continue even through breaks in communications. The new rush of
activity was planned to stiffen the resolve of the Italians to defend their
homeland, but many of the static coastal troops looked longingly over their
shoulders at their cosy villages and rural towns and wished for nothing
more than to go home.

Kesselring met Gen Guzzoni, C-in-C Italian Sixth Army during June, to
finalise a defence plan. All the senior formation commanders on the
islands were present. Kesselring and Guzzoni went over the measures in
detail, agreeing actions for every eventuality. The German field marshal
then emphasised that all formations were under direct Italian control and
had to be prepared to act immediately. He told his German commanders
they were to move against the Allies the moment that an invasion fleet was
spotted and its objectives were ascertained, no matter whether or not they
had received orders from Guzzoni's headquarters at Enna on Sicily. These
orders well suited the aggressive GenLt Conrath, commander of the
Hermann Göring Division: 'If you mean go for them, field marshal,' Conrath
growled, 'then I'm your man.'[12]

Kesselring left the island with a feeling of apprehension, as he later
noted in his memoirs: 'With the fall of Lampedusa and Pantelleria on 11
and 12 June, the last doubts that the enemy had over the landfall of the
next Allied invasion were removed.' He made one final tour of the defences
in Sicily and went back to his headquarters in Italy. 'I deliberately retired
into the wings,' he later recorded, 'seeing that the defence of their native
soil was pre-eminently the Italians' business.'[13]

CHAPTER 6

Invasion: The Airborne Landings

In the bright early evening sunshine of 9 July, all along the dusty airstrips at Kairouan, gliders and their tugs were lined up ready to take to the air. At 1842 hrs the first of the Halifax-towed Horsas began its bumpy ride down the airfield and bounced aloft, swinging wildly on the end of its tow; Operation 'Husky' had begun. Other aircraft followed at one-minute intervals, Halifaxes towing Horsas and C-47 Dakotas towing Wacos, until the last took flight at around 2020 hrs. As the glider/tug combinations became airborne, they settled down into formations around the airfields then headed north towards the sea. Just off the coast, over the Kuriate islands, the aircraft assembled into streams and set course for Malta, flying over the island of Linosa en route. The American C-47s flew in echelons of four at one-minute intervals, their leaders navigating the way. The British bombers, as was their custom for night flights, flew individually.

During take-off and shortly thereafter, a few glider pilots aborted their mission for various reasons and turned back, so that once out over the sea and well into the 300-mile journey the main force numbered 137 gliders. The great fleet of aircraft flew at a very low altitude, most of them below 500 feet, to avoid detection on enemy radar. Radio silence was absolute and the only communication between tug and glider was by intercom along tiny wires lashed around the tow rope. At best conversation between pilots was very faint, at worst it was inaudible. Once over the searchlight beacon at Malta – six beams rising vertically to help navigation – the air convoys took a half-turn to port, heading to pass south of the southern tip of Sicily at Cape Passero. By this time all was not well with the great air fleet. High winds buffeted the aircraft combinations making it very difficult to keep station. The first turn along the route caught some pilots off guard and a few tugs and gliders began to fall out of formation. Those that had slipped away from the main fleet now had to do their own navigation, and some of them had had little practice in this exact art.

When visual contact was made with Cape Passero, there was to be turn to the north to pass 5 miles to starboard of the cape, then a straight 18-mile run-in to Syracuse. Tug aircraft now began to climb, gradually aiming for the 1,800-foot altitude required before release of the gliders. Just to the south of the port the Maddalena Peninsula jutted out across the route with the two main landing zones located just beyond its shoreline. By this time the gliders would have been released to glide in over the low cliffs to touch down. The landings zones for the *coup de main* parties were 3 miles further inland, slightly to port.

The leading aircraft approached Cape Passero at around 2220 hrs. Beneath them were the dark shapes of the invasion fleet carrying British Eighth Army. Anti-aircraft gunners in the vessels below heard the roaring sound of scores of aircraft passing low overhead and held their fire, just as they had been ordered to do. They had been well briefed to expect this fly-in of friendly aircraft. Up above them some pilots were anticipating their final change of direction, others were not. More and more of the aircraft fell out of line and began to drift across the sky searching for the correct landmarks. The tight formations which started out from Tunisia were becoming seriously dispersed. Those tugs in the rear columns that had kept station began over-running stragglers in front of them. Little could be seen but the occasional exhaust of the next C-47 up ahead. To avoid collisions, some aircraft tried to climb above slower ones in front. It was all too much of a new experience both for the tug planes and for the gliders; no one had been trained for this. Then the enemy began to put up anti-aircraft fire. Tracer, exploding shells, searchlights and flares streaked across the sky; smoke added to the haze of battle. Confusion was everywhere as tug aircraft began taking evasive action.

Up at the front of the air fleet the leading combinations had made their run-in exactly on time and in place, before the enemy had reacted. With a clear sky ahead of them, they slipped over the coast and set course for their landings. Behind them was total disorder. Pilots found it difficult to judge their positions or even to see the shore through the exploding flak. Aircraft were above and below them as tugs tried to gain height to release their tows and gliders swooped down to land. Some C-47s veered away and let go their gliders wherever they could, seeking an escape from the mêlée. The release of a glider was supposed to be a mutual decision between glider and tug pilot, either by visual signal or by intercom. The reality was that a number of C-47s cast off their gliders without warning and a number of glider pilots failed to signal to the tug up ahead and let loose their aircraft.

Most of the glider pilots could not see the coastline let alone identify their landing zone. Lt-Col Chatterton at the controls of his glider pulled the release lever to disengage the tow when he saw his tug plane turn and dive. For a moment he was completely blinded by a great bank of dust that had been blown in by the high winds. The moon was covered and he was plunged into almost total darkness. His glider plummeted through the black night, his target totally obliterated. Then the sky was lit up by rounds of tracer snaking towards him. Several cannon rounds ripped through his port wing. The glider went into a turn and began to fall. Chatterton remembers seeing the black sea rush up to his windscreen and then he was awash with water pouring into the cockpit. Momentarily stunned, the next thing the colonel recalls was struggling with his harness when two hands grasped him and helped ease him out of the glider up onto the roof to join Brigadier Hicks and the rest of his passengers, some on the wings, some still in the sea. Dazed and a little disorientated by the crash, Chatterton saw a searchlight beam sweep across the water and catch the downed glider in its shaft of brilliant light. A few seconds later a ribbon of small shells, interspaced with white-hot tracer, snaked towards the doomed aircraft. Helpless, devoid of cover and unable to fire back, the two senior commanders and their companions clung impotently to the wreckage. Soon the colonel had had enough. 'It's no good staying here,' he said to Brig Hicks, 'Shall we swim for it?' 'I think that's best,' replied Hicks. 'Come on everybody,' he called and led his men into the dark sea. The shore was a good half mile away.[1]

From the sky above gliders seemed to be crashing down all over, some ripped apart by flak, some slipping down into the water when they ran out of momentum. Few of the Waco gliders made it to land; fewer still landed intact or on target. The off-shore wind, the premature cast-off by tugs, and the deadly flak had thrown the glider attack into chaos. Those that landed close to the island were peppered by small arms fire from the Italian coastal troops and their passengers had to swim ashore. Those that landed far from land, with their airborne infantry clutching precariously to their wings, heaved up and down on the rise and fall of a rough sea until they succumbed to the waves. The lucky few were found by the incoming invasion armada and their troops taken off; the unlucky many sank without trace.

A few successful landings were made. Against all odds Staff Sergeant Galpin brought his Horsa glider in to land on its correct landing zone close to the bridge. This was the only glider of the *coup de main* party that landed on target and got its troops into action. Another glider piloted by Capt Denholm came close, but it crashed right into the river bank near the bridge at speed. The force of the impact detonated a bangalore torpedo inside the Horsa and the subsequent explosion and fireball killed all inside.

Everyone in Galpin's glider was fortunately uninjured, although the leader of the airborne troops, Lt Lawrence Withers, sprained his ankle. To everyone's surprise the Italians defending the bridge did not fire. Lt Withers was able to gather his platoon of the South Staffordshires together and move towards their target unmolested. There was no sign of any other gliders in the vicinity, so Withers decided not to wait for reinforcements but to assault the bridge with the men he had. He swiftly formulated a plan and whispered instructions to his men. He and five others would swim across the river and canal to the far side and, on a prearranged signal attack the pillbox guarding the north side of the crossing. The rest of his men would put in an attack on the south side at the same time.[2]

The attack was executed in fine style: grenades exploded, Sten guns chattered and determined men with blackened faces screamed at the top of their voices as they raced forward. The noise and violence came at the Italians from both sides of the bridge. A few rifle shots rang out in return, even a machine gun got off a few stuttering rounds, before the dazed defenders threw down their arms and surrendered. The Italians were quickly rounded up and locked into the stone guardhouse near the end of the crossing while Withers's men split into groups to search for the demolition charges which they knew would be wired onto the structure of the bridge. These were easily located and removed, the bundles of explosives dropped silently into the water below. Lt Withers and his small band of men had achieved the work of a whole airlanding brigade; they had captured the bridge over the Simeto River and canal intact. They now had to hold the Ponte Grande against the inevitable enemy counter-attack. One questioned remained, where were Brig Hicks and the other 1,200 men of the Airlanding Brigade?

The answer was that the missing troops were either spread over miles of the Sicilian countryside or clinging to wreckage out to sea. In the first two hours of Operation 'Ladbroke', the glider-borne attack, Brig Hicks had lost a third of his force. Most of those who had reached a landfall had gone wildly astray, some up to 12 miles from where they should have been, and it took hours for them to find their bearings and take some part in the action. They disrupted communications, set about Italian positions and generally made a great nuisance of themselves, but only one in fifteen of them actually took part in the events at the Ponte Grande.

Maj-Gen Hopkinson was one of those who had to be dragged from the sea by part of the invasion fleet; the glider carrying him had come down miles from land. Cursing profusely, the wet and bedraggled general damned the American pilots who had cast off their towed gliders so far from the shore. Brig Hicks and Col Chatterton had adventures of their own. They met up with a group of the SAS landing close by and by the end of the night had attacked several pillboxes and strongpoints, capturing over a hundred prisoners, most of whom thought that they were to be shot out of hand. With the coming of daylight Chatterton and his party came across many gliders with bodies scattered around, lying where they had been killed in the landings or shot by the Italians. A feeling of despondency gradually crept over the survivors as the scale of the disaster became evident.

As the night progressed, Lt Withers's small band increased to eight officers and sixty-five men. A small defence perimeter was placed around the crossing with outposts covering the approaches. Arms and ammunition available to the small band were woefully inadequate. The heaviest weapon they had was a 2-inch mortar.

Just before dawn the Italians had sealed off the bridge with a perimeter guard which stretched completely around the area. No more airborne stragglers were able to get through to the now isolated defenders; they were on their own. The Italians began to snipe and machine-gun any sign of life on the bridge and plaster the structure with mortar bombs. One by one the exposed British troops were picked off. Then shell fire started to home in on either end of the structure. The defenders retaliated, but ammunition stocks were low. The mortar had to be used sparingly, only firing when a target was pinpointed exactly. The early morning passed slowly for the exposed men, but the sound of battle and the rumble of naval guns could gradually be heard from 5th Division's landings well under way 8 miles to the south. Lt Withers looked at his watch; it was now 0400 hrs. The link-up with 5th Division should take place around 0730 hrs. He and his men had to hold on for just a few more hours.

The men of the American 82nd Airborne Division were also in action that night, leaving their airfields in North Africa shortly after the British glider force. Their flight plan was to take the American division east from Tunisia towards Malta, flying over the tiny island of Linosa as a landmark. Having passed over Malta, the C-47 transports were to make a dog-leg turn to port and fly northwards to make landfall along the south coast of Sicily. The island would be seen on the right of the aircraft.

Few of the paratroopers had any real idea of where they were going and the news that Sicily was to be their destination was given to them on a slip of paper as they boarded their aircraft. Each man gave his equipment a final check – rifle, rations, water, knife, grenades and compass. Here and there a man would have the responsibility of carrying a bazooka. The hand-held rocket launcher was the only anti-tank weapon carried by the paratroopers, giving them some small ability to engage enemy armour should they be unfortunate enough to come up against any.

The 36-year-old Col Jim Gavin, commander of the 505th Parachute Regimental Combat Team – 'Slim Jim' to his men – recalls being loaded and ready in his aircraft just as the C-47 was about to roll out onto the runway when an airman from the airfield weather station ran up calling his name. Gavin answered, to be greeted with the news that there would be a stiff wind blowing over the drop zone in Sicily when he and his men jumped. 'Thirty-five miles an hour, blowing west to east,' Gavin was told. 'I thought you'd want to know about it,' said the airman. The news hit

Gavin like a thunderbolt. As training jumps were normally cancelled when winds reached 15mph, and as few had jumped in winds of more than 25mph before, the news foretold disaster. Steeling himself to the fact that there was nothing he could do about it now, the colonel sat back and let the aircraft roll.[3]

As anticipated, the strong winds disrupted the airborne armada and some confusion resulted. Many of the aircraft missed Malta altogether, overflew the dog-leg turning point and found themselves flying up the south-east coast of Sicily with the coastline on their left. Insufficient practice in night flying in V-formation caused the break-up of many of the groups; planes began to straggle and disperse. The more intrepid of the pilots turned back to find their way around to their correct drop zones along the south coast. Others gave the green light to their paratroopers and dispatched them over the area controlled by the British. A few unfortunates shed their loads into the sea, drowning all that made the jump.

The results of the airborne drop were chaotic; the 3,400 paratroopers from Gavin's command were scattered all over south-eastern Sicily. In all, 33 of the sticks dropped in British Eighth Army's area; 53 were in the rear of US 1st Division's beaches and 127 sticks came down inland of 45th Division's sector. Out of all this, only the 2nd Battalion of the regiment landed relatively intact; unfortunately, it came down 25 miles from its designated drop zone.[4]

One of Gavin's battalion commanders, Maj Mark Allen, himself almost perished out at sea along with his battalion: Allen saw the red warning light come, on alerting him and his men to be prepared to exit. The paratroopers all stood up to make ready for the jump. Allen looked down from the open door and saw they were still over the sea. The green light then came on and his men tried to surge forward out into the night air. Allen forced them to stop and went forward to speak to the pilot, asking him what the hell he was doing. The pilot sheepishly replied, 'Sorry, the co-pilot was in too much of a hurry.'[5]

The flight bringing Col Gavin and his regimental headquarters team was off course. Gavin knew that things were going wrong when no sight was made of Linosa or Malta, even though they had been told that the larger of the two islands would be well lit as an aid to navigators. More unease was felt when the aircraft began flying across the line of great lanes of shipping, all steaming their way towards the invasion isle. Gavin knew that his men were going astray, for their flight path should have taken them parallel and between the American fleet on the left and the British on the right. Realising their mistake, the pilots of the transport aircraft all turned to port and began flying along the path of the great seaborne armada. Soon, up ahead, Gavin could see the great flashes of pre-invasion bombing along the coast. At least he and his men would make landfall of some kind, even though it would be more than 20 miles south-east of where he expected to be.[6]

Col Gavin landed in a Sicilian field to a mixed reception. Sporadic small arms fire could be heard but nothing could be seen of the enemy. Also scarce on the ground in the dark were his men. The high winds had dispersed his regimental combat team over a wide area, along with most of his regimental headquarters group. After an hour of searching for stragglers, the colonel managed to assemble a group of around twenty men and decided that he would have to make some attempt to reach his objective, even though he had no idea where he was and what direction he ought to take. Looking to the north-west, Gavin could see the occasional flame of bursting shells along the dim horizon. That was where the battle was being fought and, using the old West Point battle axiom of moving toward the sound of guns, that was the direction in which the colonel moved with his small band of men.[7]

The drop by the 505th Parachute Infantry was a mess. Fewer than 200 paratroopers actually made it to the main rendezvous point at Piano Lupo. The scattered nature of the landings had made it difficult for the troops to find out exactly where they were, let alone organise themselves and attack their objectives. Direction was completely lost. Bands of paratroopers began roaming through the rear areas of the Italian coastal forces, ambushing small parties, cutting enemy communications and creating confusion among Italian commanders who were unable to establish just where the location of the main airborne landings was sited.[8]

CHAPTER 7

Invasion:
The British Landings

General Guzzoni, commander Italian Sixth Army, received word of the airborne landings soon after midnight on 10 July. He was sure that the scattered drop of parachutists and gliders signalled the start of an invasion. By 0145 hrs, he was convinced that the Allies were coming and telephoned both his XII and XVII Corps headquarters to expect landings on the south-eastern coast and in the Gela Bay. An hour later, the leading waves of Allied 15th Army Group came ashore.

The first Allied troops to land were the special forces ordered to eliminate the Italian gun batteries overlooking XIII Corps' landing beaches: No. 3 Commando to tackle the guns behind Cassibile and Lt-Col 'Paddy' Mayne's 1st Special Air Service Regiment the guns on the extreme right at Capo Murro di Porco.

Lt-Col Durnford-Slater's 3 Commando was carried to its unloading point by the transports *Dunera* and HMS *Prince Albert*. The Commando's run in to its landing beach was through a pitch-black night over a sea criss-crossed with vessels of all types. There were several near misses as ships meandered around trying to find their correct positions. A few hundred yards from shore a pillbox opened up on the tiny landing craft with machine-gun fire. The commandos replied with bursts from the Vickers K guns mounted in the bows of the boats. The pillbox fell silent. The colonel

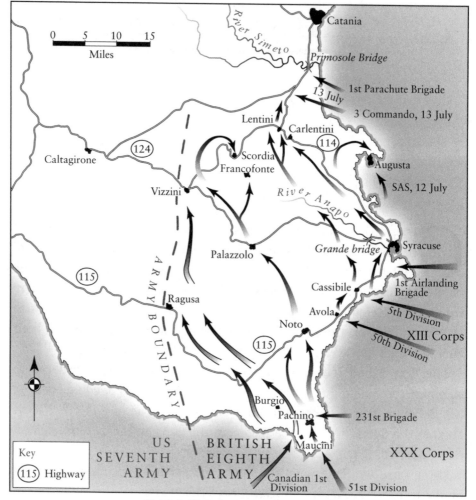

British Eighth Army Landings

was the first to land, leading his men up the beach at around 0305 hrs, 20 minutes late. 'We were faced by masses of wire and many pill boxes, all useless unless manned by determined troops,' Durnford-Slater later recalled. 'We were soon through.'[1]

While Maj Young tidied up the Italian defences, the remainder of the Commando passed inland. They formed up a few hundred yards from the beach and began their timed advance. The colonel was impatient to keep up the momentum and urged his men forward. As they approached the battery the commandos heard it open fire. The invasion fleet had been spotted. Soon they arrived at a dry river bed directly under the line of the Italian guns. Here the 3-inch mortars were set up along with four Bren guns while half of the group were sent round to the rear of the battery. A few others formed a small party on the flank of the defended site. The colonel gave the order and the whole of the gun site was brought under devastating light machine-gun and mortar fire. After 5 minutes of this harassing fire, the colonel signalled the rear party to attack. He then led his party into the wire surrounding the site. They came at the Italian defenders from all angles, blowing the wire in front of them with bangalore torpedoes. The commandos dashed through the gaps, firing from the hip. The defenders replied with heavy automatic fire but once the commandos were inside the perimeter it was clear the battery was lost. The attack was soon over. It just remained to secure prisoners and blow up the guns. Durnford-Slater looked at his watch. Eighty-five minutes had passed since he stepped ashore, 5 minutes less than he had estimated to the corps commander at the planning stages of the operation.

The second attack on Italian gun batteries in 5th Division's sector was the task of 1st SAS. The location of its target, the gun battery of the Capo Murro di Porco, was right under the flight path of the gliders carrying the airlanding brigade. The landings by the SAS were timed to take place just after the gliders had flown in so that the attention of the Italian defenders would be diverted skywards when Mayne's men came ashore from their craft. The raiders would then land, scale the cliffs and eliminate the guns before they could open fire on the invasion fleet.

Lt-Col 'Paddy' Mayne's unique band of special forces had been re-titled the Special Raiding Squadron for the operation as some sort of security ruse, but the change of name did little to undermine the exceptional opinion that its men had of their abilities. Paddy Mayne had built up a formidable reputation for his raids behind enemy lines in North Africa and his association with Col David Stirling and the Long Range Desert Group was legendary.

Mayne's force was carried over to Sicily in the *Ulster Monarch* and disembarked into small landing craft assault (LCAs) just off the coast. The rough weather had made the task of transferring to the attack craft hazardous and the operation began to fall behind schedule; there were even some doubts if the attack would go ahead. The raiders were, however, able to take heart when bombers of the RAF swooped in to attack their target and machined-gunned the length of the shoreline on which they were to land Most of the men inside the small craft were seasick and wanted for nothing more than to be on dry land. All of them wished that their raid had been by air, as the title of their regiment suggested, until, that is, they saw what was happening in the sky above them.

The gliders were late coming in, but when they did arrive it seemed like the world had gone mad. One after another they were crashing down into the water. As Mayne's craft ploughed through the choppy sea they passed a number of these crippled gliders with their crews and passengers clinging desperately to them. Cries for help seem to come from every quarter. Mayne was now in a fix; should he stop to help or continue with his task to silence the guns?

'It was a terrible thing to have to do,' he wrote later, 'But a further delay of just a few minutes would have thrown out the timing of the whole operation.' He was right, of course; the main invasion fleet would be at the mercy of the guns should they not be eliminated. Casualties as a result would have been many more than those holding on for dear life on the gliders.[2]

Mayne scanned the jagged shoreline for the flashing light of his guide. Men from the Combined Operations Pilotage Parties (COPPs), a naval officer and a rating, had come ashore earlier in a rubber dinghy from a submarine to pinpoint the landing place for the Special Raiding Squadron and now signalled to Mayne's landing craft as they began their run-in to the beach. The landing place was exactly as described in photographs and models during rehearsals with high cliffs rising from the rear of the beach. Just beyond the cliff edge was the gun battery.

A little apprehensive, Mayne's men began the long climb, not knowing what awaited them at the top. The first man up saw a figure in the gloom and let off two bullets from his carbine. It was a statue. The edgy troops behind him could not suppress a snigger. That was it, the only shots fired in the attack. The gun battery was deserted. Closer inspection among the underground chambers was to find the whole of the garrison cowering in a corner, paralysed with fear. The accurate bombing by the RAF had driven them below ground and they refused to have any part in the battle.

Engineers among Mayne's troops laid charges on the large guns and blew them. The resultant explosion terrified the Italian prisoners even more. They were a pitiful sight and disgusted the battle-hardened men of the SAS even more. They recalled that Italians in the desert could be remarkably cruel and many British troops reserved a special hatred for their cowardly exploits. However, Mayne insisted that everyone behave properly and rounded up the prisoners and put them under guard.

It seemed that the operation was over but, just as it was getting light, another battery of large guns opened up nearby and began firing on the convoys out to sea. Mayne immediately grouped his men and led them off to fight another battle to eliminate it. After a brief, but fairly intense battle, the enemy emplacements were over-run and the guns put out of action. The colonel then led his men southwards to join up with 5th Division.

While the special forces units and the airborne assaults were tackling the Italian defenders on Sicily, spreading alarm throughout the south-east of the island, British and American seaborne assault waves were closing rapidly on the invasion beaches. British XXX Corps' landings stretched around the Pachino Peninsula, from the Special Service Brigade's beach west of Punta Castellazzo on the left, round to 231st Brigades beaches near Pachino on the east. Between the two, Canadian 1st Division's landings were grouped around the Costa dell'Ambria on the west of the peninsula with 51st (Highland) Division's concentrated along the tip.

Just before 0300 hrs, almost 30 minutes later than planned, 40 and 41 Royal Marine Commandos of Brig Bob Laycock's Special Service Brigade approached the shore just west of Punta Castellazzo on the left flank of the Canadian 1st Division's landing beaches. In the distance the low outline of the land was lit up by the bombing and fires that had begun during the night.

41 RM Commando was the first ashore, drenched by the spray from a strong swell, landing amid confusion in the wrong place. At the top of the beach Lt-Col Bruce Lumsden assembled his men among the dunes. He

soon realised that their landings were too far to the right and led his men off at a gallop towards their planned objectives. Lumsden and his men were among the Italian positions sorting out machine-gun posts and isolated pillboxes before 40 RM Commando came in on its scattered landing beaches. By the time they were assembled and organised and set about their objectives, the eastern sky was gradually being lit by the first rays of dawn. The commandos set about their tasks in the semi-darkness only to find out that the heavy gun batteries identified by the planners and assigned to Lt-Col J.C. 'Pop' Manners's 40 RM Commando, were in fact machine-gun posts. They were soon eliminated and patrols were sent out to contact the Canadians to the east to join up the beachhead.

Earlier that night, Maj-Gen Simonds had seen the transports carrying his Canadian 1st Division anchor 7 miles off shore after their long journey from England. The assault waves of the 1st Brigade's Royal Canadian Regiment leading companies were late disembarking and finally left their transport at 0400 hrs. The troops were carried to the shore in DUKWs inside tank landing craft and when the larger vessels grounded on a sandbar near the shore, the amphibious vehicles inside – seven fully loaded DUKWs in each of them – motored down the ramps and roared across the short stretch of water onto the shoreline. Making good use of their momentum the DUKWs continued up the sand to deposit their troops dry-shod in the dunes at the top of the beach. It was 0530 hrs. Coming ashore nearby on the left, albeit at the much earlier time of 0445 hrs and rather dispersed over a wide area of Roger Beach, was the Hastings and Prince Edward Regiment. Over to the extreme right, Canadian 2nd Brigade landed its two battalions virtually without incident.

Opposition to the Canadians was slight and both brigades had their assault companies quickly off the beaches. The weight of the naval bombardment and the success of the landings by the commandos had persuaded the Italian defenders to withdraw from the seafront. Some desultory machine-gun fire occasionally burst across the water and a few salvos from the gun battery north of Maucini splashed in the water, but by 0645 hrs Maj-Gen Simonds was able to signal to Leese at corps HQ that his division had captured all of his initial objectives.

Over the next few hours the reserve battalions of the assault brigades began to land and the Canadians moved inland. Arriving two hours after the assault craft were the much larger tank landing ships (LSTs) bringing the Sherman tanks of the Three Rivers Regiment into the beachhead. By late morning the reserve battalions were ashore along with a regiment of self-propelled artillery. Just before midday the 142nd Field Regiment RA (Royal Devon Yeomanry) could signal that its Bishops – 25-pounder guns on Valentine tank chassis – were landed ready for action.[3]

Initial objectives for the 1st Brigade were the gun battery near Maucini and the airfield at Pachino. The village of Maucini was reached and cleared with little effort. Then the lead company moved out to surround and take the gun battery which had fired sporadically on the landings. A sergeant up with the main body fired a rifle shot at what he thought was one of the enemy. The volley seemed to act as a signal to the Italian defenders within the compound and three officers and thirty-five other ranks filed out of a shelter behind a white flag.

The airfield at Pachino, just 2 miles further on, was found to be deserted and was captured without a shot being fired. The landing ground initially appeared to be of little use, for the Italians had ploughed up the runway to make it unserviceable. This eventually had, however, been catered for in the plan, for later that morning men from the British 15th Airfield Construction Group landed on Roger Beach along with some of their equipment and sped on to the airfield. To their great credit, by the early afternoon they had bulldozed a working landing strip capable of serving as an emergency field.

The other lead battalion of 1st Brigade met with a little more resistance when it had cleared the area of the beach. A few miles inland the Hastings and Prince Edward Regiment ran into opposition from a barracks to the north-east of the airfield. Fire from warships out in the bay soon silenced this position. The defenders then withdrew into Pachino and were dealt with by the lead companies of the 51st Highland Division who had landed to the east of the Canadians. A further gun battery to the north of the town was attacked by the Royal Canadian Regiment and it took a short fire-fight before the garrison of 130 Italians surrendered along with their four 6-inch guns.

The Canadian 2nd Brigade landed without opposition and throughout the day was able to push its three battalions inland in a planned arc, to seize all the objectives given it during the planning stage. The only counter-attack that the Canadian landings had to deal with was really aimed at the Special Service Brigade on the extreme left flank. During the afternoon a unit of sufficiently well-led Blackshirt Militia made a brave move against the lodgement. They attacked the commandos with mortar and anti-tank fire, threatening to drive a wedge between them and the Seaforth Highlanders of Canada of 2nd Brigade. Lacking any heavy weapons, the commandos were hard pressed to hold the Italians. A plea for help was picked up by the Saskatoon Light Infantry and a heavy mortar detachment brought its weapons to bear on the Blackshirts. The 4.2-inch mortars fired over 160 rounds into the Italian positions with devastating accuracy. Behind this barrage of mortar bombs the commandos closed in on their opponents. It was too much for the Blackshirts. The weight of the commando attack forced them into a hurried withdrawal, leaving their horse-drawn guns and much of their ammunition strewn around on the battlefield.

The Canadian reserve, the 3rd Brigade, began its landing at 1100 hrs then advanced inland between the other two brigades to reach Burgio by the evening. By the end of the day the division had established firm contact with 51st Division on its right and controlled a lodgement that stretched in a curve 4 miles deep. Casualties during the first day's fighting had been modest, just 7 men killed and 25 wounded in the three brigades. Brig Laycock's Special Service Brigade had fared comparatively worse having had 7 men killed and 19 wounded in its two battalions. Its task was now over, for Canadian 2nd Brigade took over the commando positions and the SS Brigade withdrew the next day into army reserve.

To the right of the Canadian Division were the landing beaches of the 51st (Highland) Division. During the planning stages, its commander, Maj-Gen Douglas Wimberley, had taken the unusual step of rejecting the best beach along his landing sector in Portopalo Bay for lesser beaches on either side. 'The beach was too obvious,' he reasoned, 'the enemy was sure to have guarded its understandable attractions with plenty of barbed wire underwater and mines in the sand.' He decided to land his assault formation, 154th Brigade, on the flanks of the bay.[4]

The initial assault was on a four-battalion front. The whole of 154th Brigade was to land on the western beach and 1st Gordon Highlanders of 153rd Brigade on the eastern side of the bay. The two groups would then act as pincers and advance in and around the defenders guarding Portopalo Bay. Once a beachhead had been won, the remaining two brigades of the division would land and advance to clear the town of Pachino and seize the Noto–Avola road and make contact with 50th

Division of XIII Corps. The Highlanders were then to move northwards towards Palazzolo and Vizzini.

The division was split for the move to Sicily. The infantry travelling in troopships were to be landed from LCAs sailed directly from ports in Africa. Those carried in LCTs and LCIs (landing craft tank and infantry) made the move in two stages, via Malta. On 7 July Montgomery visited these troops in Malta, calling on each unit in turn. The pattern of each visit was the same. The men would be lined up along three sides of a hollow square. Monty would call on them to break ranks and gather round. He then gave them a talk, not an address, speaking quite sincerely about how their unit was one of his best and went on to outline their part, and that of the whole army, in the coming battle. His interspaced his information with jokes and remarks and proved himself to be 'a fellow of infinite jest'.[5] The historian of the 7th Black Watch summed up the effect it had on the troops: 'Each man left the parade feeling that he had spoken personally to General Montgomery. As a result of this the morale was exceedingly high.'[6] This was Monty at his best: away from political intrigues, away from his quest for glory, he could be a leader of men again, one who understood their fears and worries and one who would look after their best interests.

Despite the inclement weather, ships carrying the division made the rendezvous and arrived at their lowering point 7 miles off the coast on time. Assault craft were loaded and the attacking troops of 154th Brigade made their run for shore, touching down at approximately zero hour around 0245 hrs. Ahead of them the ground had been plastered by rocket-firing landing craft and all known or suspected enemy defences had been pounded by naval shells. The deluge of fire demoralised the Italian defenders and they mostly melted away. Little or no resistance was met on the beaches. All of the battalions got ashore without mishap and began to spread out, capturing objectives almost at will. Desultory fire came at lead companies as they pushed out from the beachhead, none of which was organised and all was ineffective. The general impression was that the Highland Division walked ashore and pushed inland with impunity. Behind them the follow-up brigades and divisional HQ landed unmolested. Soon tanks, transport and self-propelled artillery were ashore and supplies were being unloaded by scores of Italian prisoners. Inland, Pachino was taken, contact was made with both 231st Brigade on the right and with XIII Corps to the north and a ridge 7 miles inland overlooking the lodgement had soon been secured.

On the right of the Highland Division, round the tip of the peninsula to the east of the town of Pachino, were the landing beaches of 231st Independent Brigade at Marzamemi. The brigade had spent almost all of the previous four years since the outbreak of war serving on the island of Malta. It comprised 1st Hampshires, 1st Dorsets and 2nd Devons, all regular battalions, and formed part of the garrison during the long siege during which the island was bombed almost daily by Axis aircraft. In April 1943 it was selected to land as part of 'Husky' and was shipped over to Egypt to undertake specialised training. Its roots, however, remained in Malta and it was henceforth known as the Malta Brigade, taking a white Maltese Cross on a scarlet shield as its badge.

Commanding the Malta Brigade was Brig Roy Urquhart who had taken over from Brig K. Smith less than two months before. Up until then he had been a staff officer (GSO1) at Wimberley's Highland Division headquarters. Smith had led the Malta Brigade since December 1941 but became a victim of Montgomery's campaign to relieve commanders of fighting formations who were either too old or were unknown to him. Monty continued to do this throughout the war, gradually making sure that all those who served in senior positions in his army were his men. Urquhart was a good choice, well respected by everyone and of proven ability. He later commanded 1st Airborne Division at Arnhem.

The Malta Brigade had been given the task of holding the right flank of the XXX Corps sector on the Pachino peninsula. It had been enlarged by the addition of an artillery regiment, anti-aircraft and anti-tank batteries, Royal Engineer field companies and a field ambulance, so as to be able to act independently, but came under the tactical command of 51st Division. Its objectives were to establish itself on the road running north from Pachino to Noto so as to link XXX and XIII Corps' landings.

At 2335 hrs on 9 July the troopships carrying the brigade, the *Strathnaver* and the *Otranto*, split away from the main Highland Division convoy and took station off the eastern side of the peninsula, protected by the destroyer HMS *Keren*. Helping them into position was the station submarine HMS *Unseen*, lying quietly in the dark water showing its beacon light out to sea to guide them. The water here was much more sheltered than was being experienced by the other transports of XXX Corps over to the west, but there was still a sufficiently heavy swell running to make transfer from the old liners to the assault landing craft difficult. The LCAs were loaded and released and struck out for shore behind the guiding lights of motor launches. Total surprise was gained and most of the small craft touched down at the right place at the right time. As with all night-time landings, some direction was lost by a few of the craft and some landed on the wrong beaches, but the majority landed as planned. Occasional fire from the enemy started to flash along the beaches, but this was quickly silenced by two Dutch gunboats, *Soemba* and *Flores*, which were supporting the landings. The beachhead was secured against almost minimal opposition.

Of course there was opposition from a few brave Italians who resisted the landings. Certain pillboxes refused to surrender and had to be stalked and rushed by troops armed with grenades and rifles. Dug-outs had to be cleared and machine-gun posts over-run. Casualties were suffered and men died on both sides. But, compared with what was to come later, these landings could be regarded as being against 'minimal opposition'.

At around 0400 hrs Very lights were fired to indicate that the beaches had been captured by the Hampshires and the Dorsets. The 2nd Devons could now go ashore. The battalion had been at sea in its tiny landing craft for almost five hours waiting for the signal. Most of its men were horribly seasick. Brig Urquhart took his brigade tactical HQ in at 0400 hrs and set it up alongside the beach in Marzamemi. As dawn broke, more and more troops arrived from the support arms: Sherman tanks of 46th Royal Tank Regiment and 3.7-inch howitzers of 165th Field Regiment RA landed over the open beaches.

The brigade's opponents were mostly from the Italian 206th Coastal Division, which held a front of almost 90 miles. The Italian division bore the responsibility for the defence of the whole of the sector of the landings made by XIII and XXX Corps, together with part of the American beaches near Scoglitti. It was stretched very thin on the ground but had the backing of a mobile group based at Rosolini, about 12 miles from the coast at the northern end of the Pachino Peninsula. Further inland were the better-trained troops of the *Napoli* Division.

Intelligence had suggested that, if the brigade was to experience a counter-attack, it would come from the Rosolini direction and it would probably arrive in the early afternoon. Intelligence was spot on for, just after midday, the Dorsets found themselves facing a number of old French R-35 tanks and infantry. The attack was expected and the Dorsets were prepared to meet it. The Italians had no chance. Lined up against them were powerful 17-pounder and 6-pounder anti-tank guns and Sherman tanks whose shells sliced through the thin armour of the Italian tanks with momentum to spare. The Italians pressed home the attack with some gallantry, but it was a pointless effort. The superior firepower available to the Dorsets stopped them in their tracks and scattered the survivors in all directions, some to surrender and some to flee back to the north. Few people in the area knew of the isolated tank battle so soon was it over. The brigade history notes that this was the only Italian counter-attack made against it during the whole campaign.[7]

Further north, some 20 miles along the coast, were the landing beaches of Lt-Gen Dempsey's XIII Corps where the 5th and 50th Divisions were to come ashore. The goal of the corps was to capture the main initial objectives of Eighth Army – Syracuse, Augusta and Catania. Maj-Gen Sidney Kirkman's 50th (Northumbrian) Division was to anchor the southern end of the corps with landings at Avola and then to link up with the XXX Corps lodgement. Once established, Dempsey would use the division to strengthen his drive northwards. The 5th Division would come ashore at Cassibile just north of the Northumbrian Division's beachhead, establish a secure lodgement and then strike northwards for the port of Syracuse, its path already opened by the landings of the 1st Airborne Division.

The 50th (Northumbrian) Division intended to carry out its assault with just one brigade, the 151st Brigade. Its commander was Brig R.H. Senior, who was later wounded leading his brigade in the D-Day invasion of Normandy on 6 June 1944. The division's attack was to be made in the dark with touch-down planned for 0245 hrs, two hours before dawn. This brigade was to seize the beaches and secure a lodgement to allow the reserve 69th Brigade to come ashore. Shortage of shipping had dictated that the division's third formation, 168th Brigade, could not land before D+3 (13 July) when it would be carried over in troopships and landed at the docks in Syracuse.

The sector of coast allocated to 50th Division was not ideal for assault landings. Much of the shoreline consisted of cliffs around 20 feet high, scalable in places, but impassable in others. The sea offshore was rocky, making navigation difficult. In the centre was the sizeable town of Avola with around 20,000 inhabitants.

There was one good beach to the right of the town over which vehicles could be landed, although there were no exits for wheeled vehicles. Opposite the town was a small landing place which serviced local fishing boats, but this was known to be fortified. Pillboxes and trenches guarded the top of the beach and a few mines were thought to be sown along the rear. Inland from the shore the ground was flat for about 2,000 yards then gradually rose until it reached a range of steep hills about 3 miles inland.

Brig Senior planned to land two battalions in the assault to clear the beaches and mop up enemy resistance along the waterfront. A third battalion would then land and move inland onto the higher ground over-looking the beach. The decision when to land the division's reserve brigade would depend on when and where Maj-Gen Kirkman wished to deploy it. Originally it was thought that it would move to the southern flank of the lodgement to anchor XIII Corps' landings.

The ships of the convoy carrying the Northumbrian Division reached their expected release positions just after midnight in the face of an offshore wind. In reality, instead of being 7 miles out from land, they were nearer 12. This lapse of navigation was not realised until daylight which meant that the landing craft had to endure almost double the expected run-in to the beaches. At 0100 hrs the first of the attack LCAs belonging to 151st Brigade were lowered and one by one the craft circled around their mother ship until the entire first assault wave had been disembarked. The task proved to be quite arduous, for the heavy swell made all boat work difficult. Confusion and lack of control began to set in which then dogged the brigade throughout the whole of its landings. Many craft became lost trying to form up in their correct flotillas; some failed to form up at all.

The passage to shore was made almost totally blind; the pitching craft and thick spray made it difficult for the naval crews to keep station and check bearings. The lead craft of the 6th Durham Light Infantry should have touched down at 0245 hrs, but the small boats were so scattered that it was no longer possible to land in a concentrated wave. They came ashore in ones and twos, dotted along the coast in the most unlikely places more than an hour late. The first company to land arrived 3,000 yards south of its beach almost outside the beachhead position. Undaunted, the men waded ashore and set about cleaning out the beach defences of the enemy. Once the company officers had located where their landfall was, they set off to the north to find the railway station at Avola. On their way they met up with a group of American parachutists and a company of the King's Own Yorkshire Light Infantry of 5th Division who should have landed some 6 miles to the north.

This type of chaos was repeated all along the coast. Another company landed 4,500 yards south of its beaches near the fishing village of Calabernardo. The naval officer leading the boats in told the troops that they were arriving at the marina in Avola. The company commander, thinking he was at Avola, turned left for his objectives and marched for over 4 miles before he realised he was lost, but not before accepting the surrender of every Italian post he encountered. By this time his objective was now almost 7 miles to the rear. The next company fared even worse, landing on the other side of Calabernardo. In fact the nearest that the assault troops of the 6th Durham Light Infantry got to their proper beach was the last company landing 30 minutes after the others. It made landfall a modest 2,500 yards south of its correct beach.

All of this wayward navigation should have spelled disaster. That it did not was a great credit to the calibre of the officers and the training the men had been given. Each of them set about their tasks and gradually reached and cleared their objectives in and around Avola. It did of course help that the resistance put up by the Italian 206th Coastal Division was neither sustained nor organised.

The landings to the south of the town, and the vigour with which the Durhams attacked Italian defences, loosened the slight hold that the weak enemy forces had on the area. Gun-firing warships, rocket ships, aerial bombing and now the arrival of determined infantry demonstrated the strength that the assaulting division had behind it. The contest was rather one-sided. In the main, the Italian defenders fired off a few shots and then departed. This did not mean that the Northumbrian Division could storm miles inland straight from the boats, for objectives had to be taken and consolidated, roads and railway lines had to be covered by anti-tank guns, houses had to be cleared, prisoners rounded up and the beachhead purged of any likely pockets of resistance and secured.

To the north-east of the town, the other assault battalion, the 9th Durham Light Infantry, experienced a similarly chaotic landing. Its lead companies arrived one and a half hours late, mostly to the south of their approved beaches, although the battalion second-in-command's group landed too far to the north. It seemed that no one could actually hit the correct beach – Jig Green – although it was the only large beach along that sector of coast. A short time later, when the battalion commander, Lt-Col Lidwell, was coming ashore with his headquarters, he asked the naval officer in charge of the flotilla to set him down in the middle of Jig Green Beach. In reality the Navy landed his party in broad daylight 3,000 yards to the north on How Amber Beach, the left-hand beach of 5th Division. Unfazed, the colonel grouped his men and began the 3-mile march southwards to Avola town.

The navigation of the newly arriving vessels continued to be wayward even after the sun was well up and a beautiful July morning had begun. Tanks, self-propelled guns, carriers and wheeled vehicles now began to disembark, many of them in the wrong places. The divisional history explains that many of the arriving craft had little idea of their where-abouts and that the officers in the landing craft had to take a hand in the navigation, claiming that, if they had not done so, many of the boats would have beached even further from their correct places. 'It was natural,' the history explains, 'once daylight had come, that experienced Army officers who had studied maps, aeroplane photographs and models should be better able to recognise landmarks on the shore than young and often inexperienced naval officers.'[8]

The third battalion of 151st Brigade, 8th Durham Light Infantry, landed two and a half hours after the initial assaults. It had better luck in finding its correct beach. By that time, Avola had been cleared and the brigade was able to take all of its objectives. Troublesome shell fire continued to fall on Jig Green Beach and the offending battery was located in 5th Division's area, to the north of its landings. A message was sent asking for naval support and the battery was eliminated around 0700 hrs.

With the beachhead secured and exits bulldozed from the landing sites, Maj-Gen Kirkman gave orders for 69th Brigade to start its landings on Jig Green and began to make preparations to take his tactical headquarters ashore. They both began landing at 0820 hrs and Kirkman was able to see for himself that, despite the earlier chaos and upset timings, his division had the lodgement secured. By that time most of No. 34 Beach Brick (the formation responsible for controlling beach operations) had landed and taken over the close defence of the beaches, so he was now able to position his two brigades to anchor the south and west of his landings.

At 0900 hrs Kirkman contacted the corps commander to report the success of his landings.

A few miles to the north of 50th Division were the three landing beaches of Maj-Gen Berney-Ficklin's 5th Division. The division was to earn the title of the most travelled division in the whole of the British Army. It was comprised mainly of regular battalions and had begun its active service in France in 1939 as part of the British Expeditionary Force. During this period its 15th Brigade was sent on the abortive expedition to Norway. After the fall of France the division was withdrawn through Dunkirk. A period of reorganisation in England followed before 5th Division was sent overseas to India, although its 13th and 17th Brigades were diverted en route to become part of the occupation forces in Madagascar. They rejoined the division later in India, but, after sweltering journeys by road and railway and jungle training in torrential monsoons, it was decided to move the division back across India to Iraq and Persia. As part of Middle East Command it was then trained in both amphibious and mountain warfare and in combined operations. A little later it was sent to Syria. From there the division was brought down to Egypt for specialised training in order to take part in the invasion of Sicily. After the Sicilian campaign, the division fought in the Italian campaign, landed as part of the Anzio forces and then was finally recalled to north-west Europe to finish the war in Germany.

The 5th Division planned to attack with two brigades, each with two battalions in the assault. Once having established a beachhead, one of the brigades, 17th Brigade, was to swing to the right and capture Syracuse, its path along Highway 115 and over the Ponte Grande having been opened up by the glider landings of 1st Airlanding Brigade.

The first flotilla of landing craft bringing in the assault battalions of 17th Brigade landed well to the south of its beach, but was roughly on time. The following attack waves found the right beach but were up to an hour late. It was not until 0500 hrs that the beach was declared completely cleared of the enemy. By this time the lead battalions had moved off to capture Cassibile. The brigade's third battalion, 2nd Royal Scots Fusiliers, moved to the right and started out along Highway 115 bound for Syracuse.

The 15th Brigade landed its two assault battalions far from their correct beaches and nearly an hour late. The follow-up waves compounded these delays and it was not until 1000 hrs that the beaches could be given over to the build-up. Shells from an uncaptured enemy gun battery continued to pepper the shore until it was eliminated by gunfire from the destroyer HMS *Eskimo*. Once off the beaches, the 15th Brigade moved out to the left to anchor the lodgement and to make contact with 50th Division's landings to the south.

At 1330 hrs, Lt-Gen Dempsey visited Maj-Gen Kirkman at his headquarters to give 50th Division's commander new instructions and news of what was happening elsewhere. Kirkman first outlined his progress, explaining that preliminary tasks were almost complete and that his troops were out of touch with the enemy except in the area around Noto. Dempsey now instructed Kirkman that he wanted his 69th Brigade to move northwards and take over 5th Division's area south of Floridia in order to allow 17th Brigade to concentrate on its advance on Syracuse. The 50th Division would also take under command the 15th Brigade, which was holding the western side of 5th Division's beachhead, so that Maj-Gen Berney-Ficklin could focus on the moves northwards. Monty was adamant that Syracuse had to be captured that day.

Earlier on, the capture of Cassibile by the 2nd Northamptons had been achieved by 1000 hrs and the 6th Seaforth Highlanders took the small village of Casa Nuove just to the east of the town. Further to the right, 2nd Royal Scots Fusiliers struck out on its 8-mile march on Syracuse to relieve the airlanding brigade on the Ponte Grande. In the absence of much of the brigade's own transport, the enterprising fusiliers took advantage of any mobile contraptions they could find. They pressed local carts, mules, horses and donkeys into service to help carry the loads and were lucky enough to find a few Italian military vehicles. They searched in vain for civilian cars, but all had disappeared from the town. It was a tough march began at a swift pace, the officers urging the men on through the heat, the flies and the all-pervading white dust to reach the airborne troops.

The maps and air reconnaissance photographs studied before the invasion had pinpointed the location of most enemy posts, but the speed of the journey soon slowed to a crawl as each likely position was stalked and eliminated. The battalion knew it was advancing to join with the airborne troops at the bridge, but it did think that it was linking up with a whole brigade of glider-borne infantry, not racing to relieve a besieged outpost less than one company strong. Resistance to the move came mainly from sniper fire; tiresome as it was, it did not constitute organised opposition. Enemy interference was altogether slight. The Italian troops who manned the posts fired off a few shots then quietly slipped away.

Progress actually came to complete halt for a short while when a well dug-in machine-gun post proved difficult to overcome. A call went out for armoured support and a Sherman tank trundled up and blew the offending enemy position apart with two well-aimed shots. The advance continued its noisy way, with the troops in the lead firing at any likely Italian positions and being sniped at in return. The sounds of battle attracted the attention of isolated and lost airborne troops who had taken cover during the night to await the arrival of the seaborne landings. They now attached themselves to the fusiliers and joined in on the advance to the Ponte Grande. Lt Withers on the Ponte Grande had expected these land troops to reach him some time after 0730 hrs, but by late morning they were still miles from the bridge.

Up ahead at the vital bridge things were becoming desperate. The glider troops holding the crossing site had been attacked at around 0800 hrs by a group of Italians supported by four armoured cars. Enemy mortar and machine-gun fire kept the glidermen pinned down while the heavier weapons of the armoured cars tried to silence the British outposts along the canal bank. Each of these exposed positions was wiped out in turn. All morning long the airborne troops were subjected to attacks. Then a field gun started to shell the bridge and even more men succumbed to bullets and shrapnel. The guardhouse full of prisoners received a direct hit from the gun, wreaking dreadful carnage among those Italians inside. By the early afternoon, with still no relief by the 5th Division, all of the small outlying posts defending the bridge had been eliminated and the enemy had infiltrated into the glidermen's main position. Withdrawal was now the only option. One by one the British troops slipped away, each man having to look out for himself among the fierce fire which raked the bridge. Gradually the survivors were forced down the canal bank towards the sea. Here those few who had survived the onslaught uninjured, just 15 men in total, were all cornered and overwhelmed just as the sounds of the Scots Fusiliers' advance could be heard. Relief had been just 15 minutes away.

When the 2nd Royal Scots Fusiliers arrived at the bridge they found that the enemy had taken possession. The Scotsmen came storming up the road in their carriers with Bren gun fire raking the ground in front of them.

A short way behind were the Sherman tanks of the County of London Yeomanry. The Italians trying to re-establish themselves on the Ponte Grande were hit by a hail of fire from the tanks and carriers. Unable to reply with anything like the firepower required to stop the attack, they withdrew as quickly as they could up the highway towards Syracuse. Fortunately the Italians had not had time to reinstall demolition charges and the bridge was once again captured intact.

Back in his temporary headquarters in Malta, Gen Montgomery had been studying the reports coming in from Sicily. By late afternoon he could see that Eighth Army's landings were successful and that opposition seemed to be slight. Very anxious that Syracuse should be taken that day, he radioed his corps commanders to keep up the momentum. Leese was urged to get his XXX Corps moving more quickly to Noto and Avola to secure Dempsey's flanks so that XIII Corps could concentrate on its drive northwards. Monty reassured Dempsey that air reconnaissance had not shown up any movement of large bodies of troops against him. 'Operate with great energy towards Syracuse,' he urged.[9]

The advance up Highway 115 was now taken over by the 2nd Northamptons while the Scots Fusiliers established themselves around the vital river crossing until other troops could be brought forward to continue the task. Just short of the outskirts of Syracuse the Northamptons came upon a large party of Italians supported by a few pieces of artillery, forming up ready to launch a counter-attack. The arrival of the Northamptons took them by surprise and they tamely surrendered to the advancing British troops. Among the prisoners held by this group of Italians were survivors from Lt Withers's party from the bridge.

Syracuse was reached and entered by the lead battalion in the early evening, with the remainder of the brigade joining it a short time later. The process of clearing the town and port began immediately. Rather surprisingly, although Syracuse had been severely bombed during the preceding weeks, there was comparatively little damage done to the port installations. News was quickly relayed back to Dempsey and then on to Eighth Army's commander. Syracuse had been taken on the first day of the invasion, just as Montgomery said it would be.

Reflecting that night on how the battle was progressing, Montgomery felt assured of his army's performance. He believed that, if Dempsey could quickly take Augusta and then Catania and Leese drive inland to disrupt the road network crossing the island, then the campaign would become a simple matter. For his drive northwards the Royal Navy was protecting his right flank. Its ships would keep pace with the land battle and bring their guns to bear on pockets of resistance. The extreme left flank was being contained by the Americans. It seemed to Monty on the night of the 10th that all was going very well indeed.

There were a few men who knew that things had not gone well at all that day. The survivors of the Glider Pilot Regiment and 1st Airlanding Brigade believed that the day had been a complete shambles. Hopkinson's operation had been a fiasco. Already they were looking for someone or something to blame. The actual height that the gliders were released played a big part in the failure. Of the 137 gliders that had set out, only 54 had actually landed in Sicily and all but one of these had been released at 3,000 feet or above to allow them to glide to land against a stiff head-wind. Of these, 25 had been released within a mile of the shore and three others had been given an extra 1,000 feet of height. Only 9 of these gliders had been released at close to the planned altitude and distance from their correct landing zones. Most of the other gliders, those that had crashed into the sea or into the cliffs along the shore, were released at much too low an altitude or too far from land.[10]

Losses by proportion had been horrendous. Casualties were reckoned to be 605 officers and men out of the 1,200 that took part, 326 of whom were missing presumed drowned. Just 5 per cent of all the airborne troops who took part in Operation 'Ladbroke' had actually gone into action at the Ponte Grande.[11] Hopkinson blamed the pilots of US 51st Wing for not flying their missions with due regard to the objectives of the operation. Cowardice was mentioned. Others blamed Chatterton for not raising the glider release heights to compensate for the rise in the offshore wind speed. Chatterton blamed the rushed nature of the planning and the inadequacy of the preparations. Those on the bridge question why it took so long for 5th Division to advance 8 miles against negligible opposition. In point of fact, everyone blamed everyone else. Monty said in public that the capture of the bridge shortened the campaign by seven days. In private, it was appreciated that little good came of the operation, save perhaps for experience that could be put to better use in further glider-borne attacks some time in the future.

CHAPTER 8

Invasion:
The American Landings

While Montgomery's seaborne troops were storming ashore in the east, Patton's men were well into their own series of landings. Coming ashore on the extreme left of US Seventh Army's sector through heavy seas was Maj Gen Lucian Truscott's US 3rd Division. It was to land on Joss Sector astride the small port of Licata. Truscott's men had the task of anchoring the whole of the left flank of the invasion. Their main assaults would be over Blue and Yellow Beaches to the east of the town. These were broad deep beaches, excellent for landing troops. The planners were tempted to land the whole of the division over these beaches in one lift, but there was a problem. Between the beaches and the town the River Salso meandered to meet the sea and it was feared that the enemy might defend this river line and deny the early capture of the port. It was therefore decided that two regimental combat teams would land on Blue and Yellow Beaches – 30th RCT and 15th RCT – and a third, 7th RCT, would land west of Licata on a less favourable part of the shore, Red Beach. In the centre, the 3rd Ranger Battalion and the 2nd Battalion, 15th Regiment, would land on two rock-bound coves labelled Green Beach to clear a fort and coastal battery. By using all of the beaches allocated to his division, Truscott planned to envelop Licata in a wide pincer movement. Waiting for the Americans to

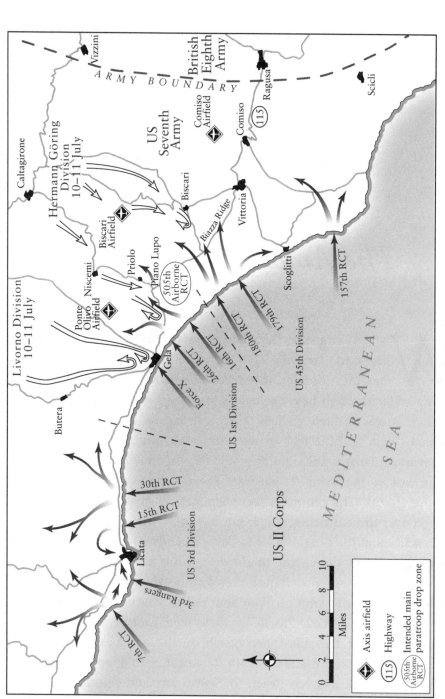

US Seventh Army Landings

come ashore was Gen Ottorino Schreiber's Italian 207th Coastal Division and a few scattered mobile units.

Truscott arrived at the lowering position on board the US Navy cruiser *Biscayne* at 0135 hrs. All around the ship were the flotillas of small craft assembling for the assault, or at least Truscott hoped they were for he could see little through the darkness and radio silence was complete. At 0200 hrs, just as the LCAs were leaving their mother ships, four search-lights swept the sea and came to a halt on the large warship. For several long minutes the *Biscayne* sat in the blinding glare waiting to see if the Italian coastal batteries to the west of Licata would open fire. Then, one by one, the lights went out and all went quiet.

Some 20 miles to the west a small crisis was developing in the sea off Porto Empedocle. The two destroyers *Swanson* and *Roe*, assigned to give naval gunfire support to the landings of the 7th RCT on Red Beach, had collided. Both were now lying still in the water as the invasion fleet gathered off Licata. The Navy responded to the situation by later sending the destroyer *Buck*, previously engaged serving as escort to part of the main convoy, across to take over bombardment duties off Red Beach. The *Buck* was later joined by the cruiser *Brooklyn*.[1]

Things remained quiet on the shore as the attack craft commenced their run-in and firing only began when the assault craft neared the beaches. Out at sea naval ships began pounding known enemy positions with their heavy calibre weapons. The two Italian railway guns lined up on their carriages along the mole at Licata were destroyed by direct hits before they could join in the fray. Further inland an armoured train mounting four 76mm guns was also knocked out by naval fire.

On paper the Italian defences around Licata were impressive, but none of them lived up to expectations. Most of the 3rd Division's assault craft came ashore just as they had done in training, with little Italian opposition to make the event much more than an exercise. There were exceptions and some craft did have to brave a considerable amount of machine-gun fire on certain sections of the shore line. The first skirmish line that most of the attacking troops met was along the top of the beaches where pillboxes and obstacles gave the enemy some feeling of protection. These were quickly overcome and once the Americans were off the seafront and moving inland, opposition faded away. Developing the landings now became a process of logistics and re-supply.

At 0440 hrs, Truscott's command signalled Patton that his battalions were all ashore, although it had not had actual confirmation that the assault on Green Beach had been successfully landed. Just to make sure that all was well, a small Piper Cub spotter plane was flown off a small runway that had been built on a tank landing ship to find out. The pilot soon radioed back that troops could be seen climbing the hill behind the shore and were approaching the fort overlooking Licata. A short while later another spotter plane was flown off. Once in the air, these aircraft could not land back on the ship so for the next two hours the brave pilots made themselves useful by reporting the progress and location of the troops advancing inland and by acting as spotter aircraft for the guns of the warships.

Soon after dawn had broken, the *Biscayne* got under way and moved in closer to the shore so that the beaches could be clearly seen. Truscott was cheered by the sight of quiet beaches with small ships and landing craft discharging their cargoes. Within just a few hours the conflict had moved several miles inland. Some long-range artillery fire sent plumes of water skywards as the enemy began to interfere with the landings from a distance. This slightly delayed the disembarkation of a flotilla of LCTs laden with tanks and guns, but Truscott quickly got the Navy to send the craft in regardless and told his men to shield the beach with smoke.

The rest of the day went as planned. Maj Gen Truscott was extremely pleased with his division, as he was later to recount:

> Careful planning and preparation, rigorous and thorough training, determination and speed of execution, had paid dividends in success. In spite of searchlights and all the activity along the coast, our assault battalions had landed before they were discovered and had quickly cleared the beaches of all resistance. In little more than an hour, ten infantry battalions including the Rangers with supporting tanks had landed and were about their business. In seven hours, these ten battalions with their supporting tanks and artillery had seized their first objectives.[2]

Just after midday the town was declared secure, the airfield occupied and the port was beginning to be organised to receive small vessels. By early afternoon the whole of the coastal area had been cleared and 2,000 Italian prisoners were being assembled ready to be shipped back to POW camps in Africa. Small Italian counter-attacks were mounted against the advancing American infantry from time to time, but none was pressed home with any vigour. By the end of the day, at a cost of no more than a hundred casualties, US 3rd Division had achieved all that was asked of it. The consensus among the men was that it was easier fighting the battle than training for it.

Over to the right of 3rd Division's landing beaches, just 10 miles to the east of Blue Beach, was the landing sector of Maj Gen Allen's US 1st Division, around the town of Gela. The division faced the strongest grouping of enemy forces on the island. Guarding the landing beaches was the Italian 18th Coastal Brigade. Just inland, deployed to defend the Ponte Olivo and Biscari airfields, were Italian Mobile Groups E and H. Twenty miles further inland was the bulk of the *Hermann Göring* Division, with the Italian *Livorno* Division on its right, poised to intervene against Gela if required. To counter these, Maj Gen Allen was landing only two of his three regimental combat teams – the 18th RCT was being held at sea as US Seventh Army's floating reserve – and a grouping called Force X, which contained two Ranger battalions (the 1st and 4th Ranger Battalions) and a battalion of combat engineers (1st Battalion, 39th Combat Engineer Regiment). The division's reserve was Col Gavin's parachute task force, which was supposed to have landed in front of 1st Division during the previous night.

Gen Allen planned to land Force X directly on the beach fronting Gela and his two regimental combat teams on the 3-mile-long beach just to the east of the town, with 26th RCT on the left and 16th RCT on the right. Col John Bowen's 26th RCT was to send one of its battalions to assist the Rangers in the capture of Gela while the remainder of his formation pushed inland to occupy the high ground 2 miles to the north. Col George Taylor's 16th RCT would land on the extreme right of the beach and move inland to Piano Lupo to join up with the bulk of Gavin's paratroopers and then advance on Niscemi.

At just before midnight Admiral Hall began bringing his Naval Task Force 81 to its unloading station, ready for the final preparations to land. Over the next hour the long columns of transports, LCTs and LCIs arrived to drop anchor on a gradually easing sea which moderated from white-topped waves into a long slow swell as the wind dropped. Ahead of the naval armada, the coastline around Gela showed up in silhouette against fires started by the pre-invasion bombing programme and a great bonfire lit near Piano Lupo by Gavin's recently arrived paratroopers from 82nd Airborne Division.

Force X was the first to go in with the two Ranger battalions leading the landings. Italian searchlights had picked out the invasion fleet and coastal artillery began opening up on the assault craft heading for shore. The lights were quickly knocked out by salvos of 5-inch gun fire from the destroyer *Shubrick*. This counter-fire was quickly taken up by the cruiser *Savannah* and all known enemy positions bombarded until the assault waves hit the beaches.

The Rangers touched down at 0335 hrs, incurring a number of casualties from machine-gun fire during the run-in. Once on the beach, more men were wounded and killed by this fire and by rifle fire emanating from the pillboxes lining the shore. Undeterred, Col William O. Darby led his men through the Italian defences and into the town. Two companies moved to the right and attacked a known battery of three 77mm guns on the western edge of the built-up area. When the Rangers over-ran the gun site they found that none of the weapons had been fired, even though an ample supply of ammunition lay stacked around the position.

The remainder of Darby's force moved through the town, clearing it of any opposition and organising a defensive perimeter around its northern and eastern sides. By 0800 hrs the whole of Gela had been captured and three companies of 4.2-inch mortars were in position along the perimeter ready to fire on any enemy counter-attacks. To the right, the 26th RCT had come ashore against negligible opposition and was moving inland to cut off Gela from the rear.[3]

On its right, 16th RCT had had a more difficult landing, suffering from Italian small arms and machine-gun fire both during its landing and for a long period afterwards. This only began to peter out some hours after touchdown when naval gunfire was brought to bear on the persistent Italian positions. From then on progress was rapid and Col Taylor sent his two lead battalions on to Piano Lupo. By the end of the morning contact had been made with a few men of the 1st Battalion, 505th Parachute Infantry, but their sparse numbers were well below the strength that was expected. By this time Allen's division was well on the way to securing its first day's objectives. Opposition had been much less than expected and things were looking good for the Big Red One.

Ten miles across to the east, Maj Gen Middleton's US 45th Division was coming ashore over beaches situated either side of the tiny fishing village of Scoglitti. The division's landing sector stretched for 15 miles along a length of sandy beaches and rocky shore, punctuated here and there by low stone cliffs. Scoglitti was the only harbour along this length of the Gulf of Gela, just big enough to land a few fishing boats. Inland the terrain was almost completely flat, with the coastal plain stretching several miles before it gradually rose into the foothills of the interior. Eight miles north-east of the western end of the division's sector was the airfield at Biscari; 10 miles from the eastern part was the Comiso landing ground.

Middleton's division would land over two separate beaches some 8 miles apart, with Col Forrest E. Cookson's 180th RCT assaulting on the extreme left and Col Robert B. Hutchins's 179th RCT to its right over beaches a little further to the east. The 180th RCT was to link up with 1st Division's landings to the west and to strike inland for Biscari. The 179th RCT's mission was to take the town of Vittoria astride Highway 115 and then the Comiso airfield, while one if its battalions turned south to capture Scoglitti.

The third of Middleton's formations, Col Charles Ankcorn's 157th RCT, was to land to the south-east of Scoglitti over two small beaches less than half a mile wide and with a depth of only 20 yards. Ankcorn's force would be separated from the rest of the division by a gap of over 9 miles. Fifteen miles to the east were the Canadian landing beaches of British Eighth Army. Ankcorn's isolation forced his combat team to act as almost an independent task force. The colonel's main objective was to link up with Col Hutchins's 179th RCT to anchor the eastern flank of Seventh Army's landings and to attack the Comiso airfield.

Enemy forces facing the 45th Division were from the Italian 18th Coastal Brigade, the right-hand elements of the 206th Coastal Division and from the nearby Mobile Group G located near the Comiso airfield, none of which posed a serious threat. The *Hermann Göring* Division was within striking distance to the north-east, but it was thought that its attention would more likely be directed against the landings at Gela. Providing that the 179th and 157th RCTs moved fast enough on Comiso and Highway 115, neither of the regiments had much to fear from an enemy counter-attack.

The assault boats of the 45th Division suffered more from missing their assigned beaches than from enemy opposition. Delays in loading and a subsequent loss of direction threatened to disrupt timetables, but the lack of any meaningful defensive fire allowed all of these mistakes to be rectified in good order. Some 300 troops from 180th RCT actually veered so far to the left that they landed on 1st Division's beaches. On 157th RCT's sector, so far to the right were its craft that none of its assault troops actually landed on the left-hand of the regiment's two beaches. Some boats never made it to either landing point, but were swept through 10-foot high surf onto a shoreline covered with rocks; one boat completely capsized and drowned twenty-seven of its passengers.[4]

From these minor mishaps the division's baptism into combat proceeded at a measured pace, allowing it to organise itself gradually into a fighting unit. Its passage inland was assisted by scattered groups of paratroopers of Col Gavin's force. Airborne stragglers had gathered together into small groups and set about reducing Italian strongpoints and seizing important road junctions and bridges, holding them until relieved by the advancing seaborne troops. By mid-morning troops were pushing inland everywhere against negligible opposition, over-running isolated objectives to form an established beachhead.

The landings had been easier and less costly than anyone had imagined. Patton's Seventh Army had got ashore against only minor resistance and was unloading tanks and artillery along the length of its lodgement. Supply dumps were being assembled, follow-up troops landed and more and more transport was entering the beachhead. Squadrons of friendly fighters patrolled the sky overhead to prevent enemy aircraft from interfering with the build-up, although the Luftwaffe did mount a few swift raids and was able to sink the destroyer *Maddox* and a minesweeper, but these raids caused few real problems with the landings. It now remained for unit commanders to earn their pay and keep the momentum of the initial assault going. There must be no let up; everyone was told to push ahead.

When Guzzoni was convinced that the invasion had actually started, he attached the *Livorno* and *Hermann Göring* Divisions to Italian XVI Corps and gave orders for these forces to counter-attack immediately, before the Americans had time to consolidate their lodgement. He also told the commander of the 15th Panzergrenadier Division to bring his formation eastwards to the centre of the island. Guzzoni decided that the main danger lay with the beachhead at Gela. Gen Conrath was ordered to attack the Gela landings from the north-east with his *Hermann Göring* Division while at the same time Gen Domenico Chirieleison's *Livorno* Division attacked from the north-west.

Guzzoni intended to launch a coordinated attack against the Gela landings, but communication among his formations had been disrupted by Allied bombing and by scattered American paratroopers during the night. As a consequence many units failed to receive orders from corps HQ and decided to act on their own initiative. Conrath himself never actually received the instruction to attack from Guzzoni and did not know that his division had been placed under Italian XVI Corps' command. When he heard of the landings he acted as he had said he would to Kesselring; he drove his formation southwards against the enemy. The result of all this was that instead of a massed harmonised drive against the Americans at Gela, this first day of the landings was countered by a series of uncoordinated attacks by various individual units scattered along the centre of the American lodgement.

Many of these attacks were supported by tanks and lorried infantry. Those against Gela itself by the *Livorno* Division managed to penetrate right into the town before they were stopped and repulsed by Darby's Rangers, backed up by fire from captured Italian coastal guns and warships at sea. Just after noon elements of the 26th Infantry Regiment, who had landed on nearby beaches, swung to the left to help the Rangers consolidate their position. The Italians withdrew with great losses. Another column of Italians was blocked for a while by a group of paratroops at Priolo just north of the vital crossroads at Piano Lupo. A fierce battle broke out later in the day around these two locations when the Axis attack was strengthened by the arrival of German units from the *Hermann Göring* Division. The position was later stabilised with the support of troops from 16th Infantry Regiment advancing up from the beaches. On the right, two columns of the *Hermann Göring* Division advanced through Biscari but were stopped by men of Middleton's 45th Division, their way blocked by the regimental combat teams of the 180th and 179th Infantry. Warships joined in with their large-calibre weapons to give support to the infantry, blasting tanks apart and scattering the accompanying panzergrenadiers. The volume of fire was such that the Germans were forced to withdraw.

None of these Axis attacks was sufficiently well organised or coordinated to counter the American build-up. For both of the Axis divisions it was their first taste of battle. Conrath was not best pleased with the performance of his division and Kesselring was not impressed by Conrath's handling of the attack. The Americans, however, were well satisfied that they had seen off two determined counter-attacks against their beachhead. Confidence was high, for each hour brought more and more men, equipment and tanks into the lodgement. The next time the enemy came at them they would have even more strength with which to resist them.

Patton knew that he needed more tanks ashore to counter these enemy moves and ordered Gen Gaffey to land his 2nd Armored Division over 1st Division's beaches just as soon as he could. This was easier said than done for several of these beaches were under long-range artillery fire and a number of anti-tank mines had been found on two of them. Patton's other major problem was the failure of the airborne landings to provide him with an extra infantry regiment inland. The arrival of enemy tanks against the beachhead now led Patton to rethink his original proposal of bringing in the second of the reinforcing airborne drops that night. He decided to postpone its arrival until the following evening.

Earlier that day, at his headquarters in southern France, Gen Kurt Student, the father of German airborne forces, heard of the Allied landings in Sicily. As commander of OKW's mobile reserve, the XI Airborne Corps, he alerted Generalmajor (GenMaj) Richard Heidrich to have his 1st Parachute Division to be ready for immediate deployment from its base in the south of France. Student contacted Kesselring and suggested that the spearhead of Heidrich's division could be parachuted into the area of the landings at fairly short notice to engage the Allies when they were most vulnerable. The idea was considered but was quickly rejected as being too risky. Instead Student was told to move the advance units of 1st Parachute Division to Italy by air and have it ready for immediate action.

The speed with which the Germans reacted with regard to deploying their mobile reserve and by moving it by air, was a measure of Hitler's determination not to give the Allies an easy time in Sicily. No one really thought the island could be held if a lodgement in force was obtained by the Allies, but Hitler was determined to try to see if Sicily really was untenable as expected, or if it could be held if he put some of his best troops onto the island. The 1st Parachute Division would help him find out.

CHAPTER 9

The Second Day – 11 July

The fall of Syracuse on D-Day was a great boost for Montgomery. Once the port had been captured and the last elements of resistance had been cleared by 5th Division from the Italian barracks in the north of the town, naval experts were shipped into the docks to get the port working. The local citizens gave the British a 'riotous' welcome according to the 5th Division's history, but this reception quickly became less affable when they learned that the conquering troops did not bring with them vast amounts of food.[1]

Maj-Gen Berney-Ficklin's division was not left to savour this victory for long, for Dempsey urged the general to continue his advance northwards to the next objective, Augusta. Early the next day Berney-Ficklin once again put 17th Brigade into the lead and sent it northwards up the main coastal road. Main road was rather a grand title for what was in effect a rather narrow, winding thoroughfare with stone walls on either side. Halfway along this highway the route passed through a thick wood by a small town called Priolo. It was here on that sunny Sunday morning that 5th Division encountered a more spirited resistance to its advance. Thus far most of the action had been against less than enthusiastic Italian troops, but at Priolo the lead battalion of the brigade, the 2nd Northamptons, met somebody quite different.

Oberst Schmalz had moved part of his battlegroup of the *Hermann Göring* Division across to bar British progress northwards. The disintegration of the Italian 206th Coastal Division and the poor showing put up by the *Napoli* Division had forced Schmalz to push his battlegroup forward to contact with the British. The 2nd Northamptons were now to feel just how good German troops could be. A few well placed machine-gun posts manned by determined Luftwaffe troops brought the advance to a halt. The Sherman tanks of the County of London Yeomanry supporting the move came forward but were unable to deploy off the narrow high-banked road to help and the division's field guns were still well to the rear. Then an 88mm gun opened up, firing over open sights from a concealed position. Three of the stalled tanks were hit and the rest of the column withdrew.

Montgomery's push to the north towards Augusta and Catania had, for the moment, come to an abrupt halt. The German position was well established and difficult to move without applying a much stronger force. Brig Waldon Tarleton came up to see what was holding up his formation and agreed that a full brigade plan would have to be evolved for an over-whelming attack to be made against the Germans. This meant bringing forward the remainder of the brigade and the supporting artillery. For the rest of the day, and through the night, a scheme was formulated which was to be put into effect at first light on the 12th. It involved a full fire-plan by the whole divisional artillery, preceded by an attack by dive-bombers. For the remainder of the day 5th Division, and the main attack towards Catania, was at a standstill.

At first light on day two of the invasion, Gen Bradley awoke on board Admiral Kirk's flagship eager to get ashore before the next inevitable Axis counter-attack against his corps. He landed from a small landing craft on a beach strewn with the debris of the previous day's assault by 45th Division. From there the corps commander hitched a lift on a passing DUKW and headed for his first command post located inside the local *carabinieri* in Scoglitti.

At Bradley's corps HQ there was bad news; the DUKW kitted out with radio equipment to act as a communications centre had not arrived. A signal lieutenant was attempting to remedy matters by trying to breathe life into a set that had been salvaged from the beach inside a radio jeep, but was having to scrounge around the town to find a soldering iron with which to make the repairs. Bradley was anxious to get in touch with Maj Gen Allen and his 1st Division, for the sound of battle was audible away to the west. He was convinced that the expected enemy counter-attack was under way. He therefore decided that, rather than wait until radio contact was made with Allen, he would go and see what was happening for himself.

What was happening was that the *Hermann Göring* Division was on the move again, southwards against the Americans. The previous evening Guzzoni still did not have a clear understanding of the situation along the coast. He knew that the British and Canadians had established beachheads south of Syracuse, but did not know that Montgomery's forces had captured Syracuse. He believed that the *Napoli* Division and the *Schmalz* Group were containing these landings and he now ordered those formations to push Eighth Army back into the sea. He also ordered the *Livorno* and *Hermann Göring* Divisions to coordinate another attack against the American centre and the 207th Coastal Division to reorganise and strike against the landings at Licata.

This time Gen Conrath was going to attack the Americans in three columns from the north-east while the *Livorno* did likewise from the north-west, again in three columns. The Italians were once more directed on Gela, while the Germans were aiming to break through to the coast to the east of the town, then move down the seafront to roll up the American landings. Two of Conrath's columns would attack south from Niscemi, the other would drive south along the eastward bank of the River Acate from Biscari. The attacks started just after 0615 hrs and were supported by attacks by German and Italian aircraft against the beaches and naval vessels lying offshore. All of the German columns and two of the Italian met American troops already advancing inland in an effort to expand their lodgement. Stiff fighting began almost immediately and spread into the mid-morning.

Gen Bradley found Maj Gen Allen at his improvised command post near the beach, some 4 or 5 miles east of Gela. Allen was tired and dishevelled from a night of having to deal with the increasingly alarming reports of Axis forces pressing against his beachhead. At 0640 hrs that morning, the division's assistant commander, Brig Gen Theodore Roosevelt, gave news that the 26th Regiment was being attacked by tanks. Few anti-tank guns had been landed and the infantry were having to deal with this armour with whatever was to hand. This meant using hand-held bazookas against thick armour. Sections of the regiment had been over-run and others were engaged in serious fighting. Help was at hand to a certain extent from the fire of warships out to sea, but it was difficult to try to cover every part of the line. The corps commander was disturbed by the situation. 'Do you have it in hand,' he asked the divisional commander. 'I think so,' replied the exhausted Allen.[2]

Gen Montgomery arrived in Sicily that morning aboard the destroyer HMS *Antwerp* at around 0700 hrs. He came ashore in XXX Corps' sector near Pachino into the beachhead won on Amber Beach by 51st (Highland) Division. With him was Lord Louis Mountbatten, head of British Combined Operations. Montgomery was greeted with the news that the whole of the Pachino peninsula had been captured by Leese's corps, together with a working airstrip.

Maj-Gen Wimberley was there to meet the party as they arrived in their naval launch. Monty was elated by the latest situation report which confirmed that the port of Syracuse had been captured intact, completely undamaged and with all of its quayside facilities still working. The news was indeed welcome, for all previous ports captured by Eighth Army from Axis forces had been totally wrecked. The army commander was now impatient to drive to Syracuse to see matters for himself and to meet with Lt-Gen Dempsey and his XIII Corps. The problem was that there was little transport ashore to take him there. His tactical HQ, which should have been loaded in advance ready to be landed within 24 hours of the assault, had not yet been discharged; its vehicles and caravans were still being unloaded and were not completely ashore and ready for use until two days later. Monty was not best pleased. Maj-Gen Wimberley stepped in and offered Montgomery the use of his personal DUKW for his tour.

Wimberley sat with Monty at the front of the vehicle as it drove round the Highland Division's area and showed the army commander the progress being made. Well satisfied, Montgomery and his group dropped the Scotsman at his HQ and set off northwards to meet Dempsey. As the DUKW disappeared into the distance in a cloud of shimmering dust, the general's ADC turned to his master and sheepishly remarked, 'Sir, I am afraid that I have left our rations for the next five days and a bottle of whisky on board.'[3]

Over in the western bridgehead, Gen Patton was also coming ashore. He and his bodyguard embarked from the *Monrovia* in Admiral Hewitt's barge and landed close to Gela. Waiting for him on the beach was a band of photographers who filmed his arrival in dramatic fashion, for a few long-range enemy shells were splashing down into the water in the background, giving the pictures an authentic atmosphere. Patton was then forced to wait impatiently on the shore while his transport was being de-waterproofed. To while away the time he inspected several abandoned landing craft that had been holed in the assault.

The army commander and his group then set out to visit Gen Allen's US 1st Division's HQ located on the coast road to the east of Gela. As they entered the town enemy artillery fire began falling among the buildings. This was soon joined by mortar fire and flashing streams of tracer. On their way through Gela the party spotted a flag indicating the direction of the Rangers' HQ. Patton decided to drop in and find out what was going on.

Col William Darby and his Rangers were once again being engaged by Italian troops from the *Livorno* Division backed by tanks. Further to the east, elements of the *Hermann Göring* Division were also advancing, trying driving a wedge between the Rangers and the rest of 1st Division. Patton arrived at Darby's command post just as the colonel was massing his mortars to meet a new assault. The general asked Darby to point out the enemy counter-attack. 'Which one do you want to see, General Patton?' the colonel replied. 'They are coming at us from everywhere.'[4]

Within a few minutes a full-scale battle had broken out. Italian tanks and infantry had reached the edge of the town and were being countered by every available defender who could be mustered: Rangers, infantrymen, paratroopers, engineers and naval personnel were all preparing to fight. Patton rushed up to the roof of the building and could clearly see the enemy moving across a field no more than 800 yards away. A few enemy aircraft then joined in the assault and bombed the town. Two planes swept low over the buildings and hit a house close by the American head-quarters. The building Patton was in was hit twice by bomb fragments.

Patton was now in his element; he was at last fighting on the front line. He joined in the fray by helping direct some 4.2-inch mortars which were firing on the enemy troops and tanks at about 900 yards' range. The mortars were firing white phosphorus bombs and the general took great glee in the sight of Italians being panicked by the explosions and burning chemical.

Although commanders on the spot were making appropriate decisions, Patton could not stop himself from issuing orders. He sent word to

Maj Gen Gaffey for the gap between Gela and the 1st Division to be closed with some of his tanks. He also radioed Maj Gen Allen to send tanks to help the Rangers. Both of these matters were already in hand. Allen's 1st Division a few miles to the east was also dealing with its own German counter-attack. Enemy tanks were now pushing hard for the coast road; they had swung to the west in open country, by-passing most of the 16th Infantry Regiment, intending to reach the sea and roll up the invasion beaches from the east.

By late morning Col Darby and his men were ready to put in their own attack. Bolstered by ten tanks that had arrived from Licata in the west and supported by the big guns of the *Savannah* out at sea, the Rangers went at the Italians. The determination of the assault and the ferocity of the supporting fire prompted the troops of the *Livorno* Division to withdraw. Patton watched the attack from his vantage point and turned to the company commander alongside him and said: 'Kill every one of the Goddam bastards.'[5] The general was enjoying his morning up at the sharp end.

With the danger to Gela seemingly over, and Truscott confirming with Patton that all was well with the 3rd Division in Licata, the real concern was now to the east and the attack against 1st Division. The main body of Conrath's forces was almost at the sea. Two battalions of Panzer III and Panzer IV tanks (90 in total), two armoured artillery battalions, an armoured reconnaissance battalion and an armoured engineer battalion had cracked open the American line. With few anti-tank weapons ashore, the lightly armed GIs in the forward positions had been over-run. Twenty tanks broke through and set themselves down the road towards Gela. Forty others swerved to their left across the fields and made for the beaches, intending to join up with the other German tanks on the coast road. Once they had joined up, Allen's division would be cut off and the beachhead destroyed piecemeal.

Allen knew that the key to the battle would be the artillery. He ordered every gun in the division to be rolled into position to meet the tanks at point-blank range. Word went out along the beaches to get the guns off the landing craft and moved forward. Inland, the battle-hardened infantry of the 1st Division stuck to their positions. They had to let the tanks roll by, but they sat deep in their foxholes and prepared to repel the panzer-grenadiers advancing behind.

For a while, things looked bleak for the 1st Division, but very steadily more and more guns began to lay down fire on the advancing tanks. Those panzers that moved along the road were hit by American artillery which had been dragged into position and now fired over open sights; those enemy tanks on the open ground further to the east were hit by heavy rounds fired by warships at sea. At the same time, an infantryman's battle raged along the northern edge of the lodgement as the GIs countered the advancing grenadiers. The forward-most German tanks got to within 2,000 yards of the beach before they were turned back. Solid though they were, the panzers were no match for the 5- and 8-inch shells fired at them from cruisers and destroyers lying offshore. The attack faltered, order was lost, confusion reigned and then the units of the *Hermann Göring* Division retired whence they had come. Their attack had been well and truly repulsed.

The Germans came on again in the afternoon. Fewer tanks and fewer grenadiers went into the attack against an even stronger US 1st Division. The result was the same. Artillery and anti-tank gun fire, naval gunfire and determined infantry once again turned back the enemy. Conrath knew that he could no longer hope to drive through to the sea. He pulled his division back to the area around Caltagirone while higher command argued about what tactics should next be employed against the Allies.

Over to the east, Col James Gavin had spent the whole of the day working westwards through enemy-held countryside to join up with the rest of his combat team of the 505th Parachute Infantry. On the way he had to contend with at least a platoon of the enemy in a farmhouse blocking his path. By then he was down to just six men. During the night he made contact with a machine-gun post of the US 45th Division. He learned that he was 5 miles south-west of Vittoria, still 12 miles short of his objective to the north of Gela. He also heard that the 45th Division was having a difficult time. His little group pressed on towards his original objective and ran into a number of men from his regiment's 3rd Parachute Battalion. Their commander, Lt Col Edward Krause, told Gavin that there were a great number of the enemy between his battalion and Gela. The colonel decided to press on and told Krause to follow with his men. An hour later they reached a railway crossing with a long low ridge behind. From the ridge small arms fire came at the paratroopers which increased in intensity the closer the Americans got to its lower slopes. Col Gavin had at last found the front line.

Gavin had come up against Gen Conrath's right-hand column, which was advancing southwards from Biscari to the east of the River Acate. In the lead were the infantry of the 1st *Hermann Göring* Panzergrenadier Regiment. Their progress had been slowed by the presence of isolated groups of American paratroopers and marauding Allied fighters. The Tiger tanks of the 1st Tank Company supporting the move were too large and too unwieldy to use in the close countryside of olive groves and terraced strips of vines, and the artillery were of little use against scattered individuals. Four miles south of Biscari the left-hand group of the leading panzergrenadiers fanned out along the Biazza Ridge, a long low feature about 150 feet high, which overlooked the advance. A few American infantrymen from the US 45th Division engaged them as they took possession of the high ground.

On the other side of the Biazza Ridge Col Gavin had heard the fighting and was bringing his paratroopers up the slopes with the intention of eliminating the enemy on top and opening his way towards Gela. As the Americans neared the crest of the feature enemy fire became unbearable. Many men fell dead as Gavin and his men struggled for cover. Unable to move forwards or backwards, they tried to dig slit trenches in the rocky soil for protection. By this time, more and more paratroopers had arrived at the railway crossing and had been joined by other lost and displaced troops including some from 45th Division, part of a company from 180th Infantry Regiment and even some naval personnel. Gavin went back down the hill to try to organise this motley group for a concerted assault on the ridge.

The planned attack went in just a short time later and, just as Gavin intended, his small force reached the top and went down the other side. Once they had crested the rise, however, enemy fire became more and more intense. Small arms fire had been joined by the bombs and shells of mortar and artillery as more of the enemy column had arrived on the far side of the ridge. Gavin now knew that he was not dealing with just a platoon action or enemy patrol, but had walked into a full-scale German attack. Inevitably, it was not long before the sound of tanks was heard.

Gavin was concerned that his right flank was in the air. He knew that the 45th Division was to his left, filling the gap between the ridge and the sea, but to his right there was probably nothing, save for isolated paratroopers still looking for their units. If the enemy column decided to bypass the ridge on the right, it could attack his position from the rear. Fortunately, more and more men had arrived from the direction of Vittoria as they heard the sound of the action and were told what was happening. Among them were some 81mm mortars and two 75mm mountain guns from his division's 456th Parachute Artillery Battalion. With this added weight of firepower, he moved a section across to the right to act as a flank guard.

Up on the ridge the battle had become quite frantic. The exposed men on the forward slope pulled back to dig in on its rear. Gavin was determined to hold the ridge even if tanks managed to come over the crest. He positioned the two guns is such a way that they could engage the lighter-armoured undersides of the tanks as they topped the rise. He instructed his men that, even if they were over-run by the armour, they were to stay put and engage the enemy infantry following behind. They were not going to give up the hill.[6]

Down on the road on the other side of the ridge the panzergrenadiers of the *Hermann Göring* Division were deploying for a fight. They had set out their artillery and were now bringing up the first of the Tiger tanks to clear the strip of high ground. The great monster began moving through a vineyard and manoeuvring itself behind a stone house to bring its 88mm gun to bear on the paratroopers. Up on the hill, one of Gavin's primitive 75mm guns was manhandled into a position from which it had a direct line of sight to engage the Tiger. Though it was not designed as an anti-tank weapon, its crew were willing to have a try at hitting the enemy armour.

Unfortunately the Tiger crew drew a bead on the American gun first and let go with one of its high-explosive rounds. There was an almighty explosion as the German shell landed in the dirt just in front of the American gun; its crew were blown in all directions. Surprisingly none of them were killed and they had the immediate presence of mind to man their gun and let fly with a round of their own. The shell hit the side of the Tiger and the resulting explosion brought down part of the stone house alongside the enemy tank. Now feeling rather exposed, the Tiger reversed out of sight.

The German commander down on the road realised that it was pointless to attack the hill with tanks and did just what Gavin feared he would do: he sent some of his armour through the vineyards around the right flank of the Americans. Fortunately, just as this attack was gathering and the noise of tracked vehicles milling around to the north of him echoed across the ridge, Gavin was joined by a young paratroop officer with a radio set. The ensign told the colonel that he was in touch with a warship at sea and was able to call for naval gunfire. Gavin was a little nervous about this as he did not know his exact location. He did, however, agree to a trial round using the level crossing below him as a fix on his position. The naval shell whined in low overhead and hit the very spot where the Tiger had been. Encouraged by the sight, Gavin called for more and more of this naval fire to be brought down on the enemy in front of him and on the enemy tanks manoeuvring to his right.

The shells of the large-calibre naval guns screamed in with the noise of an approaching express train. The resulting explosions were spectacular, blunting the German attack and disorganising their moves. Almost immediately enemy activities went quiet. More and more men continued to join Gavin's group and he soon felt he was in a position to put in an attack of his own. He felt a pressing need to destroy the enemy in front of him and to collect his dead and wounded: 'Our attack jumped off on schedule,' he later wrote, 'regimental clerks, cooks, truck drivers, everyone who could carry a rifle or a carbine was in the attack.'[7]

The enemy reacted and hit the Americans with all types of fire. The Americans pressed home the assault with resolute spirit, swarming over the top of the ridge and down among the German positions. Machine guns were over-run, mortars captured and trucks set on fire. The suddenness of the attack had taken the enemy by surprise and they melted away back through the olives and vines towards Biscari.

Bold though Gavin's attack was, it was not the only factor to precipitate a German withdrawal. Earlier that day, Gen von Senger had visited Conrath and had come forward to see the situation in front of the *Hermann Göring* Division for himself. Reports had been reaching Kesselring from his Luftwaffe HQ in Sicily about the division's inability to drive through to the beaches and repel the invasion. Back in Berlin Hitler was furious that more had not been done to throw the Allies back into the sea. Late in the afternoon von Senger drove down the road from Biscari and witnessed the action along Biazza Ridge. He realised that further attacks towards the beaches and would meet even heavier naval fire and would not result in any appreciable victory.

Conrath's division had in fact advanced well forward, much further than had been appreciated by both Kesselring and the German higher command, and had not been counter-attacked in force by the Americans. The resistance that it had met had been defensive rather than offensive. Further advances towards the beaches, however, would leave its flanks open to American counter-attacks as the bulk of the Italian formations on either side of the division had melted away. It was clear to both von Senger and Guzzoni that Axis forces in front of the Allied lodgement were now too weak to repulse the landings.

Other opportunities seemed open, however. The Gela bridgehead was not expanding at a great rate and the US 1st Division was still relatively close to the coast. The US 45th Division was much further inland. A possibility now arose for an attack by the *Hermann Göring* Division eastwards to try to cut off the advance units of the 45th Division in the area of Vittoria and Comiso. This attack would force the Americans to take defensive action and, in the meantime, the division could draw itself northwards to regroup around Caltagirone while the 15th Panzergrenadier Division moved from the west coast into the area Armerina–Barrafranca–Pietraperzia. Battlegroup *Schmalz* would remain in front of the British landings. These moves would block Allied advances northwards and herald a tactical switch from offence to defence.

At midday on 11 July, Maj-Gen Heidrich and his tactical headquarters personnel boarded a plane in southern France bound for Rome to meet with Italian Southern Command HQ at Frascati. He left behind Oberst Heilmann with orders to get his 3rd Parachute Regiment into the air to join him in Italy later that day. Following on from airfields at Avignon and Tarascon, the 10th Machine Gun Battalion and the 1st Engineer Battalion would be dispatched as soon as possible. A short time later, when the air transport had returned to France, the 4th Parachute Regiment with field artillery and anti-tank batteries would be flown south to join them. The 1st Parachute Regiment would travel by train to Naples and then be ferried over the Messina Straits to Sicily to complete the move. This last regiment would be transported by land and sea rather than by air, for the aircraft carrying the leading units of the division would be involved for several days in transporting this advance guard to the island.

After conferring with senior commanders, Heidrich was at the airfield in Rome when the Heinkel 111s carrying his 3rd Parachute Regiment flew in.

He told Heilmann that his regiment would be embarking next morning as the forerunner to the whole of the division. He and his men would be flown over to Sicily to be dropped in daylight on the plain south of Catania. The other units would follow as available over the next two days.[8]

This rapid dispatch of an elite division to Sicily was something the Allies had not planned for. It had been assumed that it would take some time for German reinforcements to arrive on the island by land, via the Messina Straits. The alacrity with which the OKW had committed 1st Parachute Division to the theatre by air, and its arrival in front of Catania in the path of Montgomery's forces, would turn out to be a shock that Eighth Army's commander had not expected.

Over on the left of the American battlefield US 3rd Division had spent the first 30 hours since the landings expanding its beachhead. By noon on the second day the division had reached the Yellow Phase Line, its planned objective for D+3. Its 15th Regiment had struck northwards to take Campobello and the 7th Regiment had swung across to the west to occupy Palma di Montechiaro. Both of these successes had been against increasing numbers of German troops. The 30th Regiment was fighting its way north-eastwards towards Riesi and had sent an armoured column eastwards along the coast to make contact with US 1st Division. It met up with Gen Patton just outside of Gela at about 1400 hrs. By the end of the day Truscott's division had enlarged its lodgement in a great curve with a front line of over 50 miles. Out in the lead, reconnaissance patrols kept in contact with the enemy. Truscott was on the Yellow Line, but had no orders as to what to do next. His general instructions were to protect the left flank of the invasion against interference from the north-west. It was known that 15th Panzergrenadier Division was in that area and it was important that the 3rd Division establish a firm base from which it could not be evicted.

Truscott was anxious to keep up the momentum of the assault and push further inland, but knew that any further moves would have to be sanctioned by the army commander. Patton was no better informed as to what the next moves should be, other than at some point Truscott's division would have to conduct operations to capture Caltanissetta, but for the moment the 3rd Division would just build up its strength and stay put.

Earlier that morning on this second day of the invasion, Patton decided that he would fly in the second regiment of the 82nd Airborne Division to reinforce the centre of his lodgement that night. On board the *Monrovia* the army commander informed Maj Gen Ridgway that he wanted Col Tucker's regiment to drop on Farello airfield, which had been recently captured by 1st Division. Still fearful of the consequences of friendly fire, after the meeting at 0845 hrs, Patton had signalled Bradley to notify all units, especially anti-aircraft units, that the airborne drop by the 82nd would take place that night.

The 11th also proved to be a busy day for von Richthofen's airmen. The German and Italian Air Forces launched almost 500 sorties that day against the invasion. Most of them were hit-and-run raids, where the Axis aircraft would come screaming in at tree-top height to machine-gun and strafe the beaches, or launch low-level bombing runs against the ships at anchor offshore. In US Seventh Army's sector the raids started just after dawn when the anchorage was bombed by a force of about twenty aircraft. At 0635 hrs another raid was so heavy that it forced a few ships to get under way and take evasive action. The fighters came back in the early afternoon to machine-gun the shoreline at Gela. Thirty minutes later, at 1430 hrs, Scoglitti was attacked, and then at 1530 hrs, thirty Junkers 88s bombed Gela.

These heavy air attacks were worrying to Patton. He confided in his diary that night that both the Army's and the Navy's anti-aircraft gunners were firing inaccurately and were very 'jumpy'. He was so apprehensive that he had tried, at 2000 hrs, to get the 82nd Airborne Division's drop to be postponed, but his staff were unable to make contact with the North African HQ over the radio. Just under two hours later, at 2150 hrs, as darkness gathered over the fleet, the anchorage off Gela was subjected to another large air raid which went on for some considerable time. Unfortunately, at that same moment, the great air armada carrying Col Tucker's 2,000 paratroopers was leaving its airfields in North Africa and heading for that same small patch of sky.

The route of the 504th Parachute Infantry Regiment carried it over the same course as Gavin's men had taken two days previously. The leading flights took the prescribed route over Malta and carried out the appropriate turns at the correct places and flew along the coast for the final run to the drop zone over Farello airfield. The first serials of paratroopers made their drop without incident and without casualties. At 2240 hrs the later flights carrying the bulk of the division took the same route or approximately the same route and came along the shore at 700 feet. This time, however, something went wrong.

Perhaps one aircraft strayed a little too near the ships or flew too low over an anti-aircraft battery; no one was ever to discover who fired the first shot or why, but somewhere a lone machine-gunner opened up on one of the C-47s. Within minutes a chain reaction had triggered the rest of the guns in the beachhead and soon even those at sea had joined in. Everyone in the whole of the invasion area began firing at the slow moving, easily identifiable, formations of Dakotas. They were sitting ducks to bullet and cannon shell and hits were taken almost immediately. Squadrons fell out of formation and twisted and banked to avoid the fire, but at such a low altitude there was little room to manoeuvre. Six planes took direct hits and plunged into the ground with all their crews and paratroopers on board. Others were riddled with bullets, killing many of the men inside. Some of the airborne troops were standing at the doorway ready to jump and managed to get out of the stricken aircraft. Others tried to jump as their planes went down but lacked sufficient height for their parachutes to deploy properly and plunged earthwards to their deaths. Out of the 144 aircraft that had left Tunisia, 23 failed to return.

Down on the ground, waiting at Farello airfield for the drop, Ridgway and Patton could not believe the horror that was unfolding in front of them. Patton kept repeating, 'Oh my God. Oh my God.' Ridgway could say or do nothing, except choke back the tears; his division was being torn apart by his countrymen before his eyes.

Col Tucker's plane came in with the third wave, flying through a night sky that was lit up with flares and tracer. A tremendous barrage of fire ripped through the aircraft but the colonel told the pilot to fly straight and level until they reached the drop zone. Tucker exited his aircraft on target with the rest of his stick. When the plane got back to Tunisia, mechanics found that it had been hit by literally hundreds of bullets. Even while the paratroopers were in the air making their descent they were still subjected to machine-gun fire, so convinced were the men on the triggers that they were killing Germans. Tucker was beside himself with rage and ordered a signal to be sent back to Kairouan telling Col Harry Lewis not to dispatch the gliders of his 325th Glider Infantry Regiment. It was to remain on the ground in North Africa until further orders.

When the roll call was later taken, 82 men were found to have been killed, 16 were missing feared dead and 131 had been wounded. Eisenhower ordered an investigation to look into the tragedy, signalling to Alexander: 'Since disciplinary action, involving American troops, may possibly be indicated, I thought it best to send the message to Patton from me personally but dispatching it through your office.'[9] Eisenhower also insisted that it be sent to Spaatz via Tedder so that simultaneous investigations could be carried out by the air units.

Alexander forwarded Eisenhower's request, but added a few barbed comments of his own:

> Before the beginning of this operation you particularly requested me to authorise this movement into your area. Consequently ample time was obviously available for complete and exact coordination of the movement among all forces involved. If the cited reports are true the incident could have been occasioned only by inexcusable carelessness and negligence on the part of someone. You will institute within your command an immediate and inexhaustible investigation into allegation with a view of fixing responsibility. Report of pertinent facts is desired and if the persons found responsible are serving under your command,
> I want statement of the disciplinary action taken by you.

Then, just to make sure that this instruction would not be 'lost' among other communications, Alexander finished with the order: 'This will be expedited.'[10]

Patton was a little disappointed with Alexander's despatch, although he knew who had instigated it. In his own mind he believed he had taken every possible precaution to prevent the aircraft being fired upon and reasoned that it was 'an unavoidable incident in combat'. Men who get bombed all day get 'itchy fingers'. Deep down, however, he knew that he was ultimately to blame, although he did not feel that he ought to be censured. In his diary he sarcastically commented about Eisenhower never having been subjected to air attack or having to experience death at first hand.[11]

Patton ordered an investigation into the incident as instructed, but this dragged on for some time with nothing conclusively settled. The blame for the incident could not be attached to any individual or group of individuals. Matthew Ridgway reluctantly agreed with the findings, reasoning that impartial justice could not be served and that disciplinary action was of 'doubtful wisdom'.

Cunningham was quick to place the blame elsewhere than at sea and replied to Alexander's despatch with a dismissive tone:

> All ships fire at once at any aeroplane particularly at low flying ones which approach them. Nothing less is acceptable without incurring grave risk of loss or damage to valuable merchant vessels or fleet units. In the preliminary discussion on the routing of the airborne troops this was constantly kept in the foreground and pointed out by my staff. It would appear, therefore, that the reason for these most unfortunate incidents must be either in bad routing or bad navigation on the part of the aircraft pilots.[12]

There was probably some truth in this statement, for the American transport pilots had been seen during the first drop to be somewhat wayward with their navigation. Nonetheless, with so much warning of the operation and with the slow speeds of transport aircraft themselves, there should have been more control over the seaborne anti-aircraft guns. The fact was that, once one of them opened up, they all opened up and nothing appeared to be able to stop them. One commander, however, knew most certainly where the blame did not lie. Montgomery signalled to Alexander: 'There is no recorded instance of our own AA shooting at our own aircraft as far as Eighth Army is concerned.'[13]

The achievements of the two American airborne drops were very disappointing, but not through any lack of bravery or determination by the men involved. The fact of the matter was that their deployment had been bungled. Poor navigation, poor discipline and poor communications had conspired to produce two separate fiascos. The cost to the 82nd Division was equally as high as that suffered by the British 1st Airborne Division. Out of the 5,300 paratroopers (British and American) who took part in the invasion, only around 2,000 of them were actually fit for action by the end of the second day. At the end of the campaign 3,883 paratroopers were finally accounted for, leaving 1,417 dead or missing.[14] As for their effectiveness, it was true that Gavin's men had disrupted enemy communications, interfered with the German counter-attack against the beachhead and helped with the capture of the vital airfields, but these slim victories came at a great price.

By late evening of 11 July Alexander could feel generally satisfied with events and note that things were progressing well: 'The bridgehead was assuming very solid proportions.' Things were looking bright in the British sector for Montgomery as his beachhead expanded: XIII Corps was driving for Augusta with 5th Division while 50th Division was advancing steadily on a parallel route towards Sortino and XXX Corps was manoeuvring north to cut the Ragusa–Augusta road with its two divisions and 231st Independent Brigade. Little serious resistance had been met since coming ashore and the few German troops who were facing 5th Division were giving no great cause for alarm. The Italian 206th Coastal Division in front of Eighth Army had begun to melt away and even the locally based *Napoli* Division was offering only perfunctory opposition. Monty's lodgement was growing at a prodigious rate in the centre and on the left, much faster and more easily than Montgomery had privately imagined before the landings. The army commander was becoming exceedingly optimistic as to future operations. He felt he had the measure of the enemy and signalled Alexander that if the Americans could press hard inland towards Caltagirone and Canicatti and block German advances from the west, his army could push northwards with a secure left flank and, if necessary, swing inland to cut off the enemy in front of Patton's forces.[15] He was feeling very optimistic indeed.

For his part, Patton was also rather pleased with events and had no intention of merely blocking German advances: Maj Gen Middleton's 45th Division had seized Comiso and its airfield; Maj Gen Allen's 1st Division had rebuffed the German attack on Gela with the help of Darby's Rangers and Gavin's paratroopers and was again pushing inland; Maj Gen Truscott's 3rd Division had consolidated its lodgement around Licata and most of Maj Gen Gaffey's 2nd Armored Division was now unloaded. All three of Seventh Army's landings had been linked into one continuous front. Patton's beachhead was solid, supplies were rolling ashore over the beaches and America's most belligerent general was now looking to advance with his army intent on killing the enemy.

On the German side of the line in front of the British at Priolo, Schmalz decided that his stand had achieved its objective of delaying British 5th Division's advance and gaining time for stronger positions to be manned in the rear. He now gave orders for his troops to withdraw. The move was detected by the Northamptons in the early hours of the 12th and the

CHAPTER 10

The Third Day – 12 July

On 12 July, Gen Eisenhower decided to visit the landings. He travelled over from Algiers in a light cruiser with his Chief of Staff Bedell Smith, Maj Gen Harry Butcher and Maj Gen Clarence Huebner, Mountbatten was also in tow. Eisenhower met Patton in his war room on board the *Monrovia*. As Patton outlined the situation on his front, Eisenhower appeared less than engrossed by the briefing. Patton later recorded that Ike was more interested in rebuking him for the paucity of his situation reports and compared his army unfavourably with British Eighth Army, which sent him hourly news bulletins. Patton quietly fumed. He had seen many of the British reports and to his mind their content often seemed to be non-essential and even imaginary. Butcher observed an air of tension between the two. When they parted, Patton ordered Brig Gen Gay to send three reports a day in addition to the 1600 hrs situation briefing that he normally provided. If Eisenhower wanted reports, relevant or not, he could have them. Patton noted in his diary that night that Eisenhower was wearing suede shoes, 'à la British'.[1]

Maj-Gen Berney-Ficklin was increasingly concerned at the gradual stiffening of enemy resistance to the moves of his 5th Division on its drive to capture Catania. The advance along the road towards Lentini was becoming more and more difficult the closer he got to the town. His right-hand column, however, was having an easier ride on its approach to Augusta. It was still meeting Italian troops, but most of them were only too willing to give themselves up after a face-saving bout of small arms fire.

The eventual capture of the port of Augusta turned out to be an almost bloodless coup. The 17th Brigade advanced along the main road to bring it around to the landward side of the old naval port, while at the same time warships escorted a seaward attack on its dockyard and waterfront.

Augusta had been an important Italian naval port until its relative proximity to the airfields of North Africa forced most of the warships based there to move to safer anchorages in the north. It was protected by quite an elaborate network of coast defences and fortifications whose weapons were mostly manned by troops of the Italian Navy. British hopes were that simultaneous assaults from land and sea would induce the Italian garrison to surrender, but nobody was sure if that would actually be the case. The landward element of this attack would be from 5th Division; the seaward party would be Paddy Mayne's Special Raiding Squadron of the SAS.

Lt-Col Mayne heard that he was to mount the attack when he and his men were celebrating what was for many Ulstermen a national holiday, 12 July. They were recovering from their exertions on the Capo Murro di Porco the previous day when Mayne learned that his unit was to attack the port of Augusta that evening in broad daylight. They were the obvious choice for the task for they were the only Special Forces unit available in the area.

The plan was alarmingly simple. The *Ulster Monarch* would once again take them to a point offshore where they would embark into LCAs that would carry them into the port. They would seize the inner harbour and hold until relieved by ground troops. Mayne and his officers had just a few hours to study air photographs of their objective and formulate a plan of attack. To every man of them, the operation seemed suicidal, but it had to be done nonetheless. After all their escapades in the desert, the long penetrations behind enemy lines and the raids against German supply dumps and airfields, the men of the unit faced their future with equanimity and decided to embark on the attack as though it were just another great adventure.

The *Ulster Monarch* picked up an escort of a cruiser and three destroyers just as it passed into the bay off Augusta. The old passenger ship steamed to a point 2 miles short of the port and began to lower the assault craft. Through his binoculars Mayne could see the port quite clearly and was able to pick out the large citadel that rose above the harbour installations. Just then a great fountain of water erupted 200 yards in front of the ship. An Italian gun battery had opened up on the small fleet. The cruiser and the three destroyers returned fire immediately, each of them sending great salvoes of large calibre shells at the offending coastal guns. Even the *Ulster Monarch* opened up with the 12-pounder gun mounted in her bows. More batteries ashore joined in the bombardment and shells were crashing down close to the now stationary transport. Mayne and his men took to the landing craft as quickly they were able and cast off, steaming at full throttle for the shore. Bullets started to ping off the front and sides of the LCAs as Italian machine guns in casemates took up the action. Behind them the Royal Navy was having a field day ranging on the enemy batteries and knocking them out one by one. Soon they all fell silent, preferring to hold their fire rather than attract more attention from the accurate guns of the ships.

At 1935 hrs, Paddy Mayne's landing craft hit the shingle at the base of the sea wall. In a moment the ramp went down and he was out, followed by more and more of his men as each of their craft shuddered to a halt along the shoreline. The tension of crouching behind thin metal as they impotently endured enemy fire during the run-in was finally released. The SAS men stormed over the sea wall fighting mad, screaming at the tops of their voices, expecting at any moment to be plunged into a frantic fire-fight. There was nothing. Nobody, no firing, nothing. The enemy had simply melted away. They looked around, still nothing. The civilians had gone; the town was empty. True there was some occasional sniping as some brave soul let off a round or two, but Lt-Col Paddy Mayne had captured a whole town, a port, a naval anchorage and a large chunk of Italian pride, without firing a shot in anger.

While his men checked the town to make sure all really was well, Mayne took a patrol to occupy the bridge that linked the spur that Augusta was built on with the mainland. With only small arms with which to repel any counter-attack, he set his troops out to guard the bridge and await the arrival of 5th Division. By early morning, the 6th Seaforth Highlanders and the 2nd Royal Scots Fusiliers had entered Augusta; by midday on 13 July, the town was full of troops and the bay was packed with ships.[2]

The fall of Augusta after so brief an action had a number of repercussions. It strengthened Montgomery's belief that the Sicilian campaign might be much easier than had been first imagined. Enemy resistance was still patchy, with Italian forces falling back each time they were pushed. The size and scope of the landings had caused the two German divisions on the island to be stretched to a point where they could only defend localities. There was no fixed front line. Nor was there was any likelihood of the Axis forces mounting a counter-attack of any size, for there appeared to be no reserve available.

In the German camp the loss of Augusta was felt keenly by GenFM Kesselring, as he later wrote:

> One disappointment followed another. The Italian coastal divisions were an utter failure, not one of their counter-attack divisions reached the enemy in time or even at all – The 'Napoli' Division in the south-west corner of the island had melted into thin air. The commandant of the fortress of Augusta meanwhile surrendered without even waiting to be attacked.[3]

It was now clear to the field marshal that the Italians had no stomach for a fight even in defence of their homeland and the campaign would have to be taken over and controlled by the Germans. Hitler was likewise unimpressed by the Italians and realised that German troops were fighting virtually on their own.

Kesselring discussed his proposals for the defence of Sicily with Hitler and Mussolini and got a broad agreement with his views. There would be a controlled withdrawal to a defence line based to the south of Mount Etna which included the Gerbini airfields and the port of Catania. These were to be defended as long as was feasible. Control of Sicily was to be strongly contested in order to extract the highest possible price in Allied casualties. At a time later to be agreed by Hitler, German forces were to be withdrawn to the Italian mainland.

At the meeting Kesselring also extracted from Hitler some agreement to the gradual reinforcement of the German garrison on the island. Reluctantly the Führer approved the release of part of the 29th Panzer-grenadier Division. Kesselring was disappointed that there would not be more troops available to him: '[Hitler] made stipulations about the immediate transfer of the whole of the 29th Panzergrenadiers – a finickiness which was to be paid for in the subsequent battles,' he was to write later. The field marshal had hoped that he would also receive the

26th Panzergrenadier Division, which was in southern Italy. Hitler would not hear of it for he was of the opinion that the Allies might at any moment land in Calabria and he was adamant that the division would remain *in situ* to deal with any such landings.

On another matter, Kesselring was well pleased. Hitler had given orders for the headquarters of XIV Panzer Corps to move to Sicily under the command of GenLt Hans Hube and for the corps gradually to take over the campaign, with Hube gently marginalising Guzzoni's command and taking control of any reliable Italian troops.[4] 'Hube was the right man in the right place, seconded by his excellent Chief of Staff, von Bonin,' agreed Kesselring.[5]

The 53-year-old GenLt Hube was an old campaigner who had lost an arm in the First World War. Between the wars he remained in the military and was a regimental commander when the Second World War broke out. He rose to command XIV Panzer Corps with great distinction at Stalingrad and was later flown out of the pocket on Hitler's orders. Hube was one of Hitler's favourites, but was also a much decorated panzer general of great ability. He was awarded the Knight's Cross of the Iron Cross in 1941, then with Oak Leaves in August 1942 and with Swords in December 1942. After the Sicilian campaign he returned to Russia to command First Panzer Army from November 1943. He was killed in a plane crash in April 1944 on his way to Hitler's retreat at Obersalzberg to become one of the few generals to be awarded the rare decoration of Diamonds with the Knight's Cross of the Iron Cross.

The 5th Division continued its advance up the road to Lentini and Catania, but had not gone far before it once again bumped into the *Schmalz* Battlegroup south of Carlentini. On this same day 50th Division was attacking towards Carlentini from the south-west. The pressure being applied from the two directions was pushing a great number of enemy troops into the area around the town and Lentini. Both divisions increasingly had to put down more and more artillery barrages and apply set-piece attacks to get past enemy rearguards. The pace of the advance towards Catania was slowing down dramatically, but progress by Eighth Army's other formations further south was still good. On the left, Lt-Gen Leese's XXX Corps had the 51st (Highland) Division driving north-west up Highway 124 to Vizzini towards the assigned junction with American forces, and the Canadians were nearing Ragusa. The whole of the south-east corner of Sicily had now been cleared. Overall, things were continuing to look good for Eighth Army.

Monty was certain that, with continued effort and a degree of luck, there was a chance that the campaign could be finished in a matter of days. The virtually unopposed landings in the British sector had given Eighth Army a momentum that had to be maintained. If the Americans could hold the Germans in front of them and protect his flank from 15th Panzergrenadier Division, Montgomery believed that he could go all out for Messina. Such an advance would cut off the escape route of all Axis forces in Sicily. He now had an idea; if XIII Corps drove northwards with speed along the coast through Catania while XXX Corps swept round behind Mount Etna along the route Caltagirone–Enna–Leonforte, his army could virtually win the battle on its own. This second move would get his troops behind the Germans facing US Seventh Army and cut the island in two.

Montgomery considered this plan to be eminently workable. The Americans, he understood, were having a sticky time down near Gela dealing with counter-attacks by enemy armour and panzergrenadiers. Eighth Army, to the contrary, was making good inroads inland and north-wards. How much better, he decided, that the British position should be exploited while the Americans continued to hold down the main opposition and protect his flank.

Montgomery now made a decision that, contrary to his expectations of winning an early victory, condemned the Allies to a protracted and bitter campaign in Sicily. What chances there were of producing a swift demonstration of Allied might and a decisive conclusion to the invasion, reducing the island in days and cornering those Axis forces defending this outpost of Mussolini's empire, were now to be thrown away.

At 2200 hrs that night, 12 July, Gen Montgomery fired off a signal to Alexander outlining his proposals. He began with an over-optimistic outline of his progress, claiming to have taken Augusta and reached a line Sortino–Vizzini–Ragusa–Scicli. (The attack on Augusta was still in progress and Vizzini was not reached until the night of 14/15 July.) He then explained that he intended that his army would now advance on two axes, one aimed directly to the north as planned, and the other on a sweeping movement to get inland behind the great mass of Mount Etna. 'Suggest my Army operates offensively northwards to cut the island in two and that American Army hold extensively on the line Caltanissetta–Canicatti–

Licata facing west.'[6] He reasoned that once XXX Corps reached the Caltagirone– Enna–Leonforte area, the Axis forces facing Patton's army would never be able to escape. To make these moves, however, Leese's corps would need the sole use of Highway 124, which ran westwards and then north-westwards through Vizzini and Caltagirone up to Enna.

Montgomery was suggesting that the Americans sidestep to the west and allow his army to pass, while they protected his flank. Only the day before he had cabled Alexander to get the Americans to drive hard for Caltagirone; now he was proposing that his army should take the town, which lay directly in the path of the advancing US 1st Division. More puzzling was his eagerness to split his army. After arguing at great length during the planning stages of 'Husky' for the need to keep his forces concentrated, and making many enemies in the process, Montgomery was now suggesting that he divide Eighth Army and dilute the strength of what everyone imagined would be the main advance. Two days into the invasion and he was ignoring the very criticism that he had levelled at Gairdner's planners at Force 141. (On 24 April when criticising Gairdner's proposals he had stressed to Alexander that his army 'must operate concentrated'.[7])

The tone of Montgomery's signal presented the army group commander with a dilemma. The moves outlined could be seen to make some tactical sense, provided Eighth Army was able to advance at speed to exploit the fluid situation. By switching his main weight down this new axis he could surprise the Germans. It was obvious to everyone that the shortest route to Messina was through Catania and a flanking attack behind Etna could take the enemy by surprise. The attack, however, would have to be swift, resolute and immediate, for much of the route was through mountainous country along narrow roads. Tank support would be minimal and difficult to coordinate; the supporting naval guns were out of range. The advance would have to rely on mobile infantry and self-propelled guns muscling their way forward before the enemy could organise a defence line.

All available support being shipped in through Syracuse would have to be allocated to these moves, leaving the Americans to remain more or less in defence. Highway 124, the route XXX Corps would have to take from Vizzini through Caltagirone up towards Enna, was a road that had been previously allocated to the Americans. Here was the real problem, for US Seventh Army was closing on that road and had definite plans to use it to enlarge its own lodgement. Taking Highway 124 from the Americans and allocating it to Monty's forces would stall any major US movement inland.

The army group commander was now in something of a fix. Montgomery was forceful in his signal, implying that he was going ahead with his plan regardless. To reel him back would involve Alexander in a good deal of antagonism. To let Eighth Army's commander have his head did, in fact, make a good deal of sense. The optimistic picture painted by Montgomery of the current situation and the possibility of a swift out-flanking movement around Mount Etna could result in a speedy conclusion to the whole campaign. Alexander therefore reacted in the way he had always done: having been given a list of Montgomery's intentions, he simply complied with them. Eighth Army could have Highway 124 and US Seventh Army could look after its flank.

This decision condemned the campaign in Sicily to degenerate into a fiasco and caused permanent resentment and suspicion between the American and British field commanders. Patton and his army had not invaded Sicily to watch the British make an 'end run' to Messina and to reap all of the glory. Nor would international pride be served while Patton stood fast and watched British Eighth Army drive past.

Without even waiting for permission from Alexander, Montgomery now instructed Leese to order the Highland Division, supported by 23rd Armoured Brigade, to push on up the road to Vizzini and then on to Caltagirone along Highway 124. He told Leese to crack on regardless; he had to get to Enna as quickly as possible and scatter the Germans and Italians in front of him and the Americans.

For Montgomery to react to events in this way so soon after the invasion has led to a great deal of debate by later historians. His main biographer cites the move as an example of Monty's 'offensive eagerness' that eventually proved to be beyond the capabilities of his troops, suggesting that tactically the move made good sense and would have been successful if US II Corps had been placed under Eighth Army's command as Montgomery had proposed during the planning stage.[8] For that to be true there would have had to have been some intention before the landings for a two-pronged movement around Etna, while of course Monty had always planned to make his main concentrated advance northwards along the coast through Catania.

It is difficult to see why Montgomery decided to split his forces after just two days of relatively easy fighting, when prior to the invasion he was adamant that he must keep them concentrated. The only reasonable conclusion is that he was over-optimistic concerning the enemy's ability to stop the expansion of his lodgement. Known to him, but not to the vast majority of those taking part in the landings, were the precise locations of the two German divisions in Sicily and he knew that they were not facing him. Montgomery and Patton were both privy to many important German signals via the Ultra code-breaking teams at Bletchley in England. So secret was this knowledge that only a few top commanders were supplied with the results of the Ultra decodes. On 12 July Monty knew that he had a perfect chance of not only advancing directly on Messina, but also of getting his troops behind the Germans by a move round the western side of Etna.

During those first two days it must have occurred to Montgomery that his well-placed army could win the campaign on its own. On the evening of 12 July everything was going his way. The only real counter-attack to be made against the landings was in the American sector by the *Hermann Göring* Division. If Patton continued to hold the Germans in the west, XXX Corps could slip past them and strike northwards while Seventh Army kept the main opposition at bay. The drive to Catania was making good progress and the road forward would be eased even further on the 13th by two proposed landings behind the Axis front to capture important bridges: commandos would take the crossing over the River Leonardo and the airborne division would seize the bridge over the River Simeto. These advance guards would then hold open the route for the motorised units of Dempsey's corps to drive through to Catania. By 14 July Montgomery would have his troops in the town ready to start the final drive on Messina. If at the same time Monty had XXX Corps racing around the far side of Mount Etna, any forces in front of XIII Corps would have to withdraw or be cut off and captured. Once Messina was reached the campaign would be virtually over. Monty was trying to relive his successful actions in the desert when his New Zealanders threw in a powerful 'left hook' to stretch the enemy's defences while the main frontal thrust along the coast road forced its way through. But this was not the desert, and XXX Corps' proposed 'left hook' was through an unforgiving mountainous region where tight olive groves, stony walls and tiny fields confined all movement to the narrow, easily defendable roads.

There were some signs that German resistance had begun to harden, but Monty was now more determined than ever that the advance would not slow down. He gave orders for the two missions to capture the bridges along the Catania road to go ahead. First, 3 Commando would land by sea behind the front line to capture and hold the bridge across the Leonardo River near Lentini and, second, the 1st Parachute Brigade would be delivered by air astride the Simeto River to seize the Primosole Bridge just short of Catania. The two assault groups were to hold these bridges until relieved by the advancing 50th Division the next morning. The operations were set to take place the following night, 13/14 July.

On the other side of the hill, Guzzoni had a visitor at his Italian Sixth Army headquarters at Enna. GenFM Kesselring had flown over to consult with him and to speak with von Senger. The German Commander-in-Chief South had found it difficult to communicate with his commanders on the island and so decided on a personal visit. Most of the information he had been receiving from the battleground had come from his Luftwaffe units and details were either too alarming or too optimistic. When he arrived he visited all the front-line positions with von Senger to see matters for himself.

After returning to Guzzoni at Enna, Kesselring had a firm grasp of the realities of the situation on the ground. When first hearing of the landings he was inclined to believe that the Allies were attempting another 'Dieppe-style' raid in force. However, after seeing the strength of the assault, he was convinced it was an invasion proper. The field marshal was depressed by the total breakdown of the Italian divisions and the tactical chaos left by their inability to stick to the agreed defence plan. Back at Enna, he none-theless approved Guzzoni's orders to withdraw the *Hermann Göring* Division to the area Caltagirone–Vizzini and for 15th Panzergrenadier Division to move into reserve around Pietraperzia–Barrafranca, blocking the left flank of any American advance northwards.

The flanks of the *Hermann Göring* Division were to be held by what was left of the *Livorno* Division on the right and the *Napoli* Division on the left in front of the British. The *Schmalz* battlegroup of the *HG* Division was to remain in the area Lentini–Augusta. Kesselring agreed that the west of the island had little tactical value and could be gradually abandoned. The focus of the defence of Sicily was now to the north of Gela and on the plains in front of Catania. It was a battle that both Italian and German commanders knew could not be won, but the general idea was to hold out for as long as possible before the island had to be abandoned and to inflict the greatest possible cost to the Allies. To do this a formal defence line had to be established. The two Axis commanders agreed that their forces would gradually withdraw to positions where the country's natural features could be used to their advantage. An initial defence line would be organised running roughly from San Stefano on the northern coast through Nicosia and Agira to Catenanuova then along the River Dittaino to the coast just south of Catania. Behind this temporary position a further stop line would be created. It would be much shorter, and therefore more easily defended, and would take great advantage of the mountainous region through which it traversed. This 'Etna Line' was to be the main point at which the Allies would be held.

Back in Berlin Hitler agreed with Kesselring's assessment and directed that the most important aim was to delay the Allied advance and then bring it to a standstill. He approved the proposal for a gradual withdrawal to the initial line of defence forward of Mount Etna while the main line to the rear was prepared. He also sanctioned 29th Panzergrenadier Division to move south to Reggio and to be prepared to cross over to Sicily under his orders. Hitler was not yet ready to commit the division until it was certain whether or not sufficient supplies were available on the island for its deployment. He also wanted to see how the Allies would interfere with seaborne traffic across the Strait of Messina. Unless crossings could be guaranteed, he was reluctant to commit any more forces to the defence of the island. There was, however, good news on the way, for Heidrich's 1st Parachute Division was moving by air to the area south of Catania and its leading troops were scheduled to drop into Sicily that evening. Its arrival would strengthen the eastern side of the line in front of the British.

Some respite for Guzzoni's hard-pressed army was also being given from an unlikely source. Montgomery's intended seizure of Highway 124 for his own forces was to result in US 45th Division being halted south of the road, just as its advance units were pressing into the area Grammichele–Vizzini. In front of them were the disintegrating remnants of the *Livorno* Division holding the flank of the *Hermann Göring* Division. Had Middleton's division been left to pursue its original advance, the troops of the 45th might well have sliced through the *Livorno* Division and turned the flanks of the Luftwaffe division with who knows what outcome.

Earlier on 12 July, while Maj-Gen Heidrich was making ready in Rome, the first of the regiments from his 1st Parachute Division were preparing for their progress to Sicily. One of Heidrich's staff officers flew off to the island in advance of the transfer to select a drop zone for the move. Hauptmann Stangenberg arrived in Sicily during an air raid and was bombed again when he reconnoitred the ground south of Catania for a suitable site. He found one in the area Statione di Passe–Martino and quickly telephoned the map coordinates back to Rome. Heidrich agreed with the location and passed it on to Oberst Heilmann who was waiting with the men of his 3rd Parachute Regiment in their aircraft ready to fly out. With the order to move given, just four and a half hours after Stangenberg had himself taken off from Rome, the Heinkel 111 transports began to roll down the runways bound for Sicily, via a refuelling stop at Naples.

The German paratroopers dropped onto the island at around 1815 hrs with Heilmann the first one out of the leading aircraft. Following behind came the 1,400 men who made up the regiment. The drop was completed without setback as though it were an exercise. Unmolested during the whole of the descent, the colonel was able to gather his men and within 45 minutes had them marching in order southwards to a rendezvous with Hauptmann Specht. The captain had arrived earlier in the day with Stangenberg to make arrangements for the regiment's fly-in. Specht had also rounded up all the transport he could find and arranged to have the vehicles driven to Catania for Heilmann's men to pick up.

British Eighth Army's drive north of Augusta had been seen as one of the main threats to the Axis defence of the island, so the newly arrived paratroopers were to come under the command of the *Schmalz* Group to help bolster the left wing of the front. Heilmann's regiment was sent to Lentini and was told to take up a position between Carlentini and the sea to the north of Augusta, blocking British 5th Division's advance. When Oberst Schmalz arrived at Lentini he decided that the pressure being applied towards Francofonte by the 51st (Highland) Division required that this sector also be strengthened. He sent Heilmann's 2nd Battalion to bolster the defence of that part of the front. This move filled the gap between Lentini and the *Hermann Göring* Division at Vizzini.

Observing the fly-in with von Senger after his meeting with Guzzoni was GenFM Kesselring: 'I watched the first masses of the paratroop division land south of Catania,' he later wrote, 'an operation continued in the days that followed as the British fighters' rigid timetable gave us repeated opportunities to risk the move.'[9]

On the fourth day of the landings, Patton went to lunch around 1250 hrs with members of his staff. Twenty minutes after sitting down, he was roused from his meal with the news that Alexander and his entourage had arrived to see him. A somewhat apprehensive Alexander joined Patton in his command post and outlined the future plan of operations for the conduct of the campaign. It was a body blow to Patton. Alexander was proposing that Montgomery use the two main routes to Messina: XIII Corps would continue its advance on Catania up the coastal route while XXX Corps would now take Highway 124 and drive through Enna to get round Mount Etna. The British zone of operations would shift westwards to take the highway for its exclusive use. US Seventh Army would be relegated to the task of holding the left flank of Montgomery's advance. Messina was the only real goal for the Allies in Sicily, for it controlled the one escape route for Axis forces back to the mainland. Once Messina had been captured, all enemy resistance would have to cease. This prize had now been handed over solely to Montgomery. Not surprisingly, the Americans were outraged.

Patton was horrified by this turn of events, but restrained himself admirably. He accepted Alexander's orders, even though he was reluctant to impose the role of flank guard on his army. He knew that his force had to be more involved in the campaign so he now sought Alexander's permission to advance along the coast 25 miles westwards to take Agrigento and its port, Porto Empedocle. Such a move would, however, take the Americans outside the specified line for the front of Seventh Army and the army group commander was anxious that Patton's force should not get involved in an offensive battle. Patton countered Alexander's reservations by stating that possession of the port would ease Seventh Army's supply problems. At present all of its materials were coming through the port of Syracuse – a 140-mile round trip – and over the open beaches; neither method was convenient nor were they smooth running. If Seventh Army had a port of its own, Syracuse could be given over entirely to British Eighth Army. Alexander was swayed by Patton's argument and gave permission for the limited advance, but stressed that Seventh Army was not to get itself involved in heavy fighting. Its main role now was to

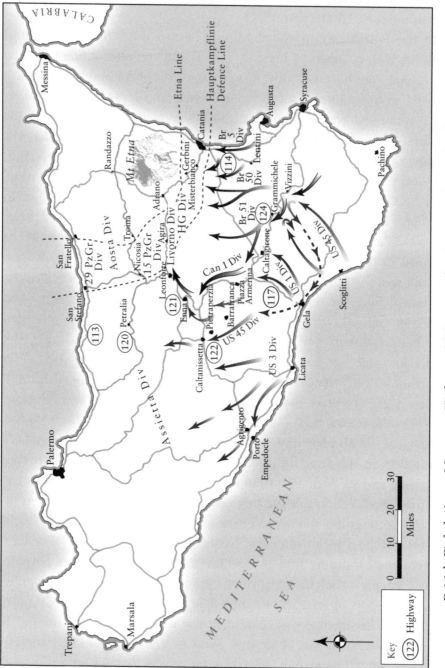

British Eighth Army Moves up Highway 124 across the American Line of Advance

anchor the western flank of the Allied lodgement while Axis forces were pushed northwards to the top of the island and annihilated.

There is little doubt that everyone in Seventh Army's camp regarded the latest decision as being a slight against American capabilities and one which brought the ability and battle-worthiness of their troops into question. Both Alexander and Montgomery seemed to be unaware of the impact such a pronouncement could have on Patton's team. It would appear that the British, and more especially Alexander, were not as yet convinced of the effectiveness of American arms; the shadow of the Kasserine defeat still hung over them. Montgomery clearly felt that he and his forces were more than capable of finishing off the campaign, providing that the Americans played ball by protecting their flank. Alexander for his part was content to agree with the strategic expertise of Britain's most important battlefield commander. It seemed quite a simple step to Alexander to coordinate the direction of the campaign to fit with Monty's wishes. What he did not seem to understand was that such a decision created a huge blow to American pride.

Patton was livid with Alexander's directive, but accepted it as an order. As far as he was concerned, the new instructions were the results of a judgement made by his immediate commander and he was obliged to implement them. Maj Gen Lucas, Eisenhower's deputy, was upset when he heard the news and believed that Patton should have expressed his views more firmly to Alexander. A British liaison officer at the American HQ had explained to Lucas that in the British Army a subordinate might disagree with his superior when he thought that the latter was wrong and put his own point of view forward for consideration. In the US Army, however, an order was an order.

The next day Patton visited Lucian Truscott at the headquarters of the 3rd Division in Licata. He outlined the new instructions and expressed a wish to take Agrigento and its port without having to put in a full-scale attack. Could he do it by bluff? Truscott replied that he would make what regulations called a 'reconnaissance in force', if that was what was wanted, consisting of 'local attacks with limited objectives' so as to keep the high command satisfied, explained Truscott with a knowing smile. Perfect, thought Patton, and departed back to Gela.

Truscott's division began attacking Agrigento and Porto Empedocle the next day through a clever encirclement by 7th Infantry Regiment while the Navy shelled the two places – requests for bombers to take part were resisted by the air authorities, for no word from Alexander had been given that the American front had been extended beyond the Yellow Line.[10] With the Italians' attention diverted by the bombardment, the 3rd Ranger Battalion slipped into the port unmolested. Some resistance was met during the action and three Italian tanks put in an appearance during the assault, but there was little heavy fighting. By the end of the first day 6,000 prisoners had been taken, 100 vehicles and tanks destroyed and 50 pieces of artillery captured.

On 13 July US II Corps was within artillery distance of the Vizzini–Caltagirone road. Possession of the road would open the way towards Enna and put Patton's army on the route north to Messina; at least that was what its commander thought that morning. Everything was going very well for Bradley's corps, although Patton had felt the previous day that 1st Division needed a little more urging to keep moving. All this was now about to change, for around mid-morning Bradley received a message asking him to report to Seventh Army HQ in Gela.

Bradley arrived in the town after driving down to the sea through great convoys of oncoming traffic all bringing supplies forward to an army on the move. He found Patton at his advance headquarters set in an imposing mansion on a headland just to the east of the town. The army commander was poring over a large map, drawing deeply on a cigar. He was obviously in a foul mood. 'Brad, we've had a directive from Army Group,' he explained. 'Monty's to get the Vizzini–Caltagirone road.'

Patton explained that Montgomery was now to use the formerly 'American' road for his own advance to outflank Catania and pass around the west of Mount Etna. Bradley's 45th Division was to pull back and come round behind US 1st Division and then slot itself into the line to the west. Bradley was dumbfounded. 'This will raise hell with us,' he pleaded. 'It will slow up our entire advance.' If the road was to be given to the British, could he at least use it for a while to shift his 45th Division over to the left of the 1st? Not possible, Patton explained; the change-over was to have immediate effect.[11]

Bradley was staggered by the enormity of the new directive. Middleton's division would have to be pulled back from its positions overlooking the vital road all the way to the coast, then passed round the rear of Allen's division. The switch would involve all the transport being diverted from its proper role of re-supply to make a move that would do nothing for the American effort. It would take days to get the division going again and to re-balance II Corps to take advantage of an enemy who was falling back in some disarray. Bradley was, in effect, being asked to disassemble his front and then patch it together again just when his units should be making a determined advance. All Patton could do was to shrug his shoulders; those were his orders. One might wonder what Montgomery would have said if he had been ordered to make such a manoeuvre.

In the event, 45th Division made the moves in remarkably good time. The Americans had the advantage of being supplied with very good transport, much of it four-wheel-driven. Their 2½-ton truck could haul good loads rapidly over poor roads and even cross-country. The Americans' ability to move divisions at speed never failed to impress the British. Although seething at the waste of effort, Middleton efficiently shifted his division back southwards almost to the sea then side-stepped it across to the west, through Maj Gen Allen's lines of communication, to bring it back into the line just to the east of Caltanissetta. Seventh Army now lined up from west to east, 3rd Division, 45th Division, then 1st Division. The Vizzini–Caltagirone road was now the property of Leese's XXX Corps.

Oblivious to the bad feeling he had created within US Seventh Army, Montgomery now gave his attention to running the sharp end of what he saw as his campaign. He instructed Leese to send the Highland Division and 23rd Armoured Brigade up Highway 124 towards Enna.

The architects of Operation 'Husky': *(seated from left to right)* Anthony Eden, Britain's Foreign Secretary; Field Marshal Alan Brooke, Chief of the Imperial General Staff; Prime Minister Winston Churchill; Gen George Marshall, US Army Chief of Staff; Gen Dwight Eisenhower, Supreme Commander North Africa: *standing left to right,* Air Marshal Arthur Tedder; Admiral Andrew Cunningham; Gen Harold Alexander; and Gen Bernard Montgomery.
(IWM NA 3286)

The grey-haired Lt Gen George Patton, 'an old man of about sixty', as Gen Montgomery first described him, takes lunch with HM King George VI in Algiers before the invasion of Sicily.
(IWM NA 3608)

Top: The two main protagonists of the Sicilian campaign share a joke on an airfield near Syracuse. Generals Montgomery and Patton were poles apart when it came to how a battle ought to be fought, neither of them having great regard for the other's ability or strategic vision. *(IWM NA 5013)*

Above: Admiral Cunningham, Naval Commander-in-Chief for Operation 'Husky', poses with Vice Admiral Kent Hewitt, US Navy commander for the invasion of Sicily. *(IWM NA 3030)*

Left: Men of British 51st (Highland) Division wait on the quayside at Sousse in North Africa ready to embark on landing craft for the invasion of Sicily. *(IWM NA 4075)*

Right: The leaders of the Eastern Task Force: Air Vice-Marshal Harry Broadhurst, Gen Montgomery, Vice-Admiral Bertram Ramsay. *(IWM NA 4089)*

Below, main picture: Troops of US 3rd Division come ashore near Licata on the first day of the landings in Sicily. *(IWM NAP 259178)*

Top left: Monty's two main critics during Operation 'Husky': Admiral Andrew Cunningham (*left*) and Air Marshal Arthur Tedder. Both of these senior officers were incensed by Monty's attitude during the planning stages of 'Husky'. *(IWM NA 3033)*

Top right: Gen Harold Alexander (*left*), the ground force commander for 'Husky', in conversation with Gen Dwight D. Eisenhower, the Allied Supreme Commander in the Mediterranean. *(IWM NA 3039)*

Right: A captured Italian coast-defence gun guarding Syracuse harbour. The gun was taken intact by British commandos and pressed into Allied use to guard the anchorage against enemy raiders. *(IWM NA 4602)*

Left: Paratroopers of 505th Parachute Regiment, US 82nd Airborne Division. The three men had been dropped miles from their target in the American sector early on 10 July and had met up with British troops as they came ashore. *(IWM NA 4347)*

Left: Gen Montgomery tours the British beachhead on the day after the assault landings. Monty is riding in Maj-Gen Wimberley's personal DUKW as his own transport was late arriving and was yet to be unloaded. British 51st (Highland) Division's formation sign, a prominent combined 'HD', can be seen on the front of the vehicle near the driver's position. *(IWM NA 4381)*

Right: Primosole Bridge just south of Catania, captured and then given up by British 1st Parachute Brigade after several fierce counter-attacks by German paratroops. *(IWM NA 4787)*

Above: A battery of British 25-pounder field guns firing in support of an infantry attack south of Catania. *(IWM NA 5910)*

Above right: American infantry share a joke with a Sicilian farmer during US Seventh Army's move inland. *(IWM NA 5893)*

Right: British and American forces join up near Randazzo on their drive through the centre of the island. Maj-Gen Vivian Evelegh, Commander British 78th Division (*with map case*) and Brig 'Copper' Cass, Commander British 11th Brigade, meet with Col Paddy Flint (*left*), Commander 39th Infantry Regiment, US 9th Division, and a representative officer from US 1st Division. Col Flint was a larger-than-life character, a cavalry officer and contemporary of Patton, who had 'AAA-O' stencilled on his helmet to signify 'Anything, Anytime, Anywhere, Bar Nothing'. He was killed by a German sniper in Normandy in 1944. *(IWM NA 5896)*

Above: Gen Montgomery in conference with Lt-Gen Dempsey, Commander British XIII Corps, in a Sicilian orchard on 13 July. In the foreground, two men are brewing a cup of afternoon tea for the senior officers. *(IWM NA 4417)*

Left: A forlorn General Gotti-Porcinari stares blankly at the photographer after his capture. The commander of the Italian *Napoli* Division was taken by troops of British 50th Division in an ambush near Sortino on 13 July, along with some members of his staff. *(IWM NA 4526)*

Above: A formidable German Panzer VI (Tiger) tank knocked out by the Canadians near Caltagirone along Highway 124. The 60-ton Tiger was more than a match for any Allied tank, but in the early years of its development it was slow-moving and unreliable, suffering as many losses from breakdowns as from Allied action. *(IWM NA 4743)*

Right: Lt-Gen Miles Dempsey, Commander British XIII Corps (*left*), with Maj-Gen Guy Simonds, Commander Canadian 1st Division. *(IWM NA 5915)*

An American mule train carries supplies through the rubble of a Sicilian village. From their experience in the mountains of Tunisia, US Seventh Army knew how vital mules were to the movement of supplies across difficult terrain. *(IWM NA 5894)*

Patton met Monty *(above left, IWM NA 5007)* on an airfield near Syracuse to discuss the latter half of the Sicilian campaign. They carved up the island between them using a map on the bonnet of Monty's staff car. Alexander, their boss, and Eisenhower's Chief of Staff, Maj Gen Walter Bedell Smith, arrived later *(above right, IWM NA 5016)*. Alexander was displeased that Monty and Patton had already agreed their future strategy before he joined the meeting.

The Allied advance was plagued by demolitions. Here American engineers are clearing mines from the area near a damaged viaduct. German tactics were to create road blocks along the main route then mine the paths of likely diversions around the obstacles. *(IWM NY 3469)*

An infantryman of US 3rd Division receives blood plasma after being wounded on the drive to Messina. A few Sicilian women look on with concern. *(US National Archives)*

Tanks of US 2nd Armored Division are greeted as conquering heroes by the civilian population of Palermo. Before the invasion it was thought that Allied troops might receive a cold reception from the Sicilians, but once they arrived it soon became clear that the locals were tired of the conflict and wished for peace to return to their island. *(IWM HU 92065)*

Palermo residents seem unconcerned that they have just been occupied by the enemy and pose for a photograph with US troops. *(IWM NY 3465)*

Lt Gen Patton meets with Lt Col Lyle Bernard, commander of 2nd Battalion, US 30th Infantry Regiment, after the amphibious landings near Brolo. Bernard's exposed battalion held out for over 24 hours, 10 miles behind the German line, against numerous counter-attacks, until it was relieved by the advancing ground troops of US 3rd Division. *(US National Archives)*

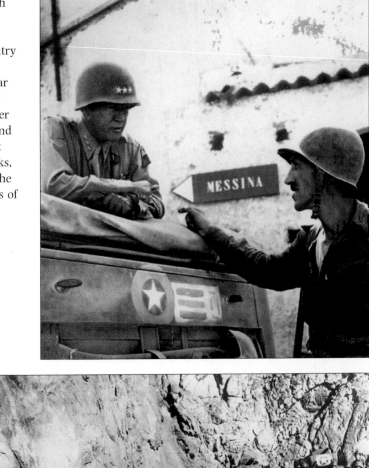

Troops of US 3rd Division attempt to negotiate their way across German demolitions along the narrow cliff-hugging coastal route of Highway 113. *(IWM NYS 2077)*

The winning team at Montgomery's HQ in Taormina at the end of the campaign.
Eisenhower and the Americans were there to invest Eighth Army's commander with the
highest order which America can bestow upon a soldier of a foreign nation, that of
Commander of the Legion of Merit. *Seated, from left to right:* Patton, Eisenhower and
Montgomery; *standing:* Bradley, Truscott, Gay (Patton's Chief of Staff), Keyes and Dempsey.
(IWM NA 6106)

CHAPTER 11

Primosole Bridge and the Commando Landings

On the third day of the landings, Lt-Col Durnford-Slater was called to XIII Corps HQ in Syracuse to receive orders for a new attack that would go in that night. He met Monty, Dempsey and Admiral Rhoderick McGrigor (Commander Naval Force B) on the quayside outside the old Italian naval officers' quarters. The senior officers were in a good mood. Monty was very pleased with the exploits of his special forces and wished to use them again to help keep up the momentum of the advance.

Dempsey explained that they had a new operation for Durnford-Slater's commando: 'It's an ambitious one, but I think you will like it.' Both 3 Commando and 1st Parachute Brigade, commanded by Brig Gerald Lathbury, would be landed behind enemy lines that night to seize important bridges that would help speed up XIII Corps' advance. The commando would be landed at Agnone, advance inland and take and hold the road bridge over the River Leonardo, the Ponte dei Malati, while the paratroopers did the same 5 miles to the north at the road bridge over the River Simeto, the Ponte dei Primosole. Possession of these bridges would help Eighth Army's advance up the main road to Catania and break through the enemy defence lines based on the two rivers.

Durnford-Slater's commandos were all tired from their previous action at the battery north of Cassibile, but faced the new operation in a confident mood. Intelligence optimistically suggested that the beach chosen for the landing was lightly held by 'half-hearted Italians' and thought that no Germans would be encountered. Time was short, however, for by the time that the orders had been promulgated down through 3 Commando, there were only three hours available to plan and brief the men who were to carry out the operation. Monty exuded confidence and, as Durnford-Slater left the briefing, he remarked, 'Everybody's on the move now. The enemy is nicely on the move. We want to keep him that way. You can help us do that. Good luck, Slater.'[1]

The landings were timed to take place in two phases: Nos 1, 2, 3, 4, and Headquarters Troops would touch down in the first wave, with 5 and 6 Troops arriving later. Headquarters and 2 Troop would hold the beach while 1 and 3 Troops were to push forward to seize and hold the bridge. Once a firm base had been established on the shoreline, 5 and 6 Troops would land and pass through to reinforce the commandos holding the bridge. No. 4 Troop would organise two patrols, one to contact the airborne troops attacking Primosole Bridge to the north, the other to link up with 50th Division advancing towards 3 Commando up the Catania road. The leading units of Maj-Gen Kirkman's division planned to reach the area of the bridge by first light the next day, 14 July.

Further up the road, just 5 miles short of Catania, was the target for British 1st Parachute Brigade that night, the Primosole Bridge over the River Simeto. The plan to capture the river crossing, Operation 'Fustian', was conceived well before the invasion. Parachutists had been training for the assault for many months and had been grouped around the airfields near Kairouan in Tunisia for weeks. In theory it was the perfect use of airborne troops. They would be dropped at night just as 50th Division attacked Lentini 10 miles to the south. The airborne brigade would seize the bridge and hold it until Kirkman's division had advanced over 3 Commando's bridge, then up the main road to relieve them.

On 12 July final briefings began for the operation. Then there was disappointment as the attack was postponed because Monty's troops had been delayed south and west of Augusta. The next day, things changed and the operation was back on again. Montgomery's army was not making significantly better progress, but its leader was determined to go all out for Catania, urging his commanders to take all risks to get the momentum back into the advance before the enemy could consolidate their defences.

At 1630 hrs on 13 July the final OK was given; the attack would go in that night.

For the airborne attack US 51st Troop Carrier Wing would once again carry British airborne troops into action in 105 of its C-47 transport aircraft. This number was reinforced by 11 British Albemarles from 38th Wing RAF. A total of 1,865 paratroopers, engineers and medical staff from the 1st Parachute Brigade would be carried in these transports. Added to this number were 19 gliders – 8 CG-4As and 11 Horsas – which would be towed by more Albemarles and Halifaxes from 38th Wing. The gliders were to transport 77 artillerymen, ten 6-pounder anti-tank guns and 18 jeeps. This time the airborne troops would take with them some decent firepower to ward off enemy counter-attacks.[2]

The plan called for simultaneous landings by three parachute battalions on four drop zones all within 2 miles of the bridge, with gliders arriving at the same time over two landing zones, one within a few hundred yards of the target, the other three-quarters of a mile away. Lt-Col Alastair Pearson's 1st Parachute Battalion would capture the bridge itself, Lt-Col John Frost's 2nd Battalion would land and hold the southern approaches to the crossing place and Lt-Col Yeldham's 3rd Battalion would hold the northern approaches. At 2200 hrs on 13 July, the aircraft began to roll down the dusty airstrips at Kairouan.

The previous day, 50th (Northumbrian) Division's advance had begun against little opposition, mainly Italians from the *Napoli* Division. The lead battalions of 69th Brigade had pushed forward to reach Sortino. The men were exhausted and expected some rest after their exertions. Just after dawn Maj-Gen Kirkman came up to see the brigadier and discuss the next moves. Intelligence suggested that there was little enemy strength in front of the brigade. Kirkman was all for carrying on: 'You're not going to sit down and rest?' he asked Brig Edward Cooke-Collis. 'There's no one in front of you at all. The place is empty.' He then told the brigadier that his troops were to push on until they dropped if necessary. They were to use their carriers as tanks and push on towards Lentini. Occupy this ground today, he urged, because you will have to fight for it tomorrow. 'Get 'em all on the move, go on, go on – now is the time to go on.'[3]

The urgings that the divisional commander made to his brigadier were given at the appropriate moment, for a little later that day Kirkman was called back to Dempsey's HQ. Montgomery was there and outlined the

airborne attack that was to go in that night on the Primosole Bridge and
the landings by 3 Commando to capture the bridge over the Leonardo. The
Northumbrian Division had to fight its way forward to relieve them at all
costs. It was now Monty who was urging 50th Division's CO to get his men
moving. 'Go on at all possible speed,' the army commander ordered.

Kirkman arrived back at his headquarters just after midday with the
news of the vital advance that his division must make. The 5th Division
was to continue its attack on the right, clearing the coastal area and the
approaches to Augusta, while the 51st Division pushed forward on the left
against Francofonte. Kirkman's drive from his positions outside Sortino, to
relieve the paratroopers on Primosole Bridge by the morning of the next
day, would involve the 69th Brigade in an advance of two bounds: the first,
10 miles from Sortino to Lentini through Carlentini; the second, another
10 miles from Lentini, through the 3 Commando positions to Primosole. It
was a tall order, but opposition still seemed to be coming from dispirited
Italians.

Waiting at Kirkman's HQ, standing sheepishly by the door ready to be
taken away were Gen Porgini, the commander of the *Napoli* Division, and
his chief of staff. They had been captured earlier that morning by 6th
Durham Light Infantry when their staff car had been ambushed as it was
leaving Sortino. With its commanding general now captive it was virtually
the end of the *Napoli* Division. This, at first sight, seemed to be thoroughly
good news for Kirkman. However, the enemy line had to be held together
somehow and it was German troops of a much higher calibre who moved
in to repair the damage opposite the 50th Division, just as 69th Brigade
was piling on the pressure to get to Lentini and on to Primosole.

All afternoon and into the late evening the brigade pressed forward. Gen
Kirkman and Brig Cooke-Collis gathered at the rear of their lead battalion
as darkness was falling to watch another of its attacks. The general urged
the men on, but the brigadier could see that the position in front of
Carlentini would need a full-scale attack to get past it. Even then the whole
town would have to be assaulted and cleared before Lentini could be
entered that night. The advance was rapidly falling behind schedule. This
worrying news was radioed back to XIII Corps HQ. Dempsey took the news
badly; it was too late to postpone the airborne and commando operations
so Kirkman's brigade would have to press on regardless. A postponement
was also tactically undesirable, for if 50th Division was able to take Lentini

the next morning, the road to Catania would be open and the enemy would be sure to blow the two bridges. No, it was decided, the two assaults would go in as planned and capture the bridges and 50th Division would have to get forward at all speed to relieve them.

There was nothing for it but for Kirkman's tired battalions to press on. More support was brought up and the weary infantry attacked towards Carlentini behind a rolling barrage. A dogged advance coupled with bloody-minded aggression cleared the first of the enemy positions barring the way by 2200 hrs, just about the same time as 1st Airborne Brigade's aircraft were leaving the runways in Tunisia. By this time the troops of the lead battalion had had enough. It was now the turn of the 7th Green Howards to have a go.

This fresh battalion put in a set-piece attack, backed by the divisional artillery and the Vickers machine guns and heavy mortars of the 2nd Cheshires, but it did not actually get going until 0830 hrs the next day. Fire from Monte Pancali held up a lot of the preparation work and it took longer than expected to get the two supporting field artillery regiments into place. The artillery blasted the hill, the machine guns and mortars swept the whole of the feature and the infantry advanced. The hill was taken and the enemy evicted. Then came the clearing of the eastern slopes and, eventually, a resumption of the advance into Carlentini. It was 1300 hrs, roughly about the time the division was expected to have reached at least one of the *coup de main* parties on the bridges.

The infantry assault ship HMS *Prince Albert* carrying the lead troops of 3 Commando had reached its lowering position 5 miles off Agnone at 2130 hrs the previous night. The passage from Syracuse had not been without incident, for the ship had come into close contact with a German E-boat. Two torpedoes had been fired at the *Price Albert* by the fast enemy craft and it was only by swift manoeuvre that a disaster had been avoided. Although all was now calm and clear on the water, the coastline was lit up by flashes and explosions as Axis positions were bombarded by long-range artillery fire from ground troops. Catania to the north was burning and Syracuse to the south was ringed by anti-aircraft and tracer fire. Assault craft were lowered, commandos embarked and the small boats were winched down into the water where they formed into assault formation. At 2200 hrs the craft pointed their bows westwards and began their run-in to the shore.

Ahead the landing place was still in total darkness in front of a background of flashing lights and coloured tracer fire emanating from Eighth Army's land battle. Overhead the drone of countless C-47s drowned the chugging noise of the landing craft engines as low-flying aircraft carried 1st Parachute Brigade on their approach to the Primosole Bridge.

Fire came at 3 Commando about 200 yards from shore when machine guns in two pillboxes opened up on the small craft. The men out on the water responded immediately and each of the two fortifications was raked with small arms fire, silencing them for a short while. Further enemy opposition did little to interfere with the disembarkation and the commandos quickly took control of the beach. The shore was lined with sandy cliffs topped with barbed wire. Bangalore torpedoes were used to blow gaps in the wire and one by one the troops slipped through the openings and began forming up ready for the tasks ahead. While the men of 2 Troop spread out to deal with the local opposition, Maj Peter Young gathered 1 and 3 Troops for the advance inland to the bridge.

'We passed off the beach in a ragged half-column, without many casualties, although I saw one man dragging himself along on his hands with his legs behind him,' recalled Lt Butler later.[4] The route through the darkness to the objective was tortuous: 5 miles of close countryside covered with cacti and scattered shrubs, dissected with numerous ravines and steep hills and covered by scattered groups of Germans. To the surprise of the attackers, the enemy they bumped into turned out not to be the disillusioned Italians Intelligence had predicted, but determined men of the German 1st Parachute Division and the *Hermann Göring* Division. A group of stray paratroopers from 1st Parachute Brigade who had been jettisoned well to the south of their correct drop zone was also met on the way and an offer was made for them to join in the commando attack, but they declined and pressed on to join their unit at the Primosole Bridge to the north. Maj Young and the advance guard arrived in the area of the River Leonardo at around 0300 hrs. In front of him the long outline of the Ponte dei Malati and its causeway stretched out in the darkness across a shallow valley for over 250 yards. In the course of the next few hours more and more men from 3 Commando joined as the second wave arrived on the beach and advanced to the objective.

At the north-east end of the bridge were two pillboxes. Surprise had been achieved for there was no sign that the Italians guarding the bridge knew of the presence of the commandos. Lt Butler attacked the first of these with a hand grenade and knocked out its defenders. Maj Young attacked the other with rifle fire through its observation slit. Within 15 minutes all opposition at the north-east end of the crossing had been eliminated and 3 Commando had established itself in a position that completely blocked the main road leading up from Eighth Army's front. By this time Lt-Col Durnford-Slater had come up to the bridge and now ordered Maj Young to form another bridgehead at the south-western end of the bridge.

Thus far all the action had been on one side of the river; the opposite bank was still in Italian hands. When 3 Troop tried to cross the shallow waterway to seize the defences on the far side it soon became clear that the earlier fire-fight had attracted more opposition. The troop encountered heavy resistance from the far side and the commandos had to take refuge beneath the bridge. A German tank began shelling them from its concealed hide in an orchard. Small arms fire also came at Durnford-Slater's men from many places along the banks of the river. The Italian defenders at the bridge had been reinforced by the stiffened resolve of German troops. No. 3 Troop was extracted from its predicament with a barrage of fire laid down from the captured side of the river.

Durnford-Slater was now suffering the effects of having to implement a rushed mission. Both ends of the bridge should have been seized simultaneously. The little time available to his team before the operation for detailed preparation, and the scarcity of accurate maps and air photographs from which to evolve an attack plan, had resulted in a stalled effort. The small force the colonel had with him, about 200 men armed only with light weapons, meant that he could not now take the far end of the bridge in the face of stiff enemy resistance. However, all was not lost for demolition charges had been removed from the bridge and there was little danger that the enemy could now destroy the structure. Durnford-Slater decided that his small gathering would continue to hold the north-east end of the bridge, bar enemy movement along the main road and wait for 50th Division to come up and relieve them.[5]

The enemy on the other hand were not content to sit it out and took steps to remove the commandos. Increasingly heavy fire from the tank and from mortars and small arms plastered the commando's positions. Dawn came with no let-up in the enemy fire and no sign of 50th Division. An hour later the situation had worsened. Casualties were mounting and the time would soon come when the commandos would have to withdraw. Durnford-Slater decided to pull back steadily with the most mobile of the wounded onto a small steep hill about 800 yards to the south-east until the lead troops of Eighth Army arrived. After 30 more minutes Durnford-Slater reluctantly gave the order and Sergeant-Major Lowe went on ahead with a section of men to establish a defensive position on the summit of the hill into which the survivors of 3 Commando could withdraw.

Little by little the tired and exposed commandos slipped away from the area of the bridge. At this point many more fell victim to enemy fire. The more serious of the wounded were left in the anticipation of them getting immediate medical treatment as prisoners of war. The colonel had hoped to make a stand on the hill until relieved, but the Germans were intent on removing what could be a grave threat to their rear. German artillery now shelled the hill, making 3 Commando's positions untenable. The number of casualties began to grow even further. Durnford-Slater realised that there was nothing more that could be done. He gave the order for his men to scatter. It was every man for himself, whether he chose to hole up until the advance guard of 50th Division arrived or to try to make it back to the beach and to the British line on his own. Most chose to slip away in small groups, hoping to infiltrate through the enemy lines. Each had an unanswerable question troubling his mind: where was 50th Division?[6]

Earlier the previous night, the aircraft carrying Brig Lathbury's 1st Parachute Brigade onto its drop zones suffered the same fate as had met the American pilots on earlier missions. First, many of them were hit by anti-aircraft fire from Allied ships as they neared the coast, then by the enemy barrage. To the paratroopers crammed onto the long bench seats along the sides of the C-47s it seemed that they were flying though a wall of coloured tracer. The Dakota transports pitched and fell violently as their pilots took evasive action, throwing the airborne troops inside all over the plane. Here and there an aircraft took a hit, burst into flames and keeled over, plunging earthwards like a fiery beacon with its passengers trapped inside. Other aircraft broke formation and veered away from their correct flight paths and, anxious to get away from all the flak, released their paratroopers over a wide area. Some sticks were dropped as far away as Mount Etna; others allegedly landed in southern Italy. A few of the more unfortunate paratroopers landed in the sea and were drowned. Less than

20 per cent of the brigade were dropped according to plan, and nearly 30 per cent were returned to base. Of these, nine aircraft had turned back because they had been hit by anti-aircraft fire, mostly from Allied warships. Some came home because their pilots claimed they were unable to find the drop zones. A later roll call determined that only 12 officers and 283 other ranks, out of the total of 1,856 men who started out from Tunisia, actually took part in the battle.[7]

In Lt-Col Alistair Pearson's aircraft the paratroopers were becoming weary of their pilot's flak-dodging antics. The colonel observed that the plane seemed to be flying up and down the coast. Pearson resolved to bring matters to a head. He unhooked his parachute and made his way to the cockpit where he found the American navigator had completely lost his nerve and was unable to give directions to the pilot. Pearson was furious. He patted his holster and said, 'That bloody man ought to be shot,' then turned to the pilot and ordered him to take his plane in over the island. Satisfied that at least they would be able to exit the plane, Pearson returned to his seat. Moments later the jump lights came on. The C-47 then went into a steep dive as the airborne troops shuffled to the door. There was no slow and level run into the drop zone to allow a tidy exit; in fact the aircraft's speed increased quickly as the pilot tried to lose height. Even before the last of the tailenders managed to get out of the plane there was insufficient height to permit their parachutes to open fully before they hit the ground. Jumping from the aircraft that day was Joe Smith: 'There was no attempt to throttle back and on exit my kitbag was literally torn from my leg.'[8]

The C-47 aircraft seemed either to come in too low or too high; few of them made successful approaches from which their paratroopers could emerge together at the correct height onto the correct drop zone. Lt-Col John Frost was one of the luckier ones; he was dropped in the right place and had a successful descent, albeit with a twisted knee from a heavy landing. The remainder of his 2nd Battalion was, however, widely dispersed, although the stick dropping with him landed close by. The colonel waited at the pre-arranged rendezvous point south of the bridge until all the aircraft had disappeared, but could only muster around a hundred men of his unit.

Undaunted, Frost and his men set off onto the high ground south of the bridge to form a perimeter. On the way he passed the brigadier at his headquarters. Lathbury had been dropped in the wrong place and had only just arrived. There was no sign of his signallers so communication with the other two battalions was impossible. Lathbury had no idea what was happening elsewhere, but the sound of firing coming from the area of the bridge at least showed that the 1st Battalion was in action around the main objective.

The 19 gliders carrying the artillerymen, guns and jeeps to support the brigade took off from Kairouan into clear and calm weather. When the airborne fleet reached Malta the sun had set and a half-moon gave clear uninterrupted visibility. There was to be no repeat of the poor weather that had contributed to the disaster in Operation 'Ladbroke'. The airborne chaos of that operation was nonetheless repeated when the aircraft flew over the Allied ships below, for they opened fire. Planes dipped and dived, twisted and banked, as they took evasive action. Once again cohesion was lost: tugs and gliders went off route, tows were cast and by the time that the glider formations crossed the shore, a third of them had been lost. Those that ploughed on were scattered: one landed north-east of Lentini, another came down in the river, yet another crashed killing and injuring all on board.

Some intrepid pilots got their charges down safely, a few on target, but many too far away to be of use in the battle. It was a difficult task to try to get guns and jeeps out of crashed Horsas, and some of them proved to be completely immovable. When the crews had finally broken open their loads and towed them up to the bridge, only two mortars and three anti-tank guns could be mustered to join in with the defence.

Lt-Col Pearson jumped into an inferno. Enemy machine-gunners on the ground raked the descending paratroopers with long bursts of fire. Many were killed before they came to earth. Pearson landed into complete chaos with few of his men around him, but he was soon to learn that Capt Rann had attacked the Primosole Bridge with about 50 men and captured it. Few difficulties had been encountered, and the Italians defending the crossing place had surrendered easily. Pearson now set his men out to consolidate their gains and by first light had mustered around 100 men under his command. One thing, however, troubled him: early reports showed that they were not just facing Italians, but that crack German paratroopers were also in the area.

The demolition charges placed on the bridge were located by engineers and removed, slit trenches were dug around both ends of the bridge and the roads blocked on either side. A dump of German Teller mines was found in one of the blockhouses. Engineers now fused them and dispersed the explosives among the outlying positions to place across the approach roads. The blockhouses and pillboxes at either end of the bridge also contained useful weapons. Several Breda heavy machine guns together with a plentiful supply of ammunition remained in position guarding the approaches. Covering the roads were two Italian 50mm guns and one German 75mm anti-tank gun, each housed in a concrete emplacement. These weapons supplemented those that had been brought in by air and gave the defenders some measure of security. Pearson now waited for the inevitable counter-attack and the arrival of the relief column from 50th Division.

To the north of the bridge, Col Yeldham's 3rd Battalion had been scattered over a wide area during its descent. Few of its troops were concentrated and able to reach their objectives. A runner reported back to Lathbury that the battalion was badly scattered and down to no more than around 100 men. The brigadier sent orders for the battalion to draw closer to the bridge and form a bridgehead around the northern end of the crossing place.

Lt-Col Frost's 2nd Battalion was the first to feel the enemy counter-attacks. The colonel had formed defences around two of the three hills overlooking the southern approach road to the bridge with the men he had available. With only about 140 paratroopers at his disposal, almost 50 per cent more than each of the other two battalions had mustered, he was not able to form quite the defensive position that he had hoped. The first attack started at 0600 hrs. By this time the sun was up and visibility was good. German parachute troops attacked the southernmost feature with machine-gun fire, but kept at a respectful distance. Thirty minutes later, mortars were brought into play. The 2nd Battalion had few effective weapons with them to counter this fire, which became more and more accurate as the morning progressed.

Frost was becoming concerned at the growing number of casualties and so decided to send out a fighting patrol to try to silence the enemy at the bottom of the hill. Unfortunately, this patrol was intercepted and armoured cars on the road caused it to withdraw with even more casualties. The firing set long grass on fire and soon the lower slopes were blanketed by billowing smoke that acted as cover for the increasingly confident enemy troops. Taking advantage of the heat and flames, the Germans improved their positions and finally put down such a level of fire that they made the hill untenable for Frost's men. The colonel ordered a withdrawal from the outpost and consolidated his hold on the rear hill overlooking the bridge.[9]

Down at the bridge, the enemy waited until almost 1000 hrs before putting in an attack from the north. From their vantage points along the high banks of the river, the paratroopers could see the Germans forming up across the flat plain that led to Catania. The battle started with German Focke-Wulf 190 fighters shooting up the area around the crossing, strafing the British positions with small-calibre cannon shells. Then came the fire of enemy 88mm guns, firing air bursts at first to find the range. A short time later, shells began crashing down on and around the bridge, then machine-gun fire and then small arms fire as the German paratroopers began their assault on the outlying positions of the 3rd Battalion north of the bridge.

The men of the 1st Parachute Brigade replied with a barrage of fire of their own and the attack was beaten off. But this was only the first of many, for the Germans resolutely tried again and again throughout the morning and well into the afternoon using the same pattern of attack. Heavy firing successfully repulsed each attempt, but only at the cost of a great deal of ammunition, a fair number of casualties and a little bit more of the perimeter ground. Gradually the Germans worked their way close to the bridge and onto the reed-covered banks.

By late afternoon, Brig Lathbury had decided it was time to pull back the remnants of the 3rd Battalion across the river and abandon the northern end of the bridge to reinforce the southern end. The enemy would be kept at bay by the river obstacle itself. For a while the move produced a stronger position with more concentrated firepower, albeit after the bridge itself, the single object of the whole operation, had been abandoned.

Way back down the road towards Lentini the 7th Green Howards were on the move again. Opposition was even worse than before, but at least the enemy did not have possession of high ground overlooking the advance. The 5th Division's moves on the right had forced more of the enemy up a diverging road that met the main highway at Carlentini. This opposition had to be blasted aside with the help of artillery and tanks. Carlentini was reached and cleared and then Lentini fell to 50th Division. Brig Cooke-

Collis kept up the momentum by passing his third battalion through Lentini, urging the 5th East Yorkshires on the 3 miles to the commando bridge over the River Leonardo. When they arrived they were gratified to find that the bridge was still intact, though unfortunately under enemy ownership. A short fire-fight evicted the enemy rearguard and, just as the light was falling, the advance was taken over by 151st Brigade, which sent 9th Durham Light Infantry and the tanks of 4th Armoured Brigade on up the road to Primosole.

Earlier that day, up on the hill behind Brig Lathbury's exposed perimeter around the bridge, Frost and his men were still trying to hold back the enemy. During the late morning an artillery signaller had managed to get in touch with a warship offshore, the cruiser HMS *Newfoundland*, and called down its 6-inch shells on the enemy. The resultant blasts blew the spirit out of the German attack. Each time the enemy troops tried to restart their attack, further salvos were called down on their heads. By early afternoon they contented themselves with firing just small arms at the 2nd Battalion, sniping at anyone who showed himself. The majority of the Germans now turned their attention to the more important matters around the bridge, leaving a few men to keep Frost's paratroopers bottled up on the hill. To Lathbury and his men down at the river the lull in the firing seemed to imply that Frost and his men had been over-run and their only line of retreat towards British forces had been blocked.

From his vantage point Frost now watched the battle raging below him. It was not possible to use the naval firepower to help Brig Lathbury's attempts to stem the German attack, for the two sides were too closely locked together. The situation started to deteriorate rapidly when the Germans brought up anti-tank guns and began to take pot-shots at the pillboxes. All afternoon and into the evening the enemy peppered away at Lathbury's small perimeter around the southern end of the bridge. One by one his guns began to fall silent. Ammunition for the captured guns ran out first, then each man had to look to his own stocks and start to conserve the last few rounds he had. A Vickers machine gun which had done sterling service in keeping enemy infantry at bay, was soon down to its last belt of bullets.

A final concentrated enemy attack down both sides of the river, covered by burning reeds at the water's edge, got among the men of the Parachute Brigade. Their position was now untenable. With no sight or sound of

50th Division's advance guard coming to their rescue, there was nothing for it but to withdraw. The order was passed to as many men as possible and one by one they extricated themselves from contact with the Germans and retreated southwards in the failing light; it was just after 1930 hrs. The intention was to rendezvous on the hill still held by Frost's men. Some made it and joined up with the 2nd Battalion, including Lt-Col Pearson; others were prevented from making contact by the enemy and had to try to cross the hills to 50th Division's lines.

A very short time later, just before complete darkness, carriers from 9th Durham Light Infantry and tanks from 4th Armoured Brigade motored up the road beneath the positions of the remnants of 1st Parachute Brigade. Relief had come too late for the bridge to be held, but the arrival of the ground troops denied the Germans access to the crossing place and prevented them from laying new charges to blow the structure. During the night the other two Durham Light Infantry battalions of the brigade came up and Brig Senior was able to establish a large perimeter around the southern end of the bridge. His troops were too exhausted after their forced march to put in an immediate attack, so preparations were made for a full-blown assault across the river at 0730 hrs the next morning.

The greatest obstacle to the success of the operation was the presence of the elite troops of the German 1st Parachute Division near the bridge. This had been totally unexpected. Were it not for the determined resistance and counter-attacks carried out by these experienced paratroopers, then the bridge would most likely have been held and the bridgeheads on either side of the river consolidated, even after the chaos of the drop. The plan was a good one, setting down three battalions of parachute infantry and establishing them on the bridge, supported with enough anti-tank guns and mortars to hold on until the next morning. Certainly this was an achievable goal, if the brigade had been landed intact and if the 50th Division had captured Lentini the same night as the drop. The next day the advance of 151st Brigade supported by 4th Armoured Brigade had made the drive from Lentini, through 3 Commando's bridge up to the Parachute Brigade in good time, again as planned. The operation had failed because of the delays in taking Carlentini and Lentini the night before by the exhausted troops of 69th Brigade.

So ended another attempt to use airborne troops to seize a strategic objective. Despite amazing acts of bravery, leadership and determination by the troops taking part, it has to be seen as a failure. Reasons were many, and excuses equally profuse. The fact remains that only a small number of paratroopers, roughly about 20 per cent, actually took part in the main actions on and around the bridge. The pilots of 51st Troop Carrier Wing came in for a lot more criticism from the men of the Parachute Brigade for not delivering them steadfastly to their drop zones. Admiral Cunningham's command also had to take some of the blame, since warships and merchantmen had opened fire on the air fleet as it passed overhead, even though prior warning had been given. It was perhaps this fire that so disrupted the aerial formations of C-47 aircraft that order was unable to be restored before they met the German flak and had to make their slow and steady runs over the drop zones.

The next day Gen Alexander suspended further operations by 1st Airborne Division until there had been a great deal more inter-service training in airborne techniques. Clearly the events of the previous few days showed that there was still much to be done before all services could work together to execute successful landings. Eisenhower appointed a board of officers to review recent operations before deciding whether or not to use Allied airborne troops in the role for which they were raised. Some good results had been achieved during the invasion but these were all too few in the greater scheme of things and the cost in men and matériel was way too high. The fact was that large-scale airborne operations were too complicated for the questionable infrastructure that was in place to deliver them.

CHAPTER 12

Monty's Plan Stalls

Lieutenant General George Patton was an aggressive soldier and the task given to him by Alexander was not to his liking. His newly formed Seventh Army needed to be blooded in action. He was not at all content to have his force present in Sicily merely to protect Monty's flank and rear.

Patton had obtained permission from Alexander to take Agrigento, provided it was done with no great risk to the main effort, and Truscott's men were in the process of doing just that. Patton, however, was looking beyond this 'reconnaissance in force' – his focus was much further to the west, all the way, in fact, to Sicily's capital city, Palermo. If his American army was to be denied a slice of the glory in taking Messina, it would at least liberate the largest city and port on the island.

With Palermo in mind, Patton contemplated forming a provisional corps, with Maj Gen Geoffrey Keyes in command, consisting of 3rd Division, 82nd Airborne Division and a regiment of the 9th Division, which was shortly to arrive on the island. He would, like Montgomery, run his campaign with two corps operating on two routes: one towards Palermo and the other, Bradley's II Corps, towards the north-western coast of Sicily. He would keep 2nd Armored Division at Licata in reserve.

Patton felt that, by 19 July, the Allies would have a secure line across the south-eastern side of the island and his army would be in a position to use its strength for some meaningful purpose. However, there was still the problem of convincing Alexander of the need for such moves. He confided in his diary that he would bring the matter up 'when the time is ripe'.[1]

In the meantime, Seventh Army would carry on creating elbow room in its lodgement. Middleton's 45th Division would continue to perform the complicated about-face and sideways shift to allow British XXX Corps to cross its path. Truscott's 3rd Division would go on closing on Agrigento and the neighbouring harbour of Porto Empedocle, wresting the area from the Italians without over-extending its front. In the centre Allen's 1st Division was pushing back the right wing of 15th Panzergrenadier Division, carving out a deep lodgement through the hills to the south of Enna. By 14 July, Allen already had his 26th Regimental Combat Team within a few miles of Highway 124 between Vizzini and Enna, some 20 miles to the west of British XXX Corps. It was to take Leese's troops two more days of hard fighting along the road itself before they came level with the Americans.

After the acquisition of Highway 124 for his own needs, Montgomery intended that Leese's XXX Corps should advance north-west through Vizzini towards Caltagirone and then Enna. From here it would swing to the right and head for Leonforte and Adrano to bring it alongside the western slopes of Mount Etna. From this point the corps would be above Catania and positioned for a further drive northwards through Randazzo and on to Messina.

On 13 July, Lt-Gen Leese and his corps were actually poised to take Vizzini. The 23rd Armoured Brigade and 154th Brigade had reached the area above the town the previous evening while the remainder of the 51st Highland Division was concentrated some 5 miles back along Highway 124. Leese had ordered that Vizzini was to be captured that day, Calta-girone on the following night and the advance towards Enna continued on the 14th, with 23rd Armoured Brigade leading the way. After 51st Division had cleared up Vizzini, it was to send 152nd Brigade north-east to Francofonte to protect the corps' right flank and to make contact with XIII Corps around Lentini.

The left flank of the corps was held by Maj-Gen Simonds's 1st Canadian Division and on 13 July it was more or less immobile. It had been ordered to rest for 36 hours in Giarratania, 10 miles south of Vizzini. The division's arrival in Sicily direct from England had not allowed the men time to acclimatise to the semi-tropical conditions of the Mediterranean and they were suffering badly from the scorching heat. Cases of sunburn and exhaustion were common. The division had been in Britain for two years and this sudden immersion in battle on the parched landscape of Sicily had come as something of a shock. This, coupled with the fact that its troops had advanced over 50 miles on foot since the landings, had taken a toll on the fitness of the average Canadian soldier. Monty regarded them as being out of shape: 'They want to get some flesh off and to harden themselves,' he commented.[2]

Vizzini did not fall on 13 July, for it took another full day's fighting before a mixed garrison of Germans and Italians was forced out of the town by the Highland Division. Most of the next day was spent clearing the area before Vizzini could be declared completely secured. XXX Corps' advance towards Enna was continued on 15 July. The increase in enemy resistance caused Montgomery some annoyance and Leese to rethink his plans. The corps' right flank was meeting with a good deal of resistance in the area between 51st Division and XIII Corps and the attack on Francofonte by 152nd Brigade was proving difficult. The brigade did not take the town until 15 July. Leese decided that he would have to bring in the whole of the Canadian Division to take over the drive on Enna while he sent 51st Division and 23rd Armoured Brigade to the right towards Scordia to clear what was becoming increasingly German opposition in the area between him and Dempsey's corps. Leese had no problem with his left flank, for US 45th Division had that ground covered with its 157th Regimental Combat Team, while the remainder of Middleton's division was performing its about-turn. The 157th was sitting idly to the south of Highway 124 in the position it had reached two days before when ordered to stop by Montgomery's edict.

What Montgomery expected to be a lightning thrust on Enna against slight opposition was proving to be completely the opposite. His left hook was in danger of becoming a slow crawl, as the Canadians met more and more German rearguards, roadside demolitions, mines and difficult terrain during their advance. The drive up a single highway was easily countered by small groups of Germans. Gen Conrath was moving the main body of his *Hermann Göring* Division eastwards and was relying on small battle-groups to protect his flank and his lines of communications to the west. These rearguards were slowing down the Canadian advance, concentrating their resistance on the string of towns that lined Highway 124. Like most of the other towns in southern Sicily, Caltagirone, Piazza Armerina, Valguarnera, Enna and Leonforte were mostly sited on hilltops. It did not take a large number of troops, nor great quantities of weapons, to organise a substantial defence among their solid buildings. A few machine-gun posts and anti-tank guns covering the road into them brought the Canadians to an abrupt halt. Set-piece attacks then had to be organised to flush out the German opposition before the advance could be resumed. Once in the towns, more house-to-house fighting was required before the area was declared captured. By then Conrath's men would have fallen back to the next point of contact ready to spring the trap again.

While these rearguards delayed the Canadian advance, Gen Conrath was moving the bulk of his division into a position in front of Catania. A great reorganisation was taking place along the Axis line. Kesselring had met Gen Hube in northern Sicily and both men had agreed on the phased withdrawal to the first of a number of planned defensive lines. The *Hauptkampflinie* was the most southerly of these. It was really a line in name only, consisting of a collection of scratch positions stretching from San Stefano on the north coast, through Nicosia and Agira to Catenanuova, then mostly along the River Dittaino to reach the sea between the Primosole Bridge and Catania. Importantly it took in the Gerbini airfields on the Catania Plain, one of the express goals of Eighth Army.

Hube had also met Guzzoni and had unofficially agreed with the commander of the Italian Sixth Army that his German XIV Panzer Corps would run the land battle. Both generals established that their main purpose in carrying out a defensive campaign in Sicily was to postpone the Allied conquest of the island for as long as possible. Guzzoni had from day one of the invasion concluded that Sicily could not be held indefinitely, but would continue to try to do so until told otherwise by the Italian High Command. The strategy agreed upon was gradually to bring all the German divisions, and those Italian formations still resisting, into the north-east corner near Messina and then withdraw them from the island across to the Italian mainland. Before this final pull-out, however, the Allies must be made to fight for every foot of territory they captured.

The first move in this plan was to reduce by half the area to be defended by Axis forces, by pulling back formations into the first of the defence lines. As a result the *Hermann Göring* Division would continue its eastwards movement to come into the line alongside the two regiments of the

1st Parachute Division, with the paratroop units being placed under Conrath's command. This caused considerable annoyance to the airborne commander, Maj-Gen Heidrich, who thought it 'a wasteful use' of his specialised troops. Heidrich was to remain in southern Italy during the campaign with the balance of his division, holding the mainland side of the Messina Strait. The 15th Panzergrenadier Division, at present in front of the Americans, would withdraw north-eastwards and come alongside the *Göring* Division. Both of these divisions would leave rearguards to cover their withdrawals and to slow up the Allied advance. The western side of Sicily was to be gradually given up and all Italian forces concentrated in defence along the *Hauptkampflinie*.

This was extremely bad news for Montgomery. His XXX Corps was now trying to push through these German formations which were crossing its front. Enemy rearguards were protecting the towns through which ran the vitally important routes carrying the withdrawal. There was also unfortunate news to be had on the eastern side of the Eighth Army along the coastal route to Catania, for XIII Corps' advance was also in difficulties as it came up against a more solid enemy front line. The *Schmalz* Group had joined up with the *Hermann Göring* Division and each day brought more and more German forces into the area opposite Dempsey's corps.

Although land operations on the island were displaying some signs of not going according to plan, things were going well in the air. By 15 July, Axis airborne opposition to the invasion was well in decline. On the first day of the invasion 481 aircraft were committed against the Allies. This number fell dramatically until only 161 enemy planes were able to fly against the beachhead just five days later. Allied air forces had quickly achieved complete domination of the air war over the island, downing 103 German and 44 Italian aircraft in this same period. Twelve more German aircraft were destroyed by anti-aircraft fire.[3]

Axis ground forces also felt the effects of Allied air superiority as troop concentrations were continually set upon by fighter-bombers. Roaming to the limits of their range, British and American aircraft set about unsettling the enemy effort. Axis communications were disrupted, unit movements curtailed and known defence positions strafed during the hours of daylight. Few Axis aircraft ventured up to engage the marauding Spitfires, Hurricanes and Kittyhawks, for most enemy air activity was confined to the nights, aimed at bombing ports and ships at anchor offshore.

On 15 July, Kesselring informed Gen Hube that he could no longer look for air support in daylight. On the same day he ordered the start of the withdrawal of all serviceable aircraft, aircrews and essential ground staff to Italy.[4]

Tedder's forces had seen off the Luftwaffe and Regia Aeronautica from Sicily in a very short time, leaving the way open for their own build-up of strength. On 13 July the Advance HQ of the RAF's Western Desert Air Force opened for business on Pachino airfield with three of its Spitfire squadrons flying in from Malta. The next day more RAF fighter-bombers landed at Comiso airfield. That same day the US XII Air Support Command opened at Gela and its aircraft became operational on the aerodromes at Ponte Olivo and Licata. And so it went on, with each day seeing more and more Allied aircraft arriving on newly taken airfields until they all soon reached their capacity. Then a halt was called in the build-up until Monty's forces could take the Gerbini group of landing grounds on the plains south of Catania.

Trying to do just that was Kirkman's 151st Brigade, which had led 50th Division's drive to join up with the airborne division at Primosole Bridge while its two sister brigades were engaged with the enemy in the rear. The 69th Brigade was back at Lentini, holding the division's base and guarding against interference from the western flank by elements of the *Schmalz* Group and Heilmann's paratroopers. The 168th Brigade had landed at Syracuse on 13 July and was marching northwards to join the division along the road leading up to Lentini. Progress was slow due to the heat and occasional interference from isolated German and Italian stragglers between the main road and the sea north of Augusta. Just short of Carlentini it passed through 5th Division's 13th and 15th Brigades which were still trying to secure the area from German and Italian troops pulling back from around Augusta. The 5th Division's 17th Brigade was holding the port and city of Augusta and trying to isolate various bold Italian Blackshirts who were sniping and interfering with Allied control of the district. Of the six brigades belonging to the two divisions making Monty's main attack on Catania, just one, 151st Brigade, was therefore actually trying to force the move.

Brigadier Senior, commander of 151st Brigade, was up with his leading battalion at the Primosole Bridge during the late evening of 14 July. The 9th Durham Light Infantry and the tanks of 44th Royal Tank Regiment had arrived at the bridging site too late to relieve the airborne troops and too tired to carry out an immediate attack across the river. Senior had ordered that they secure the near end of the bridge and dig in for the night while preparations were made to carry out an assault crossing of the Simeto early the next morning. Shortly afterwards, two regiments of self-propelled field artillery came up to join the brigade and went into action on the hills overlooking the river.

On the opposite bank, a collection of various units of the German 1st Parachute Division organised a defensive screen. Opposing 151st Brigade were the Machine Gun and Engineering Battalions of GenMaj Heidrich's division, supported by part of a battery of paratroop artillery and various personnel from the divisional headquarters. A couple of 88mm guns from the *Hermann Göring* Division's Flak Regiment were being used in a ground role and the remnants of two Italian battalions made up the numbers. Behind this screen in Catania, the *Schmalz* Group was beginning to collect as more and more of its men filtered to the rear after the fighting around Lentini and a whole battalion of the 4th Parachute Regiment complete with arms was assembling ready to move southwards. Hour by hour, the force facing Senior's brigade was growing in strength.

Brig Senior decided that the attack would go in at 0730 hrs, allowing some time to be given over to a reconnaissance of the far bank in daylight. The 9th Durham Light Infantry would be supported by the guns of the 24th and 98th Field Regiments and the tanks of 44th RTR. The infantry would assault the far bank after wading across the river.

It was a predictable attack: platoons of men fording the river on either side of the bridge behind an artillery barrage. On the other side the well-camouflaged positions of the German paratroopers were waiting for them. Odd platoons managed to get across the river in the face of fierce fire, but the considerable strength of the German positions was eventually too much for the Durhams. The more determined of the men who made it across were involved in some hand-to-hand fighting only to be forced back across to the near bank and safety when the odds moved decisively against them.

Watching from the hilltop overlooking the river were some senior officers of the airborne division. Lt-Col Frost later recalled being fascinated by the full-scale infantry assault in daylight: 'We had never taken part in such an operation, and having seen this we were determined never to do so.'[5]

He was appalled by the way that the infantry plodded on remorselessly with fixed bayonets while the Germans held their fire until almost point-blank range, and then mowed down the leading troops. The same was done to the following platoons. With Frost that morning were Brig Lathbury and Lt-Col Pearson. None of the paratroop officers was impressed with the attack.

At around 1000 hrs that morning Maj-Gen Kirkman came up to the area of the bridge to get things moving again. He urged the brigade commander to put in another attack with new troops and heavier artillery support, provisionally fixing the time of the attack at 1600 hrs that afternoon. A short time later Brig Senior called an orders group with his battalion commanders and explained that he intended to order another daylight battalion assault using the same axis and method as previously. Observing the meeting were the three airborne officers. Pearson overheard the brigadier outlining his new orders and could not resist speaking his mind in words loud enough to be heard by all: 'I suppose you want to see another battalion written off too.'[6]

There was then a hurried and scandalised little sub-conference during which Lathbury persuaded all to listen to Pearson's advice. The outcome was that the attack would go in under the cover of darkness with the airborne colonel volunteering to navigate the lead troops across the river using a crossing place known to him upstream of the bridge. There was also another reason for postponing the attack until dark, for Montgomery was pressing for an even more ambitious move on Catania.

Just before midday, XIII Corps' commander Lt-Gen Dempsey had visited Kirkman's headquarters at Lentini and outlined a much larger operation to get the drive for Messina moving. It was intended that, during the following night, 16/17 July, seaborne troops would be landed north of Catania to seize the port and the ground to the south-west. Simultaneously, Kirkman's division would capture a bridgehead across the River Simeto and the 5th Division would pass through to link up with the amphibious landing. This gave 50th Division a little respite and a few more hours of preparation before it needed to carve out a bridgehead across the river. It could now attack by night with stronger support.

The operation was due to start at 0100 hrs the next morning with a barrage fired by the guns of four regiments of field artillery and one medium regiment, supported by fire from the Sherman tanks of 44 RTR and heavy machine-gun fire from the 2nd Cheshire Regiment. After

80 minutes of artillery concentration 8th Durham Light Infantry would cross the river over a ford, located by Lt-Col Pearson, some 400 yards upstream of the bridge. Here the Simeto was about 30 yards wide, 4 feet deep and with a muddy bottom. After the leading two companies had forded the river, they would turn east and move towards their objective – the far end of the bridge. Then the remainder of the battalion and the supporting arms would cross the river by the bridge and form a lodgement.

When the leading companies reached their forming-up point that night at the start of the operation, they found the route down to the river had already been taped out by Col Pearson. The troops took cover in a sunken lane and counted down the start of the barrage. At 0100 hrs the firing began and for over an hour the far side was subjected to a terrific bombardment. At 0210 hrs the Durhams made their way across the river in two single-file columns, some 50 yards apart. On reaching the other side they soon came to grips with the enemy as they advanced through thick vines and irrigation ditches. Most of this resistance was ignored and the two companies pressed on towards the northern end of the bridge. When they neared the main structure more and more German paratroopers were encountered, but these were gradually overcome with a combination of brute force, small arms fire, grenades and the bayonet. The area at the northern end of the bridge was finally taken surprisingly quickly and those enemy not killed in the attack withdrew into the vineyards and olive groves that bordered the road to Catania. The remainder of the Durhams could now cross over and enlarge the bridgehead, but there was some delay in getting news of the bridge's capture back to battalion headquarters.

Dawn came up before the rear two companies and tank support were over the river. The infantry advanced northwards and began to spread out on either side of the road to secure a lodgement. As they pressed forward to capture their objectives, withering enemy fire forced both companies to a halt. Further fire came at the Durhams from all sides until the whole of the battalion was totally pinned down, unable to move. Original plans to carve out a sizeable lodgement through which other units could pass had to be abandoned as the Durhams struggled merely to survive the onslaught. Instead, companies had to reorganise into a small bridgehead only 300 yards deep and extending just 150 yards each side of the end of the bridge. The battalion was in extremely close contact with the enemy, as the divisional history later recalled: 'Lively fire was exchanged on both sides at ranges decreasing to twenty yards.'[7]

Brig Senior crossed the river to try to find for himself out what was holding up the Durhams, only to be pinned down on the far side by small arms fire. The brigadier was unable to return to his headquarters and was still absent when Gen Kirkman arrived to find out the latest news. The two officers had to communicate with each other by radio. The main problem was the two German 88mm guns that had been sited to cover the northern exit from the crossing. Four Shermans had been knocked out by them. With these guns in action, tank support for the infantry could not be maintained and without tank support, the infantry remained pinned down. Kirkman discussed whether or not to pass another battalion over the river but decided against this as it seemed that such a move would only incur further casualties in the confined bridgehead. Supporting artillery fire for this reinforcement could only be spasmodic, for the two sides were so closely engaged. The attack had ground to a halt.

Kirkman returned to his divisional headquarters and radioed Dempsey at corps. He explained that enemy opposition was so determined that a secure bridgehead could not be established and suggested that his division would not be able to cooperate efficiently in the amphibious plan to capture Catania; the plan would have to be modified or postponed.

When news of the failure of the attack reached Montgomery he realised that his plan for a seaborne landing to outflank the opposition at Primosole had been put in doubt. Without a simultaneous drive over the Simeto, the amphibious landings would be in danger of being cut off. Reluctantly, he agreed to a 24-hour postponement to the operation. He then set off with Dempsey to see Kirkman at his divisional headquarters. The two generals arrived at 50th Division in the early afternoon and Monty made it clear that the division must secure a considerable lodgement over the river that night.

The 16th was long and hot for the troops of the 8th DLI confined in their tight bridgehead to the north of the river. Throughout the day the enemy continued to launch small attacks against the British lodgement with tanks and infantry. The attacks whittled away at the strength of the Durhams, but no penetrations were made in the line. Little reinforcement or support was available, for traffic across the bridge was kept to a minimum as the whole of its length was subject to intermittent machine-gun fire. Meanwhile, Maj-Gen Kirkman and Brig Senior pondered on just how they were going to get the division moving again.

The third attack across the river began at 0100 hrs on 17 July with Brig Senior putting the whole of his brigade into the operation. Both 6th and 9th Durham Light Infantry crossed over the 'Pearson' ford to the left of the bridge and successfully formed up on the far side. They then advanced through the tight confines of the vineyards and olive groves, stumbling through parties of German paratroopers and detachments of the *Hermann Göring* Division. Throughout the hours of darkness they pressed forward behind artillery barrages and supporting machine-gun fire until, just before dawn, they reached their objective, an arc sweeping across the Catania road 1,500 yards north of the river. They dug in just in time to beat off a counter-attack. German paratroopers, supported by tanks, attempted to break through to the bridge but were dispersed by concentrated artillery fire from across the river.

By this time tanks were over the river and supporting the leading troops. Brig Senior was soon up at the front directing this armoured support to deploy on either side of the road. Their arrival had a dramatic effect on the enemy and more and more of the less spirited defenders gave up: 'A few white handkerchiefs appeared, and soon everywhere the enemy was surrendering,' quoted the divisional history. The fighting had been a blind and confused close-quarters action that necessarily caused casualties. The cost was high: 6th DLI lost 120 men and the 9th DLI a further 100.[8]

Back at his headquarters, Montgomery was reassessing the situation. It was evident that the ground to the south of Catania now contained a good number of German troops fighting with a determination that had been missing from their Italian counterparts who had confronted Eighth Army after the landings. Intelligence indicated that new formations were also present across the river, for advance units of 15th Panzergrenadier Regiment, from 29th Panzergrenadier Division, had arrived on the island and were hurriedly sent into action in front of Catania late on 16 July. Clearly, to continue with the proposed amphibious landing that night would court disaster, for there could no longer be a swift drive up from the bridgehead over the Simeto to join up with it. The seaborne landings would have to be abandoned and a new way found to get up to Catania.

Over on the western flank of Eighth Army the Canadian Division's advance was still having trouble. It had reached and cleared Grammichele on the 15th and Caltagirone on the 16th, and by the 17th it was through Piazza Armerina, but the next day it stalled at the crossroads 6 miles to the south of Enna. This was an important junction for the Germans, for by holding it they could halt the Allied advance in two directions: north-westwards to Enna and north-eastwards to Leonforte. Montgomery signalled to Leese urging more movement:

> Operations are a bit slow and sticky on the right, and all indications are
> that enemy troops are moving eastwards and across the plain to Catania
> . . . it is now all the more important to swing hard with our left. Drive
> the Canadians hard.[9]

While things seemed to be going badly for Eighth Army in that enemy opposition was increasing in ferocity and the drives by both of its corps were finding it slow going, Montgomery remained positive that his plan would work out and continued to feed over-optimistic reports to Alexander at his headquarters in Tunisia. Alexander actually visited Montgomery in Syracuse on 15 July and found Eighth Army's commander satisfied with the general situation. Alexander in turn was content with the progress of operations.[10] On 16 July, after the 8th Durham Light Infantry had carved out the small and precarious bridgehead at Primosole, Monty signalled Alexander that he would put in another strong attack on Catania and capture the town the next day and that the Canadians had taken Piazza Armerina and would be in Enna by dawn the following day. In fact, as noted above, the Canadian 1st Division did not capture Piazza Armerina until 17 July and never got to Enna at all.

Positive about the outcome he may have been, but the reality was that Monty's race to take Catania was over. Montgomery had gambled on pulling off a quick British victory with his Eighth Army and had failed. The campaign would now be marked by prolonged periods of hard fighting, large numbers of casualties and bitter recriminations. Worse still, the hope of cornering large numbers of German troops and bringing about their capture had evaporated. The enemy was organising a defence that was proving to be almost impenetrable, a defence which would in all likelihood only be overcome by brute force and overwhelming strength, rather than by mobility and manoeuvre.

CHAPTER 13

Missed Opportunities

On 16 July, after Alexander's positive meeting with Montgomery, he issued a new directive to his army commanders. After Eighth Army had captured Catania and its airfields, and the area of the important road networks about Enna, it was to drive the enemy into the Messina Peninsula, advancing by three main lines: first, northwards from Catania, second, from Leonforte, through Regalbuto to Adrano, and third, from Nicosia, through Troina and Randazzo. This would in effect put one thrust up the eastern side of Mount Etna and two parallel thrusts around the western side of the volcano, all converging in the north of the island at the base of the Messina Peninsula. While all this was going on, Patton would protect Monty's rear by deploying in two minor phases: the first to secure the network of roads to the west of Enna, and the second to cut the main east–west road across the middle of the island (Catania–Enna–Palermo) at Petralia.

Patton received this new instruction at around midnight on 16 July and he was, in the words of the British official history, 'moved to immediate and vehement protest'.[1] In fact he blew his top in a rage of major proportions accompanied by a tirade of profanities aimed at the British and all their fellow travellers. He was enraged not only by the slight aimed at him and his army, but also at the implied ineffectiveness of the whole of the US Army. Alexander's directive resigned Seventh Army's part in the campaign to the passive mission of guarding Eighth Army's rear. An

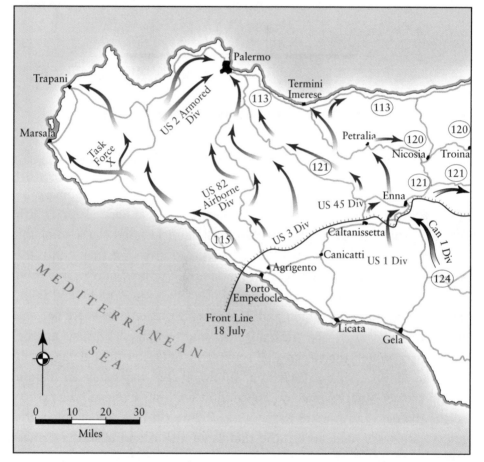

US Seventh Army's Drive to Palermo

enormous investment of American men and matériel had been placed in Sicily under the command of a British general only to be given a subsidiary role in what was the only active battlefield in western Europe. US Seventh Army and the whole of the American people needed their men in action with the enemy. Victories were there to be won and it was only proper that the Americans should win their fair share.

From a command point of view, Patton knew that tactically it was right that Montgomery should drive northwards and take Messina along the most direct route to the northern port. He also knew that his army had the strength and the mobility to play at least some part in that drive. It made little sense, therefore, that his army should virtually sit on its backside and guard another's flank. Patton confided in his diary that he was sure that neither Alexander nor his staff had any appreciation of the power and mobility of Seventh Army, nor did they have any notion of the political implications of this latest order.[2]

This time, Lt Gen George Patton Jr was not content quietly to follow orders. He gathered his senior officers around him and decided on his next course of action. Among them all was a general feeling of resentment at the task assigned to Seventh Army. Present at Patton's HQ was Maj Gen Albert Wedemeyer who was visiting the theatre as Gen Marshall's representative. He was shortly to return to Washington to brief the US Army Chief of Staff on progress in the Mediterranean. A report from him that Alexander was running the Sicilian campaign on nationalistic lines would almost certainly provoke an incident within the Allied hierarchy. Also present was Maj Gen Lucas, Eisenhower's representative at Seventh Army, and he was equally incensed. There was a consensus among the generals that to comply with the directive would be disloyal to the US Army; Alexander had to be told that American forces should be more closely involved in the battles to come. Patton proposed that he and Wedemeyer should leave the next morning for Tunisia and have a showdown with the commander of 15th Army Group. Gen Lucas said that he would fly to Algiers and protest directly to the Supreme Commander, Gen Eisenhower. Alexander had stirred up a hornets' nest among his American generals.

At 1210 hrs on 17 July, Patton and Wedemeyer flew across to North Africa, touching down at Tunis at 1309 hrs. Patton had come armed with maps explaining his idea of a using a provisional corps aimed at Palermo.

The two generals drove straight to 15th Army Group's headquarters and arrived just after the British commander had finished lunch. A meeting was hurriedly arranged at which Alexander was joined by Maj Gen Clarence Huebner, his Deputy Chief of Staff. Huebner's role at the headquarters was to advise on matters which affected American interests, although clearly on the present subject he had not forewarned his boss on the possible repercussions of his latest directive.[3] Patton and Wedemeyer conducted themselves in a polite manner and explained their mission. Although seething inside, Patton remained cool and focussed, outlining the need for American troops to be given a more active role in Sicily. He stressed that it would be 'inexpedient politically for the Seventh Army not to have equal glory in the final stage of the campaign'. Patton went on to propose how his army might be used to reduce the western side of the island and take Palermo.

At the end of Patton's presentation Alexander was clearly embarrassed by the confrontation. In his defence he claimed that he was proposing to do just what Patton asked but his Chief of Staff had failed to tell Patton this when issuing the order. (Patton later recorded that he felt this was a pretty weak excuse.) Alexander now promised Patton everything, giving him immediate permission to carry out his plan, providing that he could ensure that the Caltanissetta–Enna road network would be held securely. Patton agreed, noting in his diary that if he did what he proposed to do, there would be no need for anyone to hold anything.[4]

The whole process had been extremely unsatisfactory. Alexander's failure to take a grip on the campaign had almost led to a breakdown in Allied unity. Now, by allowing Patton to advance on Palermo, the land commander was committing half of his forces to what was reckoned by most observers to be a wild goose chase. Certainly the capture of the port of Palermo would make life easier for the administration and supply of the American effort, although Allied bombing of the harbour area had reduced the effectiveness of the docks, but the move would do little to reduce the enemy's hold on the island. The battle for Sicily could only be won in the north-east. That was where the main enemy forces were, that was where their escape route lay and that was where Patton should be going.

In complying with Montgomery's wishes on 13 July to win the battle on his own, Alexander had withheld the main strength of US Seventh Army on the advice of Montgomery. As the British official history of the campaign points out, between 11 and 17 July Montgomery six times offered Alexander his opinion on how to use Patton's army and on four of these occasions suggested using it in a holding role.[5] Now, when Alexander had at last decided to permit Patton to advance, the Americans were not directed northwards towards what could be the only ultimate Allied goal, the capture of Messina, but in the opposite direction, to Palermo. Alexander still believed that Montgomery's Eighth Army would prevail in its aims of taking Catania and also driving around the western side of Mount Etna. The positive reports that Monty was feeding him did not cause him to think otherwise. Alexander's reliance on Montgomery's excessive and unjustified confidence in Eighth Army's abilities had, as the official history points out, been a mistake.[6]

Patton lost no time in releasing his troops from their relatively passive role and switching them over to the attack. Bradley was ordered to send his II Corps forward in two columns, one pointed northwards to cut the coast road that ran from Palermo to Messina, the other directed north-west on Palermo itself. First, however, Bradley's corps was to dominate the road network in the centre of the island around Caltanissetta and Enna. On the left flank of Seventh Army, Keyes was ordered to send his Provisional Corps north and west from its Licata beachhead, to sweep up to Palermo from the south.

On 17 July Truscott had completed his 'reconnaissance in force' and his 3rd Division, with Ranger support, had captured Agrigento and Porto Empedocle. The 3rd Division was now placed under Gen Keyes's command, together with 82nd Airborne Division and the two battalions of Darby's Rangers, to form the US Provisional Corps. Keyes was to send his formation towards Palermo, using two routes, one along the coast and the other along inland highways. Maj Gen Gaffey's 2nd Armored Division was initially to follow the advance ready to 'exploit a breakthrough or extend envelopment to the west'. When the corps reached the Sicilian capital, it was to halt and prepare for a final assault under the command of Patton himself.

On 18 July Truscott gathered his unit commanders from 3rd Division together and gave them their orders. They were drive on relentlessly with two regimental combat teams in the lead and one in reserve, each with two battalions forward and one as back-up. As one was held up or began to tire, another was to take over in front. Unrelenting pressure was to be applied, allowing the enemy no respite. Truscott told his men that he expected them to be the first to arrive in Palermo in five days' time. At first light the next day the advance began.

In stark contrast to Montgomery's pitifully slow progress against the Germans in the north-east of the island, the Americans swept forward against negligible resistance. The hundred or so miles between the start line at Agrigento and Palermo were held by Italian forces, some of them from 202nd and 208th Coastal Divisions, others from the *Assietta* and *Aosta* Divisions, although these two latter divisions from Italian XII Corps had been ordered by Guzzoni to fall back to hold the new defence line from west of Nicosia to the coast. The first 40 miles were along narrow roads through rugged mountains that often rose to over 4,000 feet. The main obstacles to forward movement were mines and demolitions. Engineers up with the leading troops were able to deal with these obstructions as soon as the enemy had been cleared away. When any serious resistance was met the position was outflanked by men on foot while a set-piece attack was put in. This manoeuvre usually resulted in the immediate surrender of the Italian defenders once they had realised that the Americans had gained their rear. The advance was relentless; the attacks went in by day and by night.

To the left of Truscott's division were the paratroopers of the 82nd Airborne Division. The remainder of the division, those units that had not landed from the air, had been previously shipped over to Sicily by sea. Matthew Ridgway's complete division had formed part of the reserve around Gela but it now advanced as infantry, taking the area between the 3rd Division and the sea. Col James Gavin later recalled the advance up the western side of the island as a strange affair, little more than a road march:

> It was unlike anything else I had encountered during the war. Suddenly a machine gun or anti-tank weapon would open up, and then the white flags would appear. A shot had been fired for 'honour,' but it was just as likely to cause casualties as a shot fired in anger.[7]

The advance alternated between road marches and lifts forward by truck; the pace never slackened. An occasional roadblock was encountered which was often guarded by a bout of enemy artillery fire. The paratroopers deployed to the sides of the road for an attack, but the opposition invariably melted away. Those Italians who could not retreat fast enough surrendered *en masse*. In five days Marsala had been reached and then the fortress area of Trapani. Some slight resistance was met on the outskirts of that port, forcing the airborne troops to deploy ready for battle. They then swept down into the town bursting for a fight. What they got, however, was the total surrender of the whole of Trapani by the admiral in command, without suffering a single casualty in their ranks.

Also taking part in the drive were two of Darby's three Ranger battalions, the 1st and the 4th. These were supported by the 39th Regimental Combat Team from the newly arrived US 9th Division and a battalion of medium guns, the complete formation designated as X Force under the command of Lt Col Darby himself. X Force advanced along the seaboard side of the corps, acting as left flank guard to the main force. Again, progress was swift, with the troops alternating between marching on foot and being carried forward by truck.

Once the front line had been opened up and the three formations had burst through into open country, Gen Keyes released his armoured reserve to add punch to the advance. Gaffey's 2nd Armored Division made good use of its mobility and sped forward using any track or road that was available. By day two of the onslaught, tanks and other armoured vehicles were available to help break any bottleneck or roadblock that threatened to disrupt forward progress.

Back at his headquarters Patton was congratulating himself on forcing Alexander's hand, noting in his diary that his policy of continuous attack was the correct one, living up to the sentiment he had expressed in North Africa: 'We shall attack and attack and attack until we are exhausted, and then we shall attack again.' The further his forces progressed, the more they found enemy equipment abandoned that should not have been abandoned. Patton regarded his system of attacking all the time as being better than the British method of stop, build up and start, noting in his diary on 19 July that Eighth Army had attacked the previous day with a whole division and only made 400 yards.

Patton felt that Alexander had no appreciation of either the power or the speed that an American army was capable of, claiming rather boldly that his army could go twice as fast as the British and hit harder.[8] This was certainly true against retreating Italians, but the real test would come when they tried to push their way through determined German troops as the British were doing. That day was now quickly approaching.

The number of Italian prisoners being over-run was starting to become an embarrassment to Seventh Army. It was all very well to capture large numbers of enemy troops, but what was to be done with them? Patton's supplies were still mostly arriving over open beaches and were trying to keep pace with an army now on the move. Tens of thousands of extra mouths to feed were placing a great strain on logistics. Gen Bradley came up with a timely solution. He suggested that word should go out that any Sicilians in the Italian Army who wished to desert could go back to their homes and they would not be arrested as prisoners of war. The men could begin to put their communities back in order by gathering the now ripened crops and starting the task of rebuilding shattered villages. This move was initially disapproved of by higher headquarters, but on 28 July it was made official. Of the 122,000 POWs captured by the Americans on the island, 33,000 were Sicilians able to be paroled to their homes and farms.[9]

Not all prisoners taken in Sicily were so fortunate, for the ancient practice of killing prisoners rather than taking the time, manpower and trouble of collecting, guarding and feeding them continued in various guises, just as it still does in our own times. Some Italian formations in North Africa had reputations of being cruel to captives and German atrocities are well documented in all the theatres in which they fought. What is less well known, or indeed publicised at all, are those perpetrated by Allied personnel. One notable early occasion in Sicily is outlined in Patton's diaries. On 14 July, Gen Bradley arrived in an agitated state at Patton's headquarters claiming that a captain in the 45th Division had taken the army commander's instructions to kill the enemy too literally and had shot between fifty and seventy prisoners. What made it more horrifying was that they were shot in ranks, in cold blood. Patton told Bradley to keep the matter from the press and to prevent it becoming public knowledge. He was to certify that the dead men were snipers or had attempted to escape. Anyhow, Patton reasoned, they were dead so nothing could be done about it.[10] Other examples were recorded by both British and American war correspondents, including the case of an American sergeant who, when escorting thirty-six prisoners to the rear, machine-gunned them all down at the roadside. His excuse was that it was getting dark and he was nervous about having custody of so many prisoners.[11]

Killing the enemy was the principal role of all soldiers, and senior officers never drew back from telling their men to do so at every opportunity. Montgomery continually pressed the point in his speeches to the troops in which he asserted that the object of battle was to kill Germans, as indeed it was. Eisenhower in a letter to Gen Marshall, concerning the embarrassment of having too many prisoners to deal with, lamented: 'Too bad we couldn't have killed more.'[12] Quite often, as in the American massacre cases in Sicily, those men in the front line saw so much death that it was difficult to prevent the killing going on even after enemy troops had thrown up their arms in surrender. To his credit, Bradley had the atrocities investigated and the men were brought to task over the killings. In their defence, however, they claimed that they were only implementing the orders given by Patton in a speech before the invasion when he implied that they could kill prisoners. Several months later, Patton was interviewed by an investigator from the US War Department who was looking into the cases. He denied ever having given such an instruction to his troops. The men in question were at that time still being held in custody and it was thought best that the matter be dropped and the men were returned to their units. Both were later killed in action.

Few senior commanders have ever written about these matters, although occasionally something slips out which places questions over just what went on. In Sicily, Lt-Gen Oliver Leese announced that he was going to take hostages and shoot them if there were any more cases of isolated sniping from Italian citizens – he never followed up this threat.[13] Even Montgomery himself issued an instruction that Germans caught in civilian clothes behind the lines were to be treated as spies and shot, although when one was actually captured, he rescinded the order.[14]

While Patton's Provisional Corps was racing along the narrow lanes of western Sicily against dispirited Italian formations, Bradley's II Corps was finding the going rather more difficult. However, it was at least on the attack rather that just guarding the British flank. Bradley had been ordered to drive north-westwards to cut the Palermo–Messina road, which ran along the northern coast of the island, after he had secured the network of roads around Enna and severed the Catania–Enna–Palermo road. His two divisions drove forward against what was the tail of the 15th Panzergrenadier Division as that German formation manoeuvred into the hastily prepared defences of the *Hauptkampflinie*. The Germans initially reacted violently to the American moves, which cut across their with-drawal, but as their rearguard moved eastwards the way opened up in front of the American 45th Division pushing north-westwards to the coast. Caltanissetta was taken by the division on the 18th and Santa Caterina on the 20th. Allen's 1st Division on the right had a harder task fighting for the road network south of Enna.

In the vicinity of Enna, the Canadians of Leese's XXX Corps came close together with the advancing formations of US 1st Division. Canadian 1st Division was stalled 6 miles south of the town by stiff enemy action along Highway 124. On 17 July, Alexander gave orders to abandon the proposed move by XXX Corps along the route Enna–Nicosia–Randazzo and concentrate on a less ambitious and much tighter move around Mount Etna by way of Leonforte and Adrano to Randazzo. This new move directed the Canadians to swing to the north-east from their hold-up south of Enna, by-passing the town and moving directly to Leonforte.

As a result of the new directive Maj-Gen Simonds switched his division from Highway 124 on to Highway 117 towards Leonforte with the independent British 231st Brigade advancing along a parallel road on its right between the Canadians and 51st Highland Division. The move side-stepped Enna and outflanked those of the enemy still in the town, forcing them to withdraw lest they be cut off. As Canadian 1st Division moved to the north-east along Highway 117, Enna reverberated with the sound of German troops demolishing buildings, roads and military installations in the town that had been for so long the headquarters of Guzzoni's Italian Sixth Army.

With the Canadians now moving away from Enna, a gap began to open up along the right flank of Maj Gen Allen's 1st Division as the Americans concentrated their efforts towards the north-west. British XXX Corps had been assigned the town (which lay within its corps' boundary) and Simonds should have been covering the Americans. The Canadian main effort was now pointed towards Leonforte and not Enna, leaving open the principal roads which ran from the town back towards the rear of US II Corps. Bradley could not afford to ignore this danger and sent a signal to Leese that scarcely hid his displeasure:

I have just learned you have sideslipped Enna leaving my flank exposed. Accordingly we are proceeding to take Enna at once even though it is in your sector. I assume we have the right to use any of your roads for this attack.[15]

The amiable Leese was horrified to learn that the Americans had been compromised in this way and immediately signalled back to Bradley that he had assumed his staff had notified II Corps of the moves. Leese readily relinquished all rights to the town and the road to Bradley's formation and assured II Corps' commander that no slight was intended. Along with the message Leese quickly dispatched two bottles of Scotch to the American general to help smooth over this lapse of military judgment. For his part Simonds knew that the Germans had abandoned Enna and had ordered a patrol of just four Canadian carriers under the command of a single sergeant to 'take the town'. They arrived coincidentally with the first group of Americans from 1st Division to get there, which led to both sides later claiming to have captured the hilltop citadel.

Allen's 1st Division pushed on northwards towards Petralia and captured the town on the 22nd, while Middleton's 45th Division continued its moves towards the sea with the aim of cutting the Palermo–Messina highway that ran along the coast.

On 22 July American troops were also poised to take Palermo. Keyes gave advance warning to Patton so that the army commander could be there when the city fell. In the meantime, Truscott and Gaffey had their troops continue closing all exits from the Sicilian capital, preventing any escape for the thousands of Italians and the few Germans holed up there. Also arriving outside the city from the south-east was 45th Division's Combat Command A. On that same day the remainder of Middleton's division finally reached the northern coast at Termini Imerese and cut the Palermo–Messina road. The island was now split in two with all Axis forces in the west of Sicily cut off from Guzzoni's command in the east.

Just after noon that day, the sound of explosions began drifting up to the American troops overlooking Palermo. It was obvious that the Germans inside the port were blowing up installations in an effort to deny them to the Allies. Repeated requests were made by Truscott to Seventh Army for permission to enter the city and each of them was met with a stern refusal. At 1400 hrs, a final order from Seventh Army made it clear that no one was to cross the stop line outside Palermo until further notice. Everyone had to wait until Patton arrived on the scene before entering the city.

During the afternoon civilians representing the Palermo authorities came out to the Americans and offered to surrender the city, but the capitulation could not be accepted because Patton was not there – he was delayed in his advance up from his headquarters in Gela – and so troops and civilians alike had to wait, as did Gen Marciani and his 208th Coastal Division who were waiting in the city ready to throw down their arms. Eventually, after much pleading from the citizens of Palermo, Gen Keyes decided to allow reconnaissance parties to enter the town to protect the port. Patton finally arrived at around 2230 hrs that night at the head of an armoured column. When he met Col Perry at Keyes's HQ outside the city he found that the corps commander and Maj Gen Gaffey had beaten him to it; they could wait no longer and were already ensconced in the Royal Palace, asleep in their beds. Unable to hide his exhilaration at having taken Sicily's capital city, Patton drove down through the darkened streets looking for his generals. He felt a great thrill as his jeep sped through the captured city in the dark. He soon reached the palace and had Keyes and Gaffey roused from their sleep so that he could congratulate them. Then, from a small flask that Patton had with him, they all toasted the great achievements of US Seventh Army since the landings. Patton was on top of the world; his army had seized over half of the island, including its capital and second largest port, while British Eighth Army was stalled in front of Catania.

The taking of Palermo has, by some historians and commentators, been seen as nothing more than a rapid route march against dispirited Italians, but it was in fact much more than that. It was a splendid example of American mobility and organisation. Out of the 300 tanks taking part, only five fell out because of mechanical trouble. It is true that American casualties were minimal, just 272 against over 3,000 suffered by the Italians, and none of the fighting was anything more than skirmishes against roadblocks and protected minefields, but the unleashing of 3½ divisions across 150 miles of mountainous terrain and the capture over 50,000 of the enemy in just four days was an impressive feat of American arms nonetheless. The British official history of the campaign recognised the great achievement of US Seventh Army in clearing the western portion of Sicily 'without great trouble and at trifling cost' and commented: 'It was difficult to see why it should not have won these advantages much earlier, though no doubt with more difficulty, had Alexander allowed it to try.'[16]

With the capture of Palermo Seventh Army had the exclusive use of its own major port allowing it to shorten its lines of communication. The capture of the whole of western Sicily had cleared its flanks. On 23 July Bradley's corps was established on the coast at Termini Imerese and had severed Highway 113, slicing the island in two. There was now only one way to face, eastwards towards the enemy. Patton had proved that his army was a well-organised and competent fighting formation that could now take its place alongside the British in the drive for victory in Sicily. And it was just as well that it could, for Montgomery was in big trouble over to the east.

Further efforts in front of Catania were leading nowhere. After 50th Division's attempts to enlarge the Primosole bridgehead across the Simeto, 5th Division was brought forward to force a new crossing 3 miles upstream and to strike for Misterbianco. Montgomery remained his optimistic self, assuring Alexander on 19 July that he had the situation in hand: 'The battle for Catania and its airfields has been a dog fight of great intensity against determined Germans and I think I am shortly going to win this battle.' He went on to explain that he was no longer persisting with 50th Division's attack from Primosole as the enemy there were too strong. He was switching his main effort westwards and was using 5th Division instead; 'Five Div directed on Misterbianco. Difficulties here are mainly physical but they are being overcome and hope to be in Misterbianco by tomorrow night.'[17]

A shallow lodgement was made by 5th Division on the night of 18/19 July, and some 3,000 yards of territory was gained over the next two days during a great deal of heavy fighting against the *Hermann Göring* Division. Further plans were made to enlarge this bridgehead on 21 July and take Misterbianco, but the attack was postponed when the concentration area of the attacking infantry was devastated by enemy artillery fire. The flat plain in front of 5th Division was completely overlooked by the lower slopes of Mount Etna and German observation of the British line was absolute. By this time Dempsey knew that plans for the whole of the campaign were being rethought and told 5th Division's commander to consolidate his bridgehead for the time being and go over to the defence.

XIII Corps was now completely stalled along the southern side of the Catania Plain in positions dominated by the enemy.

Over to the west, things were little better for Leese's XXX Corps. On his left the Canadians were trying to bludgeon their way to Leonforte against 15th Panzergrenadier Division and on his right, 15 miles to the east isolated between the Canadians and 5th Division, 51st (Highland) Division was attempting to cross the River Dittaino opposite Sferro on its advance to Paterno. The Canadian 1st Division was finding the advance up Highway 117 very difficult. The rugged terrain confined all mechanised movement to the single road and this route was easily defended by accurate enemy artillery fire and small groups hidden in ambush. The obvious tactic was to take to the hills and outflank opposition, but movement across boulder-strewn mountainsides was precarious and extremely complicated. Animal transport would have been the answer, for mule trains had been organised to do this type of work with great effect in the mountains of Tunisia by Anderson's First Army just a few months previously. As a result seven companies of pack-mules had been included in Eighth Army's order of battle during the planning stages of 'Husky', but closer to the time of the invasion it was thought that the shipping of other units might be of more use. Early successes on the flat land along the coast did not require pack-mules so no requests were sent to North Africa for their dispatch. Eventually, on 17 July, at the very time that the Canadians were struggling to get weapons and equipment across the mountains in the centre of the island, Eighth Army HQ sent a signal to Middle East Command that no pack transport would be required by Montgomery's forces in Sicily during the campaign. As the author of the British official history later lamented, 'Any hope of organised animal transport now receded to the future.'[18]

Maj-Gen Wimberley's Highland Division had been given the task of crossing the Dittaino and taking Paterno. Wimberley had 23rd Armoured Brigade under command and intended to strike with his armour on the right towards Gerbini while 154th Infantry Brigade attacked 5 miles away on the left towards Sferro. The division's other two brigades were ready to exploit whichever thrust seemed to be the more promising. Opposing the division were the *Hermann Göring* Division's 2nd Panzergrenadier Regiment and the much depleted 76th Infantry Regiment of the *Napoli* Division. On call close by were 48 serviceable tanks from the two tank battalions of the German division.

The attack began on the 17th and initially made good progress against a series of German outposts, for the bulk of the enemy were still reorganising along their main defence line, which ran along the Dittaino. By 19 July the advance had reached the river and the right flank seemed the more promising. Montgomery, in his despatch to Alexander that day, had reported that the division was going well and would reach its objective on the 20th. Wimberley now switched 154th Brigade to the right side of his assault and sent it forward with tank support towards the Gerbini airfields. At the same time, 153rd Brigade carried forward the division's left-hand thrust towards Sferro. Soon all three brigades were involved in very fierce fighting as they tried to penetrate the main German line.

It seemed to Wimberley that the area around the Gerbini airfields was the anchor point of the enemy defences and he decided to try to clear the vicinity with a brigade attack supported by tanks during the night of 20/21 July. The Highlanders of 154th Brigade put in the attack as planned and in fact carried their first objective. However, sustained artillery fire and a strong counter-attack by the panzergrenadiers of the *Göring* Division regained the ground lost during the night and Wimberley's men were forced back almost to their start line. Casualties suffered by the Highland Division were considerable, with 7th Argyll and Sutherland Highlanders alone losing 18 officers and 160 men. The thrust on the left by 153rd Brigade suffered the same fate and was checked in front of Sferro. The Highland Division had been brought to a complete halt.

Montgomery's plan to finish the campaign in Sicily in quick time with Eighth Army had failed. Now, with the whole of his army virtually at a standstill, Montgomery had to admit that he could no longer win the battle with Eighth Army alone while Patton watched his rear. The invasion of Sicily was failing due to mismanagement by its senior commanders. From a very promising start, with landings more placid than could have been dreamed of by those who planned the assault, the battle for the island was slowing painfully to a crawl. Logistically, the re-supply of Allied forces had been all that had been hoped for, with sufficient men, transport and equipment landed to sustain the two armies comfortably in the field. What was lacking was competent leadership to force the campaign to a successful conclusion. This was not happening because the initiative had been snatched from the Allies by German generals who were more adept at reacting to events as they arose. The Allies had allowed the few German

CHAPTER 14

The Fall of Mussolini

The Allied invasion of Sicily was designed to achieve three main objectives: first, to continue to engage Axis forces on land so as to relieve some of the pressure being applied to Russia, second, to open shipping lanes across the Mediterranean and, third, to precipitate the break-up of the Axis alliance and eliminate Italy from the war. The first two of these intentions were accomplished with the success of the landings on 10 July; the third objective was expected to take much longer.

During the planning stages of 'Husky' in April, Allied intelligence had suggested that, if an Allied landing on the mainland followed straight after the invasion of Sicily, it could result in an immediate Italian collapse. A little later, in July, just before the Sicilian operation was actually launched, the final appreciation by the Joint Intelligence Committee suggested that the loss of the island combined with sustained air attacks on northern and central Italy might be enough to produce a breakdown in civil administration leading to an Italian request for an armistice.[1]

Every indication was that most of the Italian people were tired of the war, hated the Germans, and wished to sue for peace. Many politicians and senior military commanders were actively seeking an honourable way out of the conflict, but were handicapped by the demands of the Allies, who had indicated that only unconditional surrender was acceptable. Mussolini's fascist regime itself was crumbling from within as more and more party members were losing their determination to stick with Germany to the end.

This wavering of Italian determination had been noticed in Berlin and was the subject of many secret meetings between Hitler and his generals. Operations 'Alarich' and 'Konstantin' had already been formulated to stabilise the Mediterranean theatre should Mussolini's government collapse and pull out of the war. The Germans would take military control of Italy and remove Italian garrisons in the Balkans. German intelligence knew that there were a number of renegade Italians generals plotting with the King to overthrow Mussolini. Such a move would leave the German divisions in Sicily and in the south of the country vulnerable. Hitler decided that he would personally meet with Mussolini to try to stiffen Italian resolve and get the fascist dictator to move against those who were undermining the Axis war effort.

On 18 July, Hitler travelled south from his 'Wolf's Lair' battle head-quarters near Rastenburg in East Prussia and flew down to his Alpine retreat at Berchtesgaden for an overnight stay. The next day he travelled on to Treviso in Italy where he was met at the airfield by Mussolini. From here the two leaders took the Duce's train to a station near Feltre. Then an hour's drive in an open-top car carried them up through the mountains to the villa of Senator Gaggia where their high-level meeting was to take place. During the exhausting journey in hot sunshine the Axis leaders passed the time by exchanging polite small talk.

At noon the meeting began. Hitler started with what became a long and tiresome discourse strewn with propaganda aimed at the need to bolster Italian morale and prevent Italy seeking a separate peace with the Allies. He spoke for two solid hours. The first intrusion occurred just after he had started when Mussolini's secretary interrupted the proceedings with news that Rome was under attack by Allied bombers. The raid was primarily aimed at the vast railway network that converged on Rome. All rail traffic between northern and southern Italy passed through its great marshalling yards at Littorio and San Lorenzo. Early on the morning of 19 July, 149 USAAF B-17 Flying Fortress and 122 B-24 Liberator heavy bombers from airfields in North Africa attacked the city. In the afternoon, 249 American B-25 Mitchell and B-26 Marauder medium bombers returned to bomb the airfield at Ciampino and the Fiat and Bianchi motor works. Italian casualties were considerable and the damage done immense. But the greatest cost was to the morale of the Romans themselves. For the first time the war had been starkly brought to their very doors.

Over the next few hours more and reports were carried in to the meeting and given to the Italian leader, each more alarming than the one before. It was evident that Rome was under intense bombardment of exceptional length. The news 'charged the atmosphere with tragedy', Mussolini was later to write. Hitler tried to bolster the Italian leader with promises that things would soon change in favour of the Axis with the imminent resumption of the U-boat war in the Atlantic and the arrival of the new secret V (vengeance) weapons, but the start of the Allied bombing attacks against the capital left the Duce totally dispirited. The meeting broke up in the late afternoon and the two leaders made their way back to Treviso together. During the journey Hitler tried to get Mussolini to understand that the Italian crisis was a leadership crisis and that it was down to him to re-galvanise Italian morale. Mussolini's attention was elsewhere as he contemplated the massive Allied air bombardment that was sure to be launched against his country over the next few weeks. To Mussolini's head of armed forces, Marshal Ambrosio, the meeting reinforced his view that the Duce was a spent force. When the marshal arrived back in Rome he joined the growing numbers within the Commando Supremo preparing for Mussolini's removal. In the meantime, he would have to continue cooperating with the Germans.

Despite almost everyone at the meeting feeling that nothing had been achieved, Hitler returned to Berchtesgaden satisfied that he had lifted the Duce's spirits and impressed on him the need to carry on the struggle. It was the last time that the German leader visited the country. That evening, 19 July, Hitler's personal aide Martin Bormann, showed the Führer an intelligence report compiled by Himmler which contained clear evidence that a *coup d'état* was being planned to get rid of Mussolini and install the pro-western Marshal Badoglio as head of government. Once the Allies had completed their conquest of Sicily, Badoglio would begin peace negotiations. Hitler was appalled at Mussolini's naivety, for during the meeting he seemed unaware of the plotting that was going on around him. German sources also indicated that the Italians were stockpiling ammunition and re-occupying the fortifications that ran along their northern border.[2]

It was true that Badoglio and others were plotting against Mussolini. Two members of the royal family, the Duke of Aosta and the Prince of Piedmont, had made contact with the Allies through the Italian Consul-

General in Geneva the previous December, and Marshal Badoglio and Marshal Caviglia had been in contact with Allied agents in Berne since May 1942.[3] All of this traitorous intrigue was aimed at organising a coup with the help of the Italian armed forces and negotiating a suitable peace. On the political front, Count Dino Grandi and Ivanoe Bonomi had separately visited King Victor Emmanuel and urged him to take the lead in overthrowing the fascist regime and denouncing the Axis pact with Germany. Grandi was assuming that, with such move, a civilian government would take control with him at its head.

On 24 July events in Rome began moving towards a climax. A meeting of the Fascist Grand Council had been summoned, the first since the beginning of the war. Mussolini was now confronted by detractors emboldened by the break-down in Italian morale following the recent bombing of Rome. The meeting lasted for nine hours. Finally, after much lengthy discussion, Count Grandi felt events were swinging against the Duce. A motion was proposed for the King to assume power and a vote was taken in the early hours of 25 July, which the anti-Mussolini faction won by nineteen votes to seven. Almost unbelievably, the fascist dictatorship had been democratically voted out of office in a bloodless palace coup.

Events then moved swiftly. Marshal Ambrosio, who had been party to the coup, put his plans into action. The head of the Italian military ordered the Army, police and *carabinieri* to take over all key points in the city and at once placed Mussolini under arrest, spiriting him off to the island of Ponza in complete secrecy. Marshal Badoglio was nominated as the head of the government, ruling in the King's name. With the immediate disappearance of Mussolini from the scene and the arrival in the capital of the *Piave* and *Ariete* Divisions, the whole apparatus of the Fascist Party collapsed as ministers and officials meekly accepted the authority of the new regime.

News of Mussolini's downfall reached Hitler at the Wolf's Lair that same morning. His immediate reaction was to send paratroops to Rome to seize the monarch, arrest the traitors and reinstall Mussolini in power. Later, wiser counsel prevailed as he discussed the take-over with his senior aides. Hitler's great fear was that the Allies would take immediate advantage of the turmoil and stage a landing on the mainland of Italy. The coup had provoked a crisis in the relationship between the two Axis powers, which had to be resolved before the Allies could act. Hitler summoned all Party leaders and senior figures of the Nazi regime to Rastenburg to a war conference to discuss possible retaliation. Hitler knew that the next major Italian move would be to pull out of the war, but in order to gain time the Badoglio government would at first no doubt proclaim its intention of carrying on the fight. Hitler thought that two could play at that game. He would go along with the Italian traitors until he was ready and then drop on them in a flash, round them all up and take over their entire country. Hitler was furious that the Italian dictatorship had been swept away in matter of hours with no more than a show of hands. Gen Jodl put it bluntly when he commented that the whole fascist movement in Italy had gone 'pop like a soap bubble'. Hitler turned to Himmler and directed him to ensure that nothing went 'pop' in Germany.[4]

In the meantime some action had to be taken. The Führer believed that it was important to rescue Mussolini if he was still alive and ordered Gen Student to work out a scheme for his release.[5] GenFM Rommel was summoned to return from the Balkans and work out a scheme to take over military control of Italy if the need arose. The 3rd Panzergrenadier Division was to move to the area south of Rome and the 2nd Parachute Division was to be flown into Roman airfields from France as soon as possible. Other plans were adopted to bring more divisions to the south of France and to the border crossings in the Alps over the following few days.

This left the matter of the German troops fighting in Sicily and those stationed in southern Italy. If the Italian Army chose to act against those divisions, they would be hundreds of miles away from any immediate assistance and would have to fight their way back to the Reich border in the north. Hitler now decided that Gen Hube's command in Sicily would have to be brought out before the Italians capitulated. Kesselring was ordered to take the necessary steps to ensure that the escape route across the Strait of Messina was kept open and defended, and then gradually to give up the island in an orderly withdrawal. Arms and equipment could be abandoned if absolutely necessary; the main emphasis was to ensure that all German personnel were brought out. Hitler expected that only the men would be got away. Sicily was not to be held for longer than was necessary for the extraction of these German divisions.

In the Allied camp there was elation at the news that one of Europe's hated dictators had been removed from power. Italy's elimination from the war could now only be a matter of time. Within just a few days, just as Hitler had suspected, the new regime in Rome was in contact with British and American diplomats in Lisbon, sounding out possible peace terms. All this, however, was just behind-the-scenes diplomacy, for the Italians still professed allegiance to the Axis pact and, in public, the governments of Britain and the USA were adamant that the only terms acceptable were those of a total capitulation to Allied demands. In London, Prime Minister Churchill made a speech in the House of Commons which actually gave some comfort to Hitler. He stated that nothing short of wholesale unconditional surrender would save the Italian people from being bombed from one end of their land to the other. The Italians could 'stew in their own juice' until they submitted to Allied power, he declared. When news of the speech reached Rastenburg, Hitler knew that he had at least some time to make his arrangements for the Italian take-over while the country's leadership recoiled from the aggressive tone of the British leader's remarks. There was, apparently, still some small token pride left in Italy.

CHAPTER 15

Breaking the German Line

The downfall of Mussolini led to the abandonment of the constraints being applied to Gen Hube's actions in Sicily. There need no longer be a pretence of a dual command with all the uncertainties that existed through Guzzoni's involvement in the battle. Hube and his XIV Panzer Corps were to control the whole of the Sicilian campaign, which was now to be fought according to the needs and expectations of the German Army.

On 24 July GenLt Walter Fries arrived on the island to take command of the units of his 29th Panzergrenadier Division that had been shipped over during the previous few days. Under his command were the whole of the 15th and 71st Panzergrenadier Regiments, a regiment of artillery, Flak and engineer battalions and an anti-tank company. The division's tank and reconnaissance battalions were left on the mainland under command of 26th Panzer Division. The defence of Sicily was to be fought in the mountains where tanks and armoured cars were of limited use.

The arrival of this well-equipped formation was a great boost for Gen Hube. Although it bore the title of the 29th Panzergrenadiers, it was not the famed 'Falcon Division' that had fought with great credit in the campaigns in Poland and France and the *Blitzkrieg* invasion of Russia in 1941. That division was destroyed at Stalingrad in December 1942. The present formation had been raised in the spring of 1943 in southern France from the bulk of the 345th Reserve Panzergrenadier Division. In

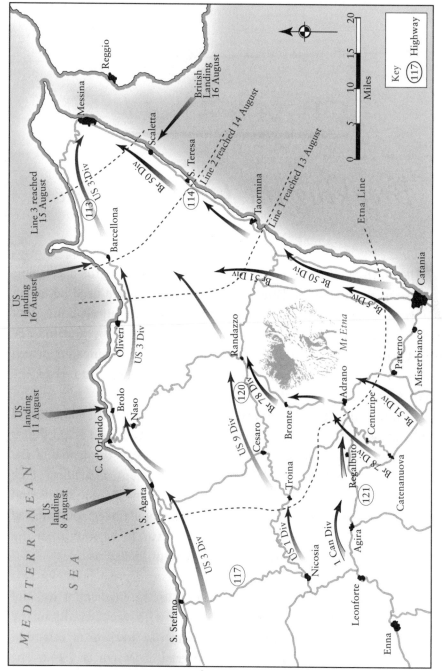

The End of the Campaign

command was 49-year-old Walter Fries, who had previously commanded a regiment of the old 29th Panzergrenadier Division.

With most of this new panzergrenadier division now available to his corps, Hube was able to man the *Hauptkampflinie* with mostly German troops. By the 25th he had in the line from west to east, 29th Panzergrenadier Division with the remains of the Italian *Assietta* Division; 15th Panzergrenadier Division and parts of the Italian *Aosta* Division; and then the *Hermann Göring* Division with the 3rd and 4th Regiments of 1st Parachute Division. The line was the first of many, for behind the *Hauptkampflinie*, Hube had located and was busy preparing two more resistance lines and three evacuation lines, each of which would play its part in slowing down the Allied advance so that the withdrawal from the island might take place under strict control. These lines stretched roughly northwest to south-east across the long peninsula leading up to Messina and each of them was shorter than the one before, allowing formations to be taken out of the line as the front contracted to be sent back to Messina for evacuation. The *Hauptkampflinie* was the first of Hube's lines and was assembled very quickly during the second week of the campaign. Behind it a much stronger line, the Etna Line, had been prepared and this gradually became the main defence line as Hube adjusted his formations to meet the renewed Allied threats.

Both of these defence lines ran through the mountains around Centuripe in the centre of the island. This hill-top town, only approachable through difficult terrain and dominating the mountainous central region, was the pivot of the German resistance. To the north-west and to the south-east, the line could fall back along both coastal flanks providing the middle held at Centuripe to anchor the central defence. As long as the Centuripe massif remained under German control, the British would be denied Adrano, and if Adrano was held then there was no way for Eighth Army to get behind Mount Etna. Without this inland route to outflank the Catania position, there would be no advance on Messina for Monty. On the northern sector, now taken over by the Americans, the village of Troina served the same strategic task. Gen Hube knew that, once Troina and Adrano had been taken, Sicily could not be held and the evacuation from the island would have to be implemented at a gathering pace. In his short time on the island, Hube had devised an impressive defensive strategy.

In stark contrast, Montgomery's strategy had stalled. The failure of 51st Division to get anywhere near Paterno and the slow progress of the Canadians against Leonforte, coupled with the lack of success south of Catania with his other two divisions, meant that his army was not going anywhere. Nowhere along his front did it have the strength to splinter the enemy line. His men were tired from almost two weeks of continuous action; what Montgomery needed now was more punch from fresh troops, but there were few to be found in Sicily.

This need for new blood resulted in several ill-equipped units being sent into the line. Most notable of these was the strange case of the 7th Royal Marines. The battalion had been shipped overseas from the UK in 1942 without any real purpose. Originally it was intended to garrison South Africa, but when it arrived, the government decided that it did not wish to use foreign troops in local defence. From there it went north to Egypt and spent months trying to find a new role. Eventually it became the core of a formation called a 'beach brick'; in fact it became No. 31 Beach Brick. At that time there were no others – the name and number were devised to fool the enemy into thinking there was a large number of such formations.

The role of the beach brick in an invasion was the same as its later equivalent the 'beach group', as used in the Normandy invasion. It was intended that it would land soon after the initial assault waves and take over the administration of the beaches and the subsequent arrival of stores, reinforcements and equipment. It carried out provost and local defence duties, guarded prisoner of war cages, and undertook countless other tasks including engineering and transport. At its peak, 31 Beach Brick had a complement of 3,400 men.

No. 31 Beach Brick arrived in Sicily behind the assault troops of 231st Brigade on the eastern tip of Cape Passero. For the next week it carried out its duties as planned until 17 July when the beach defence commitment provided by 7th Royal Marines was deemed to be over. The battalion marched inland to Buccheri to take up occupation duties with its commander, Lt-Col F.W. Dewhurst, becoming the military governor of the area. A few days later it moved up the line on foot to take over the close defence of XXX Corps HQ. This was the time that 51st Highland Division was trying to gain a lodgement across the River Dittaino and Maj-Gen Wimberley decided that he needed a diversion to draw some of the opposition away from his front. Lt-Gen Leese decided that Wimberley could use 7th Royal Marines to try to cross the river further upstream in an attempt to outflank or divert the enemy.

The Royal Marine battalion was used because it was there, right under the corps commander's nose, seemingly idling its time in the task of defending his headquarters. To the military mind it was immensely suitable for the task. The reality was it was not suitable at all. The 7th Royal Marines had been trained and landed in Sicily as a beach organisation. It had no supporting arms of its own, two of its 3-inch mortars had been lost while landing and it had no transport other than four carriers. It had not been trained in the infantry role since leaving Britain almost a year before and none of its men had seen action in the field.

When the battalion's second in command, Maj de Courcy-Ireland reported to Wimberley's HQ at 1400 hrs on 19 July – his colonel was then still back in Buccheri – he was given orders for the attack which was planned to start that evening. The battalion at that moment was stretched out along the road marching up to the Highland Division's sector. The major requested the battalion be given 24 hours to complete the move and organise itself for the attack, reminding the divisional commander that his unit lacked recent infantry training. The request was refused.

The 7th Royal Marines made the assault across the Dittaino that evening as ordered, going into the attack as they arrived at the start line, and the outcome was as might be expected. The battalion got across the river but could not hold on to the small gains that it made. Enemy fire and a sharp counter-attack forced the troops back over the river, back in fact to their original start line on the slopes of Massa Parlato. Heavy casualties were inflicted on the attacking companies. The marines were then left in position on this exposed high ground for the next nine days as a threat, unable to move at all in daylight, suffering a growing number of casualties each day from hostile shell fire. During the night they moved on to the face of Massa Parlato, and then withdrew to the reverse slopes in daylight. They just had to sit there on that barren hillside and suffer. On 28 July the battalion was pulled out of the line; nothing had been accomplished, save some minor distraction to the enemy on the first night and a marginal threat thereafter that it might launch another attack across the Dittaino.[1]

This debacle was clearly summed up in short notes for a diary entry written during the battle by of one of the battalion's company commanders, Maj Derek de Stacpoole:

A really horrible period. The CO screaming for tanks and doing nothing. Nobody was in the picture. No real co-ordination between arms. A wonderful lesson in the powerfulness of well-concealed machine guns and sniper fire. My God! When I think of the things that went wrong – the unpreparedness and the rush and hurry of the whole blasted amateurish mess up! It is no good trying to find a scapegoat, but I am certain if the battalion had gone in fresh with a well recced. co-ordinated and well prepared plan that nothing would have stopped it and that it would have held on to the gains. Disorganisation in the withdrawal I am afraid was the result of lack of control by officers and NCOs. Morale is low now. I am fed up. It makes me furious to think that with even half a day's preparation and rest we would have roared in with complete success and ever afterwards there wouldn't be a battalion on this bloody island to touch us. Poor old 7th R.M. Never have so many been buggered about by so few.[2]

A reinforcement of Montgomery's effort could only be provided by bringing more troops to the island. Eighth Army did have a reserve in North Africa, for 46th and 78th Divisions were resting and training on the beaches of Tunisia while waiting for a call to return to battle. Montgomery had hoped to use these two formations later in the Mediterranean campaign, more especially if the Allies chose to invade the Italian mainland. Reluctantly then, Montgomery now decided that he would bring one of these divisions across to Sicily to help him force his way through Hube's defences. He chose 78th Division for this task.

On 21 July Monty signalled Alexander on his new intentions. Resistance about Catania and through the foothills around Misterbianco and Paterno was great and his troops were tired fighting in the summer heat. He had therefore decided that he would hold with his right in front of Catania and continue operations with his left against Adrano. He would bring 78th Division over from Tunisia and give it to XXX Corps so that it could have greater strength in its operations northwards. These moves would require US Seventh Army to thrust along the north coast road towards Messina so that full pressure could be applied to all sectors of the German line.[3]

With this signal Montgomery finally admitted that he could not win the battle on his own; he needed the Americans involved in the drive for Messina. He would also have to use a division that was not originally from his famed Eighth Army, but one that had won its spurs in Tunisia as part of the often belittled First Army of Gen Anderson.[4]

The 78th Division was one of Britain's best divisions, a mix of regular and territorial battalions that had performed exceptionally well in Tunisia. Under the divisional badge of a yellow crusader's battleaxe, the formation took part in most of the major operations carried out by First Army. Maj-Gen Vivian Evelegh commanded the division, which had arrived in North Africa as the spearhead of Anderson's formation during the 'Torch' landings in Algeria. With armoured support it made the dash for Tunis and came within 15 miles of the capital before being stopped dead by the elite paratroopers and tanks of Oberst Koch's famed battlegroup. For the greater part of the Tunisian campaign, the Battleaxe Division fought in the hills and mountains above Medjez, earning a reputation as Britain's premier 'mountain' division.[5] It suffered, in Montgomery's eyes, from being part of the unfashionable and often criticised First Army, but now, in Sicily, he needed the division more than he cared to admit. His famed Eighth Army's divisions were unable to complete the task Monty had felt they could achieve on their own; they were stalled in the mountains and needed a boost. Evelegh's Battleaxe Division was just the outfit to get them going again.

Montgomery gave orders for Eighth Army's line to be consolidated. XIII Corps was to hold the right-hand sector and to extend leftwards to take over 51st Division's area. The Highland Division was to ease itself out of the line and concentrate for the forthcoming operation. The Canadian Division would take 231st Brigade under command and began to press towards Agira, keeping the 15th Panzergrenadiers in front of it occupied while 78th Division came into the line. The signal for 78th Division to come over to Sicily was sent on 21 July and the division began landing on the island four days later. It took another three days to complete its arrival.

The Battleaxe Division then began to move into its assembly area at Scalpello on the 26th and completed its concentration on the 30th, just one day before the opening of Monty's new offensive. It was very close-run timing.

Over on the American side of the island, Patton was also reinforcing his army and signalled for the remainder of the 9th Infantry Division to be brought across from North Africa. Maj Gen Manton Eddy's division was landed at Palermo in the first convoy to arrive at the newly re-opened port.

The 9th Division had fought in Tunisia through much of the latter half of the campaign as part of US II Corps and had provided the lead troops of the corps during the famous left-hook manoeuvre to capture Bizerte. Eddy's division had been in action right up to the Axis surrender in Tunisia.

With US Seventh Army now on the northern coast with 45th Division and in the centre with 1st Division the whole of the left-hand sector of the front line could be given over to the Americans. Alexander now ordered Patton to face north-east and drive for Messina. What had been Montgomery's exclusive goal was to be shared by both armies. Patton relished the task, believing that his army could beat the British to Messina. The race was on, although Montgomery probably never saw the Allied drive to Messina as being a contest between the two armies. Patton, however, most assuredly did. Reaching Messina first would be a prestigious victory for his new army and would go some way to avenging the slights felt by the Americans at the hands of the British. Since arriving in North Africa the Americans had the feeling that the British saw them as being somewhat inferior, much less experienced and 'unlettered in the intricate arts of combat', as Bradley later put it.[6] Patton was determined that his Americans would be seen as equals to the British, although in his own mind they were far and away superior. His troops just had to be the first in Messina.

Patton was now allocated the northern coast road, Highway 113, which ran from Palermo to Messina and Highway 120, which travelled across the mountainous centre of the island from Petralia to Nicosia then on to Randazzo via Troina. These were now to become the two axes for Seventh Army's drive on Messina. Randazzo was also the objective of Leese's XXX Corps, which intended to drive up to the town from around the western side of Etna. Depending who got there first, the others might well find themselves pinched out of the final battle.

On 25 July Alexander called a conference with both Patton and Montgomery, the first such meeting of the campaign. The three were to meet near Monty's headquarters at the airfield outside Syracuse. Patton flew to the meeting in a C-47 escorted by two Spitfires. Montgomery was waiting for him when he arrived but there was no sign of Alexander. Monty called the American general over to his car where a map was spread out on the bonnet. Marked on the map Monty had drawn boundary lines depicting the ground allocated to each army. Patton was invited to discuss the roads they would need for their next operations and was very surprised, and also a little suspicious, that Montgomery agreed to everything he wanted.

Patton was later to confide in his diary that Monty had agreed so readily that he felt something was wrong, but try as he might he could not figure out what the catch was. The Eighth Army commander also offered Patton the whole of Highway 117 (the lateral road which ran Leonforte–Nicosia–San Stefano), feeling that it was of little use to either of them so the Americans could have it. Patton now had under his control the whole of the northern coastal strip of the island and a clear route to Messina. The two army commanders had carved up what remained of the island between them.

When Alexander arrived, matters had all been settled. The army group commander was a little annoyed that he had not been in on this discussion. He became, in Patton's words, 'quite brusque' and told Montgomery to explain the plan. Monty replied that he and Patton had already decided what they were going to do. Alexander got more annoyed and insisted that Montgomery show him his plan. He then asked Patton to show him his. Alexander was clearly put out at not having been the one to initiate the plans and, in order to show that it was he who was in charge, said that there were supply difficulties and asked Eisenhower's chief supply officer, Gen Miller, to explain. The supply difficulties amounted to a cut in the number of transport ships available to Patton to thirty-five. Patton was adamant that he needed forty-five and reluctantly Miller agreed, but said it was up to Admiral Cunningham to make the final decision.[7]

The meeting then broke up and the commanders all went their separate ways. Patton thought it was ill-mannered of Montgomery not to offer anyone lunch. An hour later Patton was back in Palermo. It was with a great sense of satisfaction that he considered his two routes to the north. They were now officially his, and with them his army had been placed on an equal footing with British Eighth Army. All he had to do now was win the race for Messina. Three days after the meeting with Montgomery, Patton sent a note to the 45th Division's commander. In it he stressed to Middleton the need for speed in his advance along the coast road: 'This is a horse race, in which the prestige of the US Army is at stake. We must take Messina before the British.' Patton confided in his diary that night that he felt Bradley and Middleton were getting 'sticky' and needed spurring on.[8]

Lt Gen Omar Bradley opened the American drive to Messina with Middleton's 45th Division on the coast road and Allen's 1st Division on a parallel path 20 miles inland along Highway 120. The two drives were separated by bare mountains covered with scrub and strewn with boulders, connected by a few tortuous narrow paths. Initial progress was good until both divisions came up against the main German positions. Hube had shifted his defence line back slightly in its northern sector which allowed US 45th Division to reach and take San Stefano on the coast and 1st Division to arrive at Nicosia along the inland route. From here on both advances became embroiled in difficult fighting as they were drawn into what had developed into the main German stop line, the Etna Line. The 1st Division gradually slowed almost to a standstill as it pushed its way forward to the outskirts of the hill-top town of Troina. Here, deep in Sicily's central mountain region, the German defences were masterly. Every approach, hill and valley was under observation and could be covered with accurate and devastating artillery fire. Allen's division was brought to an abrupt halt. It was the same for Middleton's men. Just past San Stefano was the coastal anchor of the Etna Line and roadblocks, demolitions and well-sited gun emplacements completely barred their way further along the seaside highway. The days of fire and movement were over; rapid develop-ment was a thing of the past. The Americans were now having to experience the tenacious and vicious nature of good quality German troops dug in for defence, just as their British cousins had had to endure for several weeks on the other side of the island.

On 1 August Gen Patton issued a message to all the men of Seventh Army congratulating them on their first twenty-one days of ceaseless battle. He claimed that they had killed and captured more than 87,000 enemy soldiers and captured or destroyed 371 guns, 172 tanks and 928 trucks. He went on to say how Gen Eisenhower and Gen Alexander had expressed pride and satisfaction in their efforts. 'You are now closing in for the kill,' he went on, 'Messina is our next stop.' In his diary that day he once more reiterated what was becoming almost a fixation: 'We must beat the British to Messina.'[9]

Patton may have sounded upbeat to his men, but he was very aware that things were slowing down noticeably all along the American front; his divisions were getting tired and opposition was becoming increasingly difficult to overcome. Of almost equal concern were Monty's attacks on his right. On 1 August the Canadians were on the verge of taking Regalbuto and the fresh British 78th Division was closing on Centuripe, threatening to break through the German defence line. Eighth Army was on the move again and once it had got astride of Mount Etna, it would have the enemy on the run. The race for Messina was hotting up and Patton did not like it.

There is no hard evidence that Montgomery was actually participating in this race. He was oblivious to Patton's obsession with getting to Messina first. The heady days of July were long past and Montgomery had settled in for a hard slog and was looking for the campaign to reach a conclusion. He probably knew that it was unlikely that Eighth Army would actually beat the Americans to Messina; it was more likely that the two armies would have to be mutually supporting the closer they came to the city as both of their forces would converge on Randazzo in the centre. Montgomery was now heavily committed to a campaign that had lost its major headlines. The long slog through the mountains and the masterly defence put up by the Germans had made the battle tiresome. Montgomery, as his official biographer readily admits, now had his sights set elsewhere; he was fixed on leading the Allied invasion of the Italian mainland. But first he had to break through the German line.

XXX Corps' new operation against the centre of the Etna Line involved all three of Leese's divisions. The Canadians were to make the break-in with their 3rd Brigade by capturing a bridgehead over the River Dittaino at Catenanuova on the night of 30/31 July. The 78th Division would then pass through and enlarge the lodgement to form a firm base for the assault on the hill town of Centuripe planned for 2 August. At the same time 51st Division would make a move across the Dittaino downstream and capture Monte Serra di Spezia to anchor the corps' right flank. As 78th Division advanced along the main axis, the Highland Division would conform to its movements to guard the south-western side of the corps. The remainder of 1st Canadian Division would push its main body through Regalbuto and move down Highway 121, its way, it was hoped, made easier by the attack on Centuripe. Its converging attack would meet 78th Division somewhere near the River Simeto where it would then participate with the Battleaxe Division in a two-pronged attack on Adrano.

The operation got off to a good start, with both Canadian 3rd Brigade and 78th Division's 11th Brigade capturing their objectives, and the next day the 51st Highland Division, supported by the tanks of 50th RTR, formed a lodgement across the Dittaino downstream of the main effort. These attacks were made against troops of the *Hermann Göring* Division and paratroopers from the German 3rd Parachute Regiment. Unsurprisingly all of these British gains were counter-attacked by both enemy infantry and armour as soon as they had become established, but these efforts were successfully repulsed by Allied artillery and tank fire.

In the early hours of 1 August 78th Division began its attack on Centuripe, Maj-Gen Evelegh had planned to begin the assault on 2 August, but the progress made the day before allowed him to bring the attack forward by 24 hours. Problems associated with the capture of Centuripe were considerable. It was located on a slim ridge which jutted out from the main mass of hills. The town sat perched 2,000 feet up, forming a fortress-like bastion across the road to Adrano, looking down in every direction. The approach road to the town from the south wound its way through a number of hairpin bends, all of which were overlooked from every angle by the enemy. On either side of the road the hillsides were lined with terraces of olives and vines, each level rising in a sheer step, 6 or 8 feet high. Those slopes that were not cultivated were covered in loose stone or coarse grass. Each hairpin bend concealed an ambush; enemy guns covered every yard of the approaches. All culverts and bridges were blown. Craters pock-marked the road surface and man-made landslides blocked the road itself.[10]

Evelegh was anxious that Centuripe be taken as soon as possible, before the enemy could regroup from their counter-attack against the Dittaino bridgehead. He intended for his lead formation, 36th Brigade, to capture the high ground to the west of Centuripe during the hours of darkness and then launch an assault against the town from that direction at first light. His 38th (Irish) Brigade would follow through the town after its capture, advancing on down to the River Salso which lay in the valley on the far side.

The battle to capture the town took just over two days. The 36th Brigade captured the high ground to the left of Centuripe and got into the cemetery on the edge of the town, but could not move any further forward when daylight came. Enemy fire raked the ground and prohibited every movement. Evelegh reinforced his attack with two battalions from 11th Brigade, but still movement forward was slow and painful. The next day he switched his effort to the right and introduced the redoubtable Irish

Brigade into the battle. At one point Gen Evelegh had eight of his battalions all pressing at the town's perimeter. Then, during the late evening of 2 August, all of the Battleaxe Division's field guns and all of XXX Corps' medium artillery laid down a barrage of devastating fire on the town. From behind this onslaught of hot metal the Irishmen of the 6th Inniskilling Fusiliers scaled a hundred-foot cliff to get into the first of the buildings perched on top of the rocks on the eastern side while another battalion, 1st Royal Irish Fusiliers, came at the town from the direction of the cemetery, supported by the small arms fire of the 2nd London Irish Rifles perched high above on the heights to the west. Very close fighting followed as the Germans were driven from their positions house by house. By first light the town had been cleared of all the enemy.

It was a great victory for Evelegh, more especially because it was his division's first battle with Eighth Army. The relentless pressure that he had subjected the German defenders to, and the gradual ramping up of the numbers committed to the attack, demonstrated the fine tactical ability of the divisional commander and the fighting prowess of his men. Everyone in the Eighth Army camp was elated with the news of Centuripe's capture. The road was at last open to Adrano just 8 miles away.

Evelegh was determined to keep up the momentum of his advance. His engineers were filling in craters on the road up to the town even as the final attacks went in. Well before dawn he had artillery moving up onto the heights. During the next day gun positions were laid out along the ridge and their location 2,000 feet above sea level gave them a spectacular view of enemy territory. The guns were situated just below the crest, with artillery observers stationed on the summit just in front of the field guns. Their location gave them uninterrupted observation over the western side of Mount Etna and, more importantly, a commanding view of the lateral road running around its southern slopes which joined Adrano with Paterno. The British could now dominate this road with fire and interdict enemy movement along it. The time was fast approaching when Hube would have to issue the order to give up Adrano, abandon the Etna Line and withdraw to a new line to the north of the great volcano.

Over in US Seventh Army the 45th Division was becoming exhausted; it had been in almost continual action since the landings, much of this time in contact with German troops. Patton sensed that its commander looked tired and his attacks lacked drive. He spoke with Bradley and told

him that he would motor up and see Middleton the next day. On 30 July,
the army commander visited 45th Division's headquarters and told
Middleton that he and his formation were to be rested. Middleton agreed
that it was in the best interests of Seventh Army to do so, which impressed
Patton as an excellent example of 'willingness to play ball and
unwillingness to ask for help'.[11] The relief was timely, for Patton was
continuing to drive his men hard. Bradley needed fresh troops at the point
of II Corps to speed up the advance.

Middleton's 45th Division was replaced by Lucian Truscott's 3rd
Division. The change-over occurred during 1 August. As circumstances
permitted, the 45th was gradually pulled out of the line and returned to
the rear. The division had fought well during its first spell of action and
had suffered little from the disadvantage of having been brought directly
from the United States for the invasion, while other formations were
planning and preparing on the shores of Tunisia. It was now to rest and
refit ready for its next challenge, for the division had been earmarked to be
included in Lt Gen Mark Clark's Fifth Army in Italy.

The US 3rd Division had landed at Licata on 10 July, as had the 1st and
45th Divisions, but its progress through the western half of the island had
been less difficult than that of Middleton's division. It was therefore a
much fresher formation and had a suitably aggressive commander.
Truscott would continue the coastal drive while Allen's 1st Division,
supported by fresh units of Eddy's 9th Division, would take the inland
route. Patton was keeping his 2nd Armored Division as a reserve, ready to
use it to exploit any open ground once the drive got through the
mountains.

Maj Gen Truscott's arrival on the coast road brought him face to face
with the same problems that had confronted Middleton. His front was
narrow in the extreme, for the 'coastal plain' along which Highway 113
passed was no more than a few hundred yards wide at most, and often was
just the width of the road itself. The highway took a meandering course,
hugging the shape of the shore, sandwiched between the Mediterranean
and the mountains. It was often carved into the sheer rock face of the cliffs
that rose up from the sea, suspended on concrete piers or disappearing into
tunnels beneath headlands. Inland from the road the terrain was sheer
rock or rubble-strewn hillsides, passable only by men on foot or mule
trains. For the enemy, the highway took little manpower to defend, for

roadblocks, minefields and demolitions themselves slowed American progress to a crawl and German artillery and mortar fire punished any attempts to outflank these obstructions. Aiding the Germans in this area were the remnants of the Italian *Assietta* Division, although most of the fighting was actually done by the Germans.

The 29th Panzergrenadier Division made impressive use of this natural defensive topography and also organised more elaborate strong positions along the steep estuaries where mountain streams reached the sea. For the Americans, each of these required set-piece attacks in order to get past. Each position was, however, designed to be so strong that frontal attacks would inevitably be costly. Areas that might offer a chance for the obstruction to be outflanked were mined and covered by artillery, machine-gun and mortar fire. No vehicles could pass these defensive barriers without engineering assistance. The 3rd Division's rate of advance was dependent on the speed that the enemy could be cleared from observation of these obstacles so as to allow engineers to construct by-passes around them and permit artillery and transport to move through. There was, however, some extra support available to Truscott, for the seaward flank was Allied territory and supporting naval gunfire was always on call, able to bring down large-calibre shells on located enemy positions. Nevertheless, 3rd Division's coastal route was a tortuous and difficult advance, filled with frustration, danger and disappointment. Patton's love of fire and movement and impatience to get forward were going to be as frustrated as that of his divisional commanders before very long.

To the south, Maj Gen Allen's 1st Division was making equally slow progress along Highway 120, although his formation did have more room to manoeuvre. The main direction of its advance was along the highway itself, for this was the only route available for motorised transport, but the hills and mountains on either side of the road were passable to infantry and mule trains and could be used to outflank enemy positions. Nonetheless, this movement off-road was precarious and difficult, for Axis observation was complete and all movement subjected to interdictory fire.

On 1 August, 1st Division's first attempts to reach Troina were stopped dead and then hit by a powerful counter-attack, forcing it back to its line of departure. The 15th Panzergrenadiers, assisted by elements of the *Aosta* Division were holding a very formidable network of field emplacements, roadblocks and natural features. Surveillance of the whole of the contested ground was available to Axis artillery observers on Monte Pelato to the north. The strength of the rebuff was of such force that Allen immediately knew the area was more strongly held than he had thought and must be a vital anchor to the Axis defence line. The 1st Division's commander had underestimated just how powerful the Troina position was and the setback required a rethink.

Patton visited Bradley that night and asked for a progress report. On hearing Allen had been forced back he got angry and criticised the divisional commander. Bradley rose to his subordinate's defence, claiming that getting to Troina was going to be tougher than anyone thought. This made Patton even gloomier. Middleton was stalled on the coast road and Allen had been pushed back in the centre. Patton could do nothing but urge Bradley on: 'I want you to get to Messina just as fast as you can,' ordered Patton. 'I want to beat Monty to Messina.'

For the next two days, 1st Division pressed on either side of Highway 120 with two of its regiments, the 16th and 26th, assisted by 39th Regiment from US 9th Division. The attacks made only little progress, even though they were supported by bomber and fighter-bomber aircraft. Each time they tried, the infantry were thrown back and then counter-attacked. In the taking of Troina, Allen's troops were counter-attacked no fewer than twenty-four times. Bradley knew that the pressure being applied to the enemy at Troina needed to be ramped up to overwhelming strength. Fortunately, Maj Gen Eddy was at that moment assembling the remainder of his 9th Division in the area of Nicosia. To boost Allen's hand, Bradley committed a second regiment from 9th Division to 1st Division, sending the 60th Regimental Combat Team up to the Troina sector.

During these two days Patton was becoming increasingly restless. His belligerent nature and constant carping were causing open resentment among his subordinates and his fixation on Messina was bringing him into contempt. 'His impetuousness outraged his commanders,' Bradley was later to write. 'In Sicily, Patton the man, bore little resemblance to Patton the legend.'[12]

Patton's impatience led him to visit the very front line to 'butt kick' the troops into more action. He was critical of everyone he saw and thought that Allen's division was in a frightful state, suffering from a lack of discipline and a widespread disregard of authority. Allen appeared to be oblivious to this general insubordination, or unable to do anything about it. Allen's division was indeed tired and its strength was beginning to sap away under the terrific German onslaught. Even worse, more and more men were dropping out through combat fatigue and being sent back to hospitals for medical treatment. Replacements were few so every man in the line was being made to endure an ever heavier load; each man left out of battle for whatever reason was keenly felt by those left behind.

On 3 August, after a day that started well with the news that Eisenhower was to award him the DSC for his actions at Gela at the start of the campaign, nothing followed but disappointing results and slow progress reports. Patton decided, on the spur of the moment, to pay a visit to the 15th Evacuation Hospital. He often visited medical facilities throughout his army's sector. Sometimes the visit acted as a lift to his own morale; at other times it was to provide a morale boost to those soldiers who had been maimed in battle. Moving among the wounded men gave him inspiration to carry on. He felt that he sometimes needed to be reminded that the price of victory had to be paid in blood and the bandaged men lying on narrow cots gave testimony to their courage. He frequently had with him a box of Purple Heart medals to pin on the wounded soldiers. It was not unknown for him to kneel down beside some comatose figure and whisper words of encouragement in his ear, or to remain on his knees and say a prayer for the man's recovery. He did this not for any reasons of publicity, but as a genuine act of contrition for the suffering he had caused to happen.

Patton's visit that day began like those of many previous occasions. He visited the receiving tent where men of the 1st Division who had been wounded in the attack on Troina were being brought for attention. He talked jovially with the patients as he made his rounds and was cheered at finding so many wounded men still in great spirits, many of them telling him that they couldn't wait to get back to their outfit and get on with winning the war. One man had lost an arm; another soldier was missing a leg. As the general was about to leave the tent, he noticed a soldier in his mid-twenties sitting quietly on a box without evident sign of any wound. Patton went up to the man, Private Charles Kuhl, and asked him what the matter was. 'I guess I can't take it,' Kuhl replied. Patton erupted into a flaming rage at seeing what he thought was a malingerer among so many genuine casualties. His actions were later described in an official report into the incident:

> The General immediately flared up, cursed the soldier, called him all
> types of a coward, then slapped him across the face with his gloves and
> finally grabbed the soldier by the scruff of the neck and kicked him out
> of the tent.

Kuhl was picked up by medical staff and removed to another tent. He
was found to have a temperature of 102.2 degrees Fahrenheit and had a
history of chronic diarrhoea that stretched back over a month. Blood tests
showed him to be positive for malaria parasites. The final medical diagnosis
was that Kuhl was suffering from chronic dysentery and malaria. He had
been with 1st Division since 2 June.

Patton was seething mad and told the commander of the hospital, Lt Col
Leaver, not to admit the 'sonuvabitch'. He said he would not have the
'yellow-bellied bastard' stinking up such a place of honour. The general
then stormed out of the tent still yelling profanities at the top of his voice,
leaving the medical staff in stunned silence. Appalled though they were at
such outrageous behaviour, none of those present followed up the matter
with higher authorities. Kuhl later wrote home to his father that 'Patton
had slapped his face, kicked him in the pants and cussed him,' but did not
expect any further action with regard to the incident.

In his diary that night, Patton recorded how he had seen a man who
was trying to look as though he was wounded and had slapped his face
with his gloves and kicked him out of the hospital. He expressed a view
that such men who shirked their duty should be tried for cowardice and
shot.[13]

On 5 August Patton issued a memo to corps, division and separate unit
commanders within Seventh Army. In it he explained that it had come to
his attention that a small number of soldiers were going to hospital on the
pretext that they were nervously incapable of combat. 'Such men are
cowards,' he wrote. He alleged that they were using the hospitals as a
means of escaping the dangers of battle. The general insisted that
measures must be taken to stop this happening and cases should be dealt
with in the unit. He went on to say that those who were not willing to
fight 'will be tried by Court-Martial for cowardice in the face of the enemy.'
It was a strong message and one which made it clear that malingerers
would be rooted out of Seventh Army, by the use of military law if
necessary. It is ironic that Patton himself had just committed a gross

transgression of military law by striking an enlisted man, though he chose to ignore this fact in his passion to bring others to task.

The next attack on Troina was begun on 4 August. The keys to the defences were the two roads that exited the town to the rear. One road led south-east to Adrano, the other northwards through Cesaro to Randazzo. If Allen's division could get around the German flanks and cut those roads, the enemy would be forced either to wait in the town and be trapped, or to pull out. Allen now decided to go after both of these roads with simultaneous pincer movements, one to the north and one to the south. The operation opened with a 50-minute barrage fired by the guns of the 1st and 9th Divisions. This fire from 8½ artillery battalions was immediately followed by a concentrated aerial bombardment of the town and the surrounding area.

Watching the opening movements of the attack from a bend on Highway 120 near Cerami was the corps commander, Gen Bradley. He was there to witness what was the heaviest air attack in support of ground troops so far in the campaign. The artillery barrage had enveloped Troina in clouds of dust and, just as the gunfire slackened off, the Allied aircraft came in. Seventy-two fighter-bombers, each carrying a 500lb bomb, swept low over the town and buried it in an ocean of flame and smoke. Huge explosions ripped through the air, sending rubble and stone high into the heavens. As the planes banked and returned to their bases, the infantry attacked once more. And once more, just as before, the Germans resisted stubbornly then, having stopped the American advance, put in counter-attacks of their own while plastering Allen's men with well-observed artillery fire.

The next day Maj Gen Allen tried again. It was clear that, for any real progress to be made, the German observation of the battlefield from the area of Monte Pelato to the north had to be cleared. Allen decided to use the 60th Regiment for the task, supported by two battalions of field artillery and a detachment of engineers. Once again Bradley was up at the front to witness the renewed attack and the ubiquitous aerial bombardment that now seemed to go hand in hand with land operations. With the corps commander that day was Maj Gen Edwin House, Patton's tactical air commander.

The two men watched the artillery barrage with great satisfaction and waited for the friendly aircraft to arrive overhead. H-Hour for the aerial attack came and went with no sign of the fighter-bombers of US XII Air Support Command. As the two generals were about to leave their vantage position, a drone was heard high overhead and three A-36 Apache dive bombers passed over on their way back to their base in the south. Bradley turned to House and remarked, 'Holy smokes, now just where in hell do you suppose they've dropped their bombs?' 'I'll be damned if I know,' replied the air force general.

When Bradley got back to his command post he received a telephone call from XXX Corps' Oliver Leese. 'What have we done that your chaps would want to bomb us?' the British general lamented. Bradley was embarrassed and asked where the aircraft hit. 'Right on top of my head-quarters!' groaned Leese. 'They have really plastered the town.'[14]

The 60th Regiment made good progress on its trek northwards across the mountains and this move, coupled with the gains gradually being made in the south by the flanking movement of the division's own 18th Regiment, began to bring it home to the German defenders in Troina that it was time to slip away to fight another day. To the south-east the British XXX Corps was also making good progress. All this successful activity was causing Gen Hube to feel that his line was beginning to bulge.

On 6 August the 16th RCT of 1st Division entered the rubble that was Troina with little difficulty, for the battalions of the 15th Panzergrenadiers holding the place had withdrawn during the night before the net closed around them. Last to leave were the engineers whose tasks of demolitions, cratering and the laying of booby-traps helped to delay the arrival of the Americans. The battle to take the town had lasted a bitter five days and had involved five complete regiments in the worst of the fighting experienced by Seventh Army thus far. The taking of Troina was a great prize for the Allies for the town was a cornerstone on the Etna Line and at that moment the British were in the process of their own operations to take another keystone along that line at Adrano.

Montgomery was well pleased with the capture of Centuripe for it meant that XXX Corps was through the mountains and could advance around the lower slopes of Etna. Eighth Army could once again become more mobile. Adrano was still the main objective and the army commander urged Leese to keep up the momentum. Once Adrano was captured, he was to press on to Bronte and then Randazzo. At this point he should meet the Americans advancing down Highway 120 from Troina and joining his left flank. It had been decided that the drive northwards from Randazzo would then be taken up by Seventh Army and Leese's corps would swing eastwards to come round the back of Etna towards the sea to meet the advancing XIII Corps, which should by then be through Catania. From here on there was a straight run to Messina.

The 78th Division continued its advance as laid out by the corps and army commanders. Leese had ordered Evelegh to reach the River Salso on the night of 4 August, then push on over the River Simeto the next night so as to be ready to attack Adrano on the night of the 6th/7th. Other formations would attack on either side of the division to protect its flanks: the 1st Canadian Division, now through Regalbuto and advancing towards Adrano on Highway 121, would cross the Simeto further upstream on the 6th and the Highland Division would attack the village of Biancavilla below Adrano just before 78th Division assaulted the town itself.

Eighth Army's advances were achieved on time without too much difficulty, although fierce fighting and planned set-piece attacks had to be implemented to gain success. Each of the moves came with overwhelming artillery support, thanks to the aid of the artillery forward observation officers on the Centuripe ridge. The Irish Brigade led 78th Division down from the high ground and across the River Salso on 5 August. The same day Canadian mobile forces made contact with the Irishmen to link up the two advances. The next day a brief skirmish took the Battleaxe Division across the Simeto at the same time as the Highland Division occupied Biancavilla. Up ahead Allied aircraft bombed Adrano and artillery pounded its centre prior to the final attack. On the night of 6/7 August 78th Division entered Adrano unopposed.

The advance made by 78th Division and the Canadians, coupled with the sustained American pressure along Highways 113 and 120, was beginning to take a heavy toll on Gen Hube's command. The Etna Line had been pushed back in many places, although there appeared to be no possibility of an actual breakthrough. When the Americans finally took Troina on 5/6 August, the Etna Line could be deemed to be broken and another line, the new Hube Line, became the main defence. Once again it was a defence line in name only, consisting of very few permanent or field fortifications. Orders were given for a pull-back to this line, which ran from Sant' Agata on the northern coast, across Monte Pelato, through Cesaro, then Bronte and then across the rear of Mount Etna to Riposto on the eastern coast. This took the Axis defences well north of Catania and so removed the need to hold the area in front of Etna.

British XIII Corps had observed a gradual withdrawal of the German forces holding the Catania plain on 2 August, just as XXX Corps was beginning to make good progress on its left. Ammunition dumps were being blown up and forward positions were being abandoned. Exceptionally large fires were observed in the area of Gerbini airfield and Misterbianco. The gathering threat that 78th Division's moves were making to the right flank of the *Hermann Göring* Division had convinced Hube to pull back the division to the seaward side of Etna to shorten its front. Dempsey now ordered 5th and 50th Divisions to push forward to keep in contact with the retreating enemy. The 50th Division entered Catania and Misterbianco on 5 August and the 5th Division took Belpasso and Paterno on the 6th, all against little opposition. The main interference with the moves came once again from German rearguards, minefields and demolitions. The town of Catania was almost completely destroyed by weeks of bombing and artillery fire, although the harbour was mostly undamaged.

Along the northern coast road, Maj Gen Truscott's 3rd Division was still finding the way forward difficult and slow. The Germans controlled the narrow coastal strip and only relinquished ground at an unhurried and measured pace. In front of the Americans was a German battlegroup of just a few battalions, but their complete dominance of the rugged terrain gave them the power to regulate events beyond their numbers.

On the coast road the main body could not move without German troops on the high ground overlooking the advance and getting American troops onto that high ground was a deliberate and exhausting task. Mortars and small arms fire dogged the Americans over every foot of ground. Attempts were made to outflank German positions by wide encircling movements inland. These were demanding in the extreme, for the jagged mountainsides were often too precipitous even for mules and everything required had to be manhandled by hot and very tired troops. Even when such moves were successful and the men reached positions from which they could strike down on the roadblocks, the Germans would hold for as long as possible then withdraw up the highway on wheeled transport demolishing as they went, while the Americans could only follow up on foot. All this took place under perfect observation from enemy posts high up on Monte Fratello.

A later British intelligence summary described the tactics the Germans were using:

> In rear guard actions the enemy is making full use of cover provided by the mountainous and wooded nature of the ground. Positions are carefully selected. Preparation of these positions is done by Italian labour, the Germans as far as possible being rested for the actual fighting. It is practically impossible to detect these positions with the usual reconnaissance methods. Knowing this full well, the Germans wait until our troops are within point blank range before opening up with automatic weapons. Frequently when a second attack has been launched against the positions they are found to be vacated. Now the position is reversed for the Germans know the exact locations of our troops because we are holding their old defences. Mortar and artillery concentrations on our troops follow from previous registration of their guns.[15]

Back in his headquarters some 5 miles to the rear, Patton was becoming more agitated. Neither of his thrusts was slicing through the enemy positions as he had hoped and his dash for Messina had become nothing more than a slow crawl. His men were fighting not only the enemy, but also the terrain. It was just not the type of country in which one would choose to wage war. The old cavalryman within him was becoming increasingly frustrated.

Also becoming anxious concerning the slow-down of Allied progress in Sicily was the Supreme Commander. Eisenhower cabled Patton on 3 August with a stick and a carrot. First the stick:

> Because of your great depth along your difficult routes of approach you will be able to attack day and night without cessation. Thus you will not only break the enemy's morale but you will be contributing in marked degree to the success of General Alexander's whole operation.

Then the carrot:

> I personally assure you that if we speedily finish off the German in Sicily, you need have no fear of being left there in the backwater of the war.[16]

The latter part of the message was welcome news for Patton, for his great rival Mark Clark had already been given command of Fifth Army for future operations against the Italian mainland and Patton was fearful that

he might well not be taking any part in subsequent ventures. He loathed
the idea of his Seventh Army having to stay on the island on garrison
duties.

Patton's left-hand thrust did have one advantage that could be exploited
to help move his army forward, its seaward flank. The army commander
decided that he would use this feature to his advantage and sought
approval from his naval colleagues to lay on an amphibious landing behind
the enemy line to speed up Truscott's advance. On 3 August his deputy,
Gen Keyes, visited Bradley and Truscott and outlined Patton's latest idea.
The 3rd Division would land a reinforced battalion of infantry in the rear
of the German line to disrupt any enemy withdrawal while the main body
of the division attacked the Axis positions head on. Several suitable places
had been identified and Keyes left it to Truscott to coordinate the
amphibious attack with a simultaneous one by his division. It was vital
that the small force landed behind the enemy not be left isolated for too
long a period.

The operation was an excellent idea and one which made good use of the
Allies' air and naval superiority. There was little danger in using light
vessels for inshore operations and any such activity could be given suitable
air cover. There obviously were some risks from such a bold step, but it was
well worth taking such risks to bring about a speedy conclusion to the
campaign. The naval staff, however, thought otherwise and began to put
obstacles in the way. First and foremost they did not like to be told to hand
over landing craft to the army. To be fair to Cunningham, all landing craft
not actually in use ferrying supplies over to Sicily were being brought back
to North Africa to be refitted ready for the next large operation, the invasion
of the mainland of Italy. The naval commander had issued a signal
recalling all such craft to Bizerte by 10 August. There were to be no further
landing craft convoy sailings after 5 August, except authorised by him.

Patton had reached a brick wall and appealed directly to Eisenhower on
4 August for the directive to be revoked, adding at the end of the message:
'Amphibious landing rear of enemy positions vital to success of operations
must necessarily be cancelled.'[17] This last point struck home, for
Eisenhower's message to 'attack day and night without cessation' had been
sent only the day before. Eisenhower acted immediately and asked
Alexander for his views. The army group commander replied on 5 August
with a message of total support for Patton, reasoning that even though

future operations elsewhere might be delayed by the use of these landing craft, if anything was done to weaken Patton's drive on Messina and a speedy conclusion to the campaign in Sicily, then that in itself would delay future operations in the Mediterranean. His cable went on:

> I approve minimum requirement for craft for Seventh Army . . . and recommend that these craft be provided as far as they can be made available from US craft . . . Further if we do anything at this critical moment other than give Patton 100 per cent support for his difficult and hard fought battle it must have a depressing effect upon him and his troops. I have informed Patton that I will give him every support and assistance in my power, but I expect him in return to do the same by me by cutting down his craft to an absolute minimum and releasing craft immediately he can make them available.[18]

Alexander sent the same message of support to Patton, but stressed that it was his responsibility to ensure that his attack was backed by adequate air cover.

While this wrangling over landing craft was going on, Bradley's planners were working out the details of the amphibious landings. They had chosen a beach at Sant' Agata di Militello, a few miles north of a point where Monte Fratello towered above the coastline. It was expected that the Germans would have created a strong position in this area around the point where the Rivers Furiano and Ignanno reached the sea, and landings beyond these defences would place the enemy in a precarious situation. The operation was scheduled to take place on 6 August.

On 4 August Truscott made a strong move along the coast road with his 15th Infantry Regiment, attempting to drive his way forward and develop operations around Monte Fratello. He knew that it would take time and effort to get into a position where the enemy forces engaged against him would find themselves compromised when the amphibious assault went in behind them. The first day of this new attack made little progress. Three battalions of the 29th Panzergrenadier Division and several Italian units were identified holding the ground ahead of 3rd Division. Artillery fire was intense and accurate and it took another day's hard fighting before the lead units reached the Furiano and the seaward slopes of Monte Fratello. Here they found the enemy securely dug in along the far bank of the river and on the mountain itself. Machine-gun and mortar fire swept all lines of attack. The Germans had blown the bridge across the Furiano and laid extensive minefields across all approaches. So furious was the enemy opposition that no transport or guns could be got up to the leading troops, for every time a crater in the road or a demolished culvert was approached by engineers for repair, the area was plastered by shell fire.

Truscott ordered the slopes of Monte Fratello to be shrouded in smoke to try to cut down some of the enemy's observation and allow heavier support to be brought forward. On the night of 5/6 August he then sent in two battalions of his 30th Infantry Regiment to gain a ridge opposite the southern slopes of the mountain. He hoped that artillery could be brought onto this flank to support a new move down the centre. The attack failed to make any significant progress, even though supported by heavy artillery fire and attacks by fighter-bombers. As Truscott later admitted, the terrain was even more difficult than he had first supposed.

By the afternoon of 6 August the 3rd Division had six battalions in the line attempting to batter their way past the towering heights of Monte Fratello. Although no rapid progress had been made, the great weight of the American attack was applying inexorable pressure on the Axis defenders. Truscott felt that soon something would have to give and decided that the time was right to initiate the amphibious landings behind the enemy line. He gave orders for Lt Col Lyle Bernard to take his 2nd Battalion, 30th Infantry, to the waiting landing craft at San Stefano, embark his men and make a dawn landing against the enemy flank.

As the loading was taking place, disaster struck. The preparations had been detected by the enemy and air support was summoned south to deal with the American ships. The embarkation area was then subjected to a lightning bombing attack by just four enemy aircraft during which one of the valuable tank landing craft was sunk. Truscott decided that it was too risky to continue without it and another was called up from Palermo to replace the unfortunate vessel. The operation was postponed for 24 hours.

On 8 August the landings went in. The convoy was escorted by two cruisers and six destroyers and made landfall without incident. Bernard got his men ashore at 0315 hrs and began to interdict enemy traffic along the coast road, although very few vehicles were intercepted. Concurrently with the landings, still during the hours of darkness, Truscott attacked the ridge to the south of Monte Fratello again and pushed the 15th Regiment once more up the axis of the main road. At first light, he then passed the 7th

Regiment through the 15th Regiment and broke into the German positions. The intensity of the attack and news of landings in their rear prompted the Axis forces facing 3rd Division to try to fall back across the mountains and along the coastal plain by any route that was open to them. Many were trapped by the landings in their rear and were captured. The battle was soon over. American casualties had been relatively heavy, but the pincer movement resulted in over 1,500 enemy prisoners being taken, along with artillery and transport that could not be got out of the entrapment through Lt Col Bernard's roadblocks. Truscott pushed his men on in pursuit, but they only went a short distance before they met the next cratered part of the highway and encountered more roadblocks, more minefields and the incessant whine and crash of enemy shell fire.

The amphibious landings had helped to urge the Germans to speed up their withdrawal from the Monte Fratello position, but they were on the point of leaving anyway. The attack did not open up Highway 113 for Truscott, just moved his formation a few miles further on. When the advance resumed, Messina was still 75 miles away. Monty's army was a little closer; his forces were just 52 miles short of the winning post. Although both Allied armies were applying a great deal of pressure, it was the Germans who were still in control of the rate at which they advanced.

By 6 August, the Axis operations on the island had entered their last phase. The day before, Kesselring had informed OKW in Berlin that Hube's XIV Panzer Corps would withdraw sector by sector into a final line that would mark the last bridgehead in Sicily. Axis tactics from here on would be delay, disengagement and evacuation. Two days before, Hube had decided that a start could be made on the transfer over to the mainland of those men not directly involved in the fighting, together with stockpiles of surplus equipment that had been gathered in the north. Already being ferried across the Messina Strait were all unnecessary materials and non-essential personnel of the supply and support arms. Hube had also let it be known among his men that they would not be sacrificed in a futile attempt to save Sicily and that they would all be withdrawn to the safety of the mainland at the appropriate time. This gave a tremendous boost to morale, even though it went against Hitler's usual policy of every man fighting to the last. Hube's evacuation plan promised that its first priority would be the saving of all German troops on the island. After this, the greatest possible amount of equipment, supplies, stores and weapons would be transported over the strait to Italy. Anything that could not be extricated was to be destroyed.

Directing the whole evacuation process was the redoubtable Oberst Ernst-Günther Baade, one of the most colourful and idiosyncratic of German commanders. Baade had begun the war as a squadron leader in 3rd Cavalry Regiment and had gained a formidable reputation during earlier campaigns in Poland, France, Russia and North Africa. A brave and daring leader with a remarkable sense of humour, he was the idol of his men. He was sometimes known to go into action wearing a captured Scottish kilt. On one occasion in North Africa while in command of a regiment of the 15th Panzer Division, he was returning from a night raid and radioed to the British over their own net: 'Stop firing. On my way back. Baade.' But this clowning did not disguise the fact that Baade was also a very brave and independent leader of men, who had been decorated with the Knight's Cross with Oakleaves. He eventually commanded with distinction the 90th Panzergrenadier Division in Italy, most especially during the Cassino battles, and in 1945 took over a panzer corps in Germany. Tragically, he died of wounds on the last day of the war.[19]

On 14 July Baade was made German Commandant Messina Strait and controlled all the nearby anti-aircraft units, the 771st Engineer Landing Battalion and part of 616th Naval Artillery Regiment. By the end of July he had taken under his command Kapitän Kamptz, the local German naval commander and Kapitän von Liebenstein, the German officer in command of sea transport in Messina. He also enjoyed the powers of Fortress Commander Messina and was responsible for all construction, signals, transport and administrative units, as well as the battalion of 1st Parachute Division holding the mainland side of the water.

Guarding the narrow strait off Messina was a string of anti-aircraft and naval gun emplacements. By mid-August, Baade had 41 heavy and 52 light AA guns on the Sicilian side of the channel and 82 heavy and 60 light AA guns on the mainland. These guns were able to put down a wall of overlapping flak up to a ceiling of 23,000 feet. Guarding against naval attacks were four batteries of German 17cm guns and four batteries of Italian 28cm coast guns, together with two batteries of Italian 15.2cm guns.[20] The concentration of so much anti-aircraft and anti-ship artillery in such a small area made the Allies rather cautious of daylight naval and air activities in the vicinity.

For the Axis forces to get away from the island there had to be sufficient ferries to carry them across to the mainland. The craft available to the Germans were 9 Siebel ferries, 7 ferry barges, 1 small ferry, 12 landing boats, 41 assault boats and 50 small rubber boats.[21] The larger vessels were more than capable of bringing out tanks, transport vehicles and artillery pieces, while the host of smaller craft could carry large numbers of men to safety. The sea crossing in the straits was comparatively narrow, ranging from 2½ miles to 4 miles, which meant that they were vulnerable in open water for a relatively short time. The light craft were particularly elusive targets even in daylight for fast-flying aircraft trying to out-manoeuvre enemy flak, and in the dark they were virtually invisible.

By early August Baade had a firm plan for the forthcoming evacuation. His Italian counterparts, Admiral Barone and Brig Monacci, had also put into place arrangements to carry their own personnel over to the mainland. Italian forces were evacuated in an operation that was organised and directed by the Italians themselves and proved to be as successful as that controlled by Baade. It had begun much earlier than the German pull-out, as more and more of Guzzoni's men were withdrawn from the ever-decreasing front line and sent to the rear. Guzzoni had ordered Admiral Barone to start the Italian evacuation on 3 August. Two small steamers were used and the one remaining serviceable rail ferry. In just the first week, over 7,000 Italian troops were ferried across the strait under the cover of darkness.

The successes in the centre of the island that led to the fall of Troina and Adrano gave Alexander hope that the end in Sicily was rapidly approaching and that many Axis troops would soon be trying to get off the island. Preventing this and perhaps trapping some of the enemy on the island would have to be down to the naval and air forces. On 3 August Alexander signalled both Cunningham and Tedder, drawing their attention to the probability of an imminent Axis withdrawal across the Messina Strait:

> It is quite possible he may start pulling out before the front collapses. We must be in a position to take immediate advantage of such a situation by using the full weight of Naval and Air power. You have no doubt co-ordinated plans to meet this contingency and I for my part will watch situation most carefully so as to let you know the right moment to strike and this may well come upon us sooner than we expect.[22]

In this signal Alexander had alerted the other two services to be ready
for mass Axis evacuation from the island. Neither of the two commanders
replied to Alexander with their plans and intentions, so he could only
assume that they both had procedures in place to deal with all
eventualities. Tedder was aware that action was needed and signalled to
his boss, Air Chief Marshal Portal, in London on 4 August that the day
was approaching when he would be called upon to throw the whole
weight of Allied air power against the enemy in the Messina Strait.[23]
Admiral Cunningham had a more difficult problem. The stretch of water
across which the enemy planned to escape was an extremely narrow zone
in which to manoeuvre large surface vessels. It was also strongly defended
by Italian and German shore batteries and searchlights. He was unwilling
to commit his ships in order to interdict what would probably be intermittent attempts by an indeterminate number of small enemy craft. To
maintain an effective screen, ships would have to be stationed in the 10-
mile-long channel just a mile or two offshore of enemy guns. Any such
attempt to enter the Messina Strait with surface warships would almost
certainly result in heavy losses. Cunningham was of the opinion that the
task was really one for Allied air power.

The unpleasant reality was that there was no coordinated plan to stop
the enemy escaping. The known enemy batteries guarding the straits had
been left unmolested by the air force since the invasion, and with these
guns still active the Royal Navy was reluctant to go in. It is true that motor
torpedo boats had operated in the straits during the hours of darkness, but
their incursions had taken the form of hit-and-run raids which lasted for
minutes rather than hours. At no time did Cunningham's and Tedder's
staffs get together to produce a plan to subdue the coastal guns and allow
the navy to control the straits. Round the clock air raids on the ports and
inlets along the channel and the use of tactical bombers to neutralise the
batteries might have allowed surface warships into the strait to stop all
Axis craft crossing the waterway. If such a joint plan had been produced
by Tedder and Cunningham, or if Eisenhower had at least taken some
interest in what was not being done, then Baade's task would have been
much more difficult if not impossible.

After the US 1st Division had captured Troina on 6 August its men
collapsed exhausted from their long ordeal. They had almost reached the
end of their endurance after their month-long trek up from the landing

beaches, fighting the enemy for most of the way. The next day Allen's formation was relieved by the 9th Division. At the same time, there was a change of command at the top of the Big Red One when Allen was replaced. The news of Allen's relief and that of his second-in-command, Brig Gen Roosevelt, came as a shock to all those in the division and many others throughout Seventh Army. Allen had made the 1st Division his own, leading the formation in an inimitable way and creating a division with great personal pride while giving only moderate attention to discipline and conformity. Since the 'Torch' landings in November 1942, Allen's formation had been in almost continual action, always involved in the worst of the fighting and earning itself high praise. However, the hell-raising exploits of its men when on leave in Tunisia and their arrogance towards any other outfit had also singled out the division for some stern criticism. As for the men themselves, they felt that their division was the only one in Seventh Army that was carrying its fair share of the war.

In May Eisenhower had originally selected Allen for promotion to a corps command back in the States. Patton had no objection but asked if he could retain the general for the invasion of Sicily. When Allen was told of the possible promotion, he declined the offer and asked to stay with his division. Patton was happy to agree to keep one of his most experienced commanders for 'Husky'. But a few weeks after the landings, however, it was clear that Allen was becoming tired and was suffering from ill health and it also seemed that his division was gradually losing its cutting edge. Patton decided that he would replace the divisional commander and recommend that he be given an equivalent command back in the USA where his great experience could be put to use. The move was to be made without prejudice, stressed Patton, otherwise there would be no move at all. Allen's assistant commander, Brig Gen Roosevelt, was so closely associated with Allen and the performance of the division that the move was to apply equally to both the men. Patton wanted a complete change of command.

In the event, news broke of Allen's relief before he received the details from his corps commander Bradley, even though Bradley's own account suggests a different picture.[24] Allen was shocked and taken by surprise by his removal, as were his officers and the whole of the division. News circulated that Allen was being relieved of his command for reasons other than plain weariness and many people were angered by Bradley's role in the changes. The mood of the division worsened when Maj Gen Clarence Huebner, late of Alexander's staff in Tunis, arrived to take over. Huebner was a strict disciplinarian and imposed a harsh regime of training and discipline on the division. Smart uniforms, saluting officers, constant drill and expert marksmanship, all of which had been missing under Allen, became the new way of things. At first the men were resentful, both at the loss of their beloved commander and with the new man at the top. Huebner knew that his methods were unpopular, as he admitted at the time: 'The division is sorry for itself and needs someone to hate – me!'[25] Gradually Huebner's stern methods began to reap dividends and the tough new commander licked the division into shape. It was an unpleasant time but, finally, Huebner was able to earn the respect of his men. Huebner went on to command US V Corps in north-west Europe; Allen returned to the States to raise a new formation, the 104th Infantry Division, and led it in action in the same theatre.

Bradley's II Corps was still making only slow progress and each day Patton's frustration was growing. After the success of 3rd Division's amphibious landing, the army commander looked for another opportunity to use the technique again to speed up Truscott's move along the coast road. The 3rd Division was again held up by 29th Panzergrenadier Division along a new defence line behind the River Zappula on the Cape Orlando peninsula. Gen Fries had established his formation in a very strong position along the length of a natural feature, protected by extensive minefields and well served by strong artillery positions with good observation of all approaches. It looked as though Truscott's men would once again be involved in a protracted and costly battle to push the Germans aside.

To Patton the situation was perfect for another seaborne landing in the Germans' rear. If this amphibious assault went in at Brolo behind the enemy line in conjunction with a flanking attack through the inland village of Naso, then the Germans would be completely cut off and have to fight their way out. At the very least such moves would precipitate a quick Axis withdrawal; at best they would bag a great number of prisoners. On 9 August Patton summoned Bradley to his headquarters and told him to lay on the operation for the 11th.

The first amphibious operation to get around Monte Fratello had been a success because the land and the sea attacks were well coordinated, for in such an operation it was important that the main body was able to break through the enemy's front quickly enough to relieve the light forces in the rear before they were defeated in detail by the enemy. This coordination of effort had to be given to a single commander with the authority to choose the time at which he would commit his forces. This had to be the man on the spot, Maj Gen Truscott, whose division was to carry out the operation.

On the night of 9/10 August, Truscott moved his 15th Infantry Regiment with mule transport on a circuitous route across the mountains to get onto the ridge south of Naso to be ready to attack in conjunction with the landings. During that night and throughout the following day the troops struggled in searing heat to get themselves, their equipment and their guns over the precipitous and barren mountainside. By late afternoon on the 10th the task looked to be impossible to complete within the required timescale. The regiment would never be in place in time to coordinate its attack with the landings. Truscott decided to postpone the seaborne assault for 24 hours to allow the 15th Regiment time to get into position. He knew that everyone would be disappointed with the delay, but without the 15th Infantry on its start line, the operation stood little chance of success.

Patton was in an unpleasant frame of mind that day. He had earlier paid a surprise visit to another medical clearing facility and his temper had once again got the better of him. His visit to the 93rd Evacuation Hospital was a spur of the moment one while he was on the way to confer with Bradley at the II Corps command post. Patton began by touring the receiving tent, speaking in a jovial and yet concerned manner with the recent casualties waiting for evacuation, asking them about their wounds and giving them a few words of encouragement. He then came to Private Paul Bennett, a 21-year-old artilleryman from 13th Field Artillery Brigade, who sat huddled up and shivering.

Bennett had served four years in the Army as a regular soldier without any difficulties. Then, on 6 August, one of his close friends was wounded. He found he could not sleep and felt nervous all the day, becoming very jumpy every time he heard shells going over. He was sent to the rear by his battery aid man and was given a sedative by a medical officer. The next day he was ordered to be evacuated as he showed signs of dehydration, fatigue and a confused state of mind. Bennett begged the officer not to evacuate him because he did not want to leave his unit.

Patton asked Bennett what his trouble was. 'It's my nerves,' trembled the shocked private. 'What did you say?' screamed Patton. Bennett replied sobbing, 'It's my nerves, I can't stand the shelling anymore.' 'Your nerves hell,' yelled Patton, 'You are just a Goddamned coward, you yellow son of a bitch.' The general then slapped the man and told him to stop weeping. 'I won't have these brave men here who have been shot at seeing a yellow bastard sitting here crying.' Patton then struck Bennett again with such force he knocked off his helmet liner and sent it flying into the next tent. He then turned to the admitting officer and shouted, 'Don't admit this yellow bastard; there's nothing the matter with him.'

Patton was beside himself with rage. Bennett just sat there, trying to hold himself at attention, but shaking all over. The army commander was not yet done with the private for he continued cussing the poor unfortunate, telling him that he was to be sent back to the line where he might get shot and might get killed, but he was going to have to fight. 'If you don't,' yelled Patton, 'I'll stand you up against a wall and have a firing squad shoot you on purpose.' By this time Patton had completely lost it; his rage was uncontrollable. He reached for his pistol, waved it in front of the terrified man's face and yelled, 'I ought to shoot you myself, you Goddamned whimpering coward.'[26]

The commotion had brought other nurses and doctors running to the tent, together with the hospital commander, Col Donald Currier. All of them stood in stunned silence, dumbfounded by Patton's actions – most of them had witnessed the second slap. Yet still Patton was not through with the unfortunate man. He continued to berate the private as he stomped out of the tent yelling over his shoulder that the man was to be sent back to the front line. Patton carried on with his tour, but continued to talk about Bennett, stressing to Currier that he meant what he had said: the man was not to be admitted but to be sent back to his unit.

Once he was outside the army commander began to calm down and eventually continued on his way to Bradley's HQ. When he got there, he apologised to Bradley for being late and explained that he had stopped off at a hospital on the way and had to deal with a couple of malingerers there, one of whom had made him so mad that he had slapped him to try to put some fight back into the man. Patton was very matter of fact about his actions, speaking without remorse, and felt that he had probably done the private some good by bringing him to his senses.[27]

Bradley was far from being impressed by Patton's actions; he was in fact rather appalled by them. Patton seemed to him to be bragging about how he had treated the man, believing that the incident was a simple case of cowardice that had to be confronted by the man himself – if you could shame a coward you could help him gain his self-respect. Bradley reasoned that each man had a breaking point; some were low, others were higher. Those with a low breaking point were those Patton would call cowards. Patton disagreed; men who suffered from so-called nerves were in fact showing a yellow streak and had to be dealt with severely. Clearly Patton would not be swayed on the matter and Bradley was forced to suppose that the episode at the hospital that day was one more example of Patton's fiery temper and his intolerance of people he saw as being weaker than himself.

Later that evening Patton's deputy, Maj Gen Keyes, visited the 3rd Division's command post and learned of Truscott's decision to postpone the amphibious landings at Brolo. Although he was sympathetic to Truscott's problems, and knew that Truscott was the man in place to make the right decision, he also knew that Patton would not agree to any delay. Keyes had been in close contact with the army commander all day and knew that he was in a highly charged and agitated mood after the incident at the hospital. Patton was desperate to get II Corps moving at a greater pace for he could not tolerate the slow crawl to which his army had been reduced. He had also arranged for a number of war correspondents to accompany the landings and knew there would be criticism and disappointment if the operation was delayed.

The two generals decided they needed stronger support and telephoned Bradley to explain why the amphibious assault would have to be postponed and to get some agreement to the cancellation. Bradley concurred with Truscott's decision that the landings should not go in unless they were properly timed to co-ordinate with the attack by Col 'Doc' Johnson's 15th Regiment. Keyes duly reported the matter to Patton by phone and explained that Truscott did not want to carry out the landing operation. Patton erupted into a bout of fury, unable to listen to reason or to hear Truscott's explanation. 'Damnit,' he bellowed down the phone, 'That operation will go on.'

Truscott could do nothing but follow orders and, contrary to his better judgement, gave Lt Col Bernard the necessary instructions to begin loading his amphibious force for the seaborne venture. He sent a message to Col Johnson that he had to get his men as far forward as possible before daylight because the landing force was going in regardless. In the meantime Patton decided he would visit the embarkation point and see the landing craft leave on the operation. When he got there the first person he saw was Capt Davis, chief of staff to Rear Admiral Lyal Davidson, the naval force commander. Davis said that the Navy thought that the landing should be called off as it was starting an hour late. Patton told him it would go on even if it was two hours late. This pessimistic confrontation put the already upset army commander in an even fouler mood.

An hour later, Patton arrived at 3rd Division's command post and stormed into Truscott's HQ in an unpleasant temper, berating everyone he came across from military police to cipher clerks. He walked up to Truscott in a screaming rage. 'Goddammit, Lucian, what's the matter with you?' he shouted. 'Are you afraid to fight?' Truscott was taken aback by the insult. He countered Patton's bluster by pointing out that the army commander's question was offensive and ridiculous. 'If you don't think I can carry out your orders you can give the Division to anyone you please,' Truscott retorted. He then pointed out to Patton that he would be unable to find any other commander who could carry out orders of which he disapproved better than he could.[28]

Patton had gone too far and he knew it. He also knew that Truscott was a very capable and efficient divisional commander. There was no question of relieving him. Patton's manner changed immediately and his tone softened considerably. He put his arm over Truscott's shoulder and said he knew that Truscott was right. 'Come on, let's have a drink of your liquor,' he said quietly, all anger gone. Patton called Bradley to let him know that the operation would go ahead as planned and that he accepted all responsibility for any failure.

When he got back to his headquarters Patton wrote up his account of the meeting with Truscott, claiming that the attack was audacious and would by-pass the bottleneck on the Zappula, but speed was important. He would accept no postponement for whatever reason. He admitted to being 'bull headed', but he felt he was right to insist that the landings took place. He also resolved not to visit 3rd Division's front during the battle as he felt his presence might imply a lack of confidence in Truscott.[29]

The landings at Brolo had mixed results. Col Bernard's force of 650 men came ashore undetected early on the morning of 11 August. Once the troops had established themselves on the beach, they moved inland across the coastal highway to gain the top of the nearby Monte Cipolla, which dominated Highway 113 and the village of Brolo. The advance started well, but before all the force was across the road it was detected by a passing German half-track. Bernard urged his men on and battalion managed to gain the summit of Cipolla and establish itself in position just in time to meet the first German reaction to the landings.

Throughout the morning German counter-attacks tried to eliminate the exposed Americans. Bernard's positions overlooked the rear of the enemy line across Cape Orlando and dominated the only escape route to the rear. Truscott knew that the landings were sure to attract a much more violent reaction than the earlier landing at Sant' Agata and that Bernard's men would have to hold on for a much longer period before the remainder of the 3rd Division could come to their aid. Patton's insistence that the landings went ahead had placed Bernard's men way ahead of the nearest American battalion, separated by 10 miles of exposed mountainside.

At first light Truscott visited the forward positions and urged his men on. The intention now was not just to break the German positions and take the objective, but to rescue fellow American soldiers cut off and surrounded by the enemy. A new urgency was injected into the battle. The 15th Regiment attacked along the ridge south of Naso, the 7th Infantry, pushed down a line south of the axis of the coastal highway while the rest of Bernard's own regiment, the 30th Infantry, attacked along the road itself to reach their comrades. Between these formations Truscott inserted the 3rd Ranger Battalion, which had recently come under his command. The lightly armed and mobile elite Rangers were ordered to infiltrate through the German positions to link up with the men on Monte Cipolla. Truscott now had the whole of his division on the move

There were, however, still plenty of the enemy to push aside and a great expanse of barren mountainside to be traversed before the relief of Bernard's force could be achieved. In the meantime, the men on the top of Monte Cipolla had to look to themselves to keep the enemy at bay, although there was help on call from both sea and air and from the 155mm Long Tom heavy guns supporting the division firing at their maximum range. Communication with the advance force was difficult, for

Bernard had lost all of his radios in the landings and the only link with the division was via the set operated by Truscott's liaison officer accompanying the amphibious assault, Capt Millar. Throughout the day this single radio provided the only contact with Truscott, the artillery, the Navy and the USAAF.

By 0600 hrs attacks against Bernard's battalion were well under way, one of the first of which was a company-strength infantry attack from the south by some Italians still attached to 29th Panzergrenadier Division. This and many other minor assaults were beaten off during the early morning. At 0930 hrs six tanks came up the road to attack the force but were confronted by the four Shermans and eight anti-tank guns that had been landed with the infantry. As the day wore on, more and more attacks of steadily increasing strength were put in. Each time the Germans gathered for the assault, their concentration areas were plastered by naval gunfire and strafed by fighter-bombers. And so it went on throughout the day: German attacks came in, were beaten off and casualties were taken on both sides.

By mid-afternoon the situation on Monte Cipolla was becoming acute; ammunition was running low, tanks and guns were being knocked out and the gathering enemy were getting so close to the American force that support from the sea and the air was becoming difficult to arrange. At 1725 hrs, a signal from Millar suggested that the Germans were gathering at the base of the hill in battalion strength, most likely preparing for the final assault. At 1850 hrs, Millar's transmission was cut off in mid-sentence and the radio went silent. It seemed to Truscott that Bernard's battalion had been over-run. Three hours later there was still no signal from Monte Cipolla and even Truscott's leading ground troops were out of contact – they had outrun communications with the regimental command posts.

The silence and the waiting were unbearable for Truscott. He felt that he had done all that he could but it had not been enough. 'We pictured the final German assault swarming over our gallant comrades,' he was to write later. 'There were long faces in our Command Post then and more than one moist eye.' All was not lost, however, for the Rangers had in fact got through to Bernard's men and the 15th Regiment had also fought its way onto the spur behind Monte Cipolla and forced the Germans to begin their withdrawal. Chasing them down the main road were the newly arrived speed-marching troops of the 30th Infantry.

What looked like a potential disaster had turned out to be a triumph. The enemy had been forced to pull out sooner than they had wished. Few prisoners had been taken by the operation, but the road beneath and foothills around Monte Cipolla were strewn with German dead and knocked-out tanks and equipment. On the American side, the attack had cost Bernard's battalion 177 casualties – 41 killed, 78 wounded and 58 missing. Seven of its eight artillery pieces and three of its four tanks had been destroyed. Truscott motored up to see the force commander as quickly as he could during the early hours of the next morning. 'Thank God Bernard, for I am certainly glad to see you,' said Truscott when he made contact with the colonel. 'General,' replied Bernard, 'You just don't know how glad I am to see you.'[30]

Back at Bradley's headquarters the news of the successful outcome of the attack was received with a great sense of relief. The corps commander disliked Patton's interference as to the timing of the operation, but had to admit that the army commander's intransigence had enabled a very strong enemy position to be swept aside. Nonetheless, the confrontation had strained the relationship between Bradley and Patton. Bradley was later to write that when he himself became an army commander, he had learned how not to behave from his time in Seventh Army.

The 29th Panzergrenadiers had been forced to retreat on this occasion at a time of the Americans' choosing, but even then only a day earlier than Hube had set out in his timetable. Gen Fries and his division were now slightly off balance, withdrawing at a greater pace than had been originally planned. But they were very resilient for it did not take long for order to be restored well enough for them to man the next stage of the shrinking front line which now stretched across the northern end of the island from Oliveri on the north coast to a position just below Taormina on the south coast.

That same day II Corps' Chief of Staff, Brig Gen William Kean, gave Bradley a report that had been handed to him by the corps' Chief Surgeon, Col Richard Arnest. It had been written by Col Currier of the 93rd Evacuation Hospital and told of a regrettable incident that had taken place at the medical facility on 10 August during a visit by the army commander. After reading its contents, Bradley told Kean to put the letter into the safe in a sealed envelope and ordered that no one else was to open it. Bradley had been put in a difficult position by the report's arrival and decided that he would not forward it to Eisenhower. Patton was his direct superior and he would not go over his head. Bradley resolved to sit on the report and hope that the incident would soon be forgotten.

It was, however, too late for that. The unfortunate scene at the evacuation hospital had been witnessed by so many people that, within a few hours, an embellished version of the incident was making the rounds and by the end of a week it was common gossip all over Sicily.[31] When Col Arnest learned that Bradley was not going to act on the matter, he decided he would do so instead and sent a copy of the report upwards through medical channels.

While Seventh Army was hammering at the German line in the north, Eighth Army was pressing on with its own uncomfortable advance through the centre and the south. Maj-Gen Evelegh's 78th Division was pushing north from Adrano through Bronte towards Randazzo, along a single highway strewn with obstacles. The division was the only XXX Corps formation that was advancing: the Canadians had been halted on the Simeto ready for their withdrawal from the campaign to prepare for action in Italy and the 51st Highland Division was being shifted across to the XIII Corps sector.

Retreating enemy troops continued to leave roadblocks, craters and booby-traps to slow down the Allied advance, just as they had done all over the island. The narrow highway towards Randazzo was bordered on both sides by high stone walls. Off the road it was extremely difficult to deploy troops or guns because of the rough lava fields. The division was advancing over ground shaped by previous eruptions from the still active volcano of Mount Etna. The road south of Bronte had been crossed by the flows of no fewer than six eruptions during the previous hundred years. One of these was from the outburst of 1843 when a river of molten lava over 300 yards wide had flowed down to the wooded banks of the River Simeto. It had crossed the road in a mass 40–50 feet high, through which, when it had cooled into solid rock, a new passage had to be hewn. These dead flows were now causing severe problems to the advancing infantry, as was the high iron content of the lava, which interfered with the reliability of mine detectors. The advance was an infantryman's battle, a tiring hard slog.[32]

The closer that the Battleaxe Division got to Bronte, the stiffer the enemy resistance became. Eight miles beyond the town was Randazzo and the junction of Highway 120 and the road from Troina. Possession of Randazzo was important to the German plans for withdrawal, for its loss to the Allies would sever the last major lateral highway available to the Axis forces.

US 9th Division had taken up the advance from Troina and was closing on Randazzo from the west, aiming to meet up with Evelegh's 78th Division coming up from the south. Hube directed that this junction was to be denied to the Allies for as long as possible. Once Randazzo had fallen, then the withdrawal from the island would have to gather pace. The significance of the town was also appreciated by the Allies and it was subjected to an almost non-stop aerial bombardment by medium, light and fighter-bombers. By the end of the campaign, a total of 1,200 sorties had been flown against Randazzo.[33]

Over on the other side of Etna, Dempsey's XIII Corps continued towards Messina with the 50th Division moving up the axis of the coast road and the 5th Division advancing on its left on lesser parallel roads. The slowing down of XXX Corps' advance on Randazzo meant that Dempsey's corps would have to speed up.

As elsewhere the moves were plagued with enemy rearguard actions and demolitions and slowed down by indiscriminate minefields. The 50th Division was aided in its advance by the floating guns of the Royal Navy. On most days a force of several destroyers, occasionally enlarged by the presence of a cruiser or a big-gun monitor, was on call to the division for tactical support. Targets had to be selected carefully, for the high-velocity, flat-trajectory shells fired by the naval guns were not suitable for all occasions. When not in direct support of ground troops, the ships bombarded roads, tunnels and the towns and villages along the coast in front of the advancing troops.

On 10 August Montgomery rearranged his forces. He gave orders for Dempsey to pull his XIII Corps headquarters out of the battle and to hand over responsibility for the completion of the campaign to Leese and XXX Corps. The 78th Division would continue its advance on Randazzo while 51st Division came into the line on the right to relieve the 5th Division. Dempsey would withdraw his command together with 5th Division and 1st Canadian Division to ready themselves for operations in Italy. XXX Corps would complete the campaign with 50th, 51st and 78th Divisions, together with 231st Infantry and 4th Armoured Brigades.

Eighth Army planners were now at work on proposals for the invasion of Italy. Montgomery believed that his army should play the major role in the attack using Dempsey's XIII Corps and Lt-Gen Brian Horrocks X Corps, which was at present training in North Africa with many of the veteran formations that had won great victories during the desert campaign. Although a decision had been made to carry the fight over to the mainland once Sicily had been conquered, the plans as to where, when and by whom this would be carried out, were still to be finalised.

Eisenhower had, on 17 July, requested his planners to consider a number of possible separate landings. Lt Gen Mark Clark was asked to plan for a landing at Salerno, south of Naples on the western side of Italy, with his Fifth Army. Montgomery's and Eighth Army's contribution would be an assault across the Straits of Messina on to the toe of Italy with XIII Corps, with a supporting subsidiary landing in the Gulf of Gioia 30 miles to the north by X Corps. Lt-Gen Charles Alfrey's V Corps, late of First Army but now under command of Eighth Army after Anderson's army had been disbanded, would land some time later on the heel of Italy at Taranto. The timings and the strength of these attacks were dependent on the completion of the Sicilian campaign and the availability of landing craft and support.

On 27 July, Eisenhower asked Mark Clark to plan his Salerno assault on the basis of a two-corps attack, using one British and one American corps. Clark was to have one of Monty's formations for the landings, Lt-Gen Horrocks's X Corps. Eisenhower also decided Montgomery would attack across the Straits of Messina using existing Eighth Army resources only, and would do so without the subsidiary attack at Gioia. However, these plans were liable to change and so Montgomery was left to assume that he would still have all available British formations under his command.

Eisenhower was determined that there would be no repetition of the fiasco surrounding the preparations for 'Husky' when planning for Italy. He would decide the shape of the attacks and his army commanders would be told what they were to do and be expected to get on with it. This time the major attack would not be under Montgomery's command. His Eighth Army would have the subsidiary role of protecting the right flank of Clark's Fifth Army, a reversal of the British and American positions for the Sicilian invasion. While Clark attacked and made for Rome, the major object of the invasion, Monty would be chasing across southern Italy clearing away Germans and seizing the airfields on the Foggia Plain.

As the campaign in Sicily drew inexorably to a close, Montgomery was unaware of Eisenhower's decision and continued to devote most of his time to planning how he might win the battle of Italy. Alexander was of no help, for on 27 July, the day that the Supreme Commander told Clark he could have British X Corps for his landings, Alex signalled Monty that Horrocks's corps was to come under the command of Eighth Army for the landings at Gioia.[34] For the next three weeks, Monty worked on the assumption that X Corps was to remain part of his army.

Progress along the eastern coastal sector was proceeding towards its climax at a snail's pace. The usual German demolitions and obstacles were proving increasingly difficult to overcome, even though there was less and less contact with the enemy. In the centre, 78th Division's determined slog got the formation through Bronte and on 12 August the Battleaxe Division made contact with US 9th Division at Maletto, just 3 miles south of Randazzo. The next day a concerted effort forced the enemy from the town. But the troops actually leaving were merely the rearguard of the 15th Panzergrenadiers, for the arrival of the Allies within artillery range of Randazzo on 11 August had prompted Hube to begin the full-scale withdrawal of XIV Panzer Corps back to the ferry ports.

Oberst Baade's painstaking plan for the evacuation was now stepped up and the Axis flight from Sicily began in earnest. On 12 August Hube ordered a general withdrawal to the first of the 'lay back' positions, stretching from Oliveri on the north coast to Taormina on the south coast. As the line shrunk, more and more units could be pulled out and transported back to Messina for shipment across to the mainland. The withdrawal was orderly and efficient, for Baade had thought of everything. Each of the German divisions had been allocated roads to the north-east, back to their designated embarkation points. Five main ferry routes were operating and each division was directed towards one of them. A fifth route was available, but was mainly kept for an emergency. None of these routes actually left from the port of Messina itself; they were all located in small fishing villages, the main routes all to the north of the city, and embarkation of troops and equipment was from small hards and jetties.

The evacuation was to be phased over five nights, although water traffic across the strait did in fact continue around the clock. The triangular nature of the ground with its apex at Messina was of great help to German plans, allowing the length of the line to shrink naturally. Each line was to be held by a strong rearguard for a prescribed time while a planned number of troops, usually between 8,000 and 10,000 men, was withdrawn and transported to the rear. They would then assemble in allocated vehicle parks where they waited until called down to the embarkation areas on foot. When a craft was alongside, and not before, the troops would file forward to the ferry-point and depart. After an arranged period, the formations in the line would withdraw to the next 'lay back' and repeat the process.[35]

Order was to be maintained throughout the whole of the operation. Hube had earlier given instructions that anyone who showed signs of panic or indiscipline was to be clubbed or shot. From 11 August numbers passing though Messina to safety were impressive. On that day 3,631 troops and 801 vehicles crossed over to the mainland. These totals rose sharply to a maximum on 14 August when 7,424 fit men, 600 casualties, 1,380 vehicles and 42 guns passed back over the straits. Even before these final few days of withdrawal, there had been a steady flow of men and equipment being shipped over to Italy. On the two ferry routes alone that were being operated by 771st Engineer Battalion, between 1 and 15 August 14,282 fit men, 13,532 casualties, 4,560 vehicles and 35 guns were taken across to safety.[36] No one in authority believed that the whole evacuation would be completed without Allied intervention once the main withdrawal across the straits was under way. Hube most of all feared another Allied amphibious assault closer to Messina in order to seal off the escape route.

In fact plans for further seaborne landings were actually being considered by both Allied army commanders, although they were to be nowhere near as ambitious as was feared by the German general. Both armies soon recognised that the enemy had broken contact and was pulling out, but this did not mean that the way forward was clear for the chase. Ahead of the leading divisions their routes were blocked by masses of obstacles. Demolitions alone were the main brake on forward movement and new ways around these obstructions were considered. Montgomery had, at last, taken note than one of his flanks was the open sea, protected by dominating sea power. He now decided to use this maritime superiority and ordered landings to be made by a mixed force of armour and infantry.

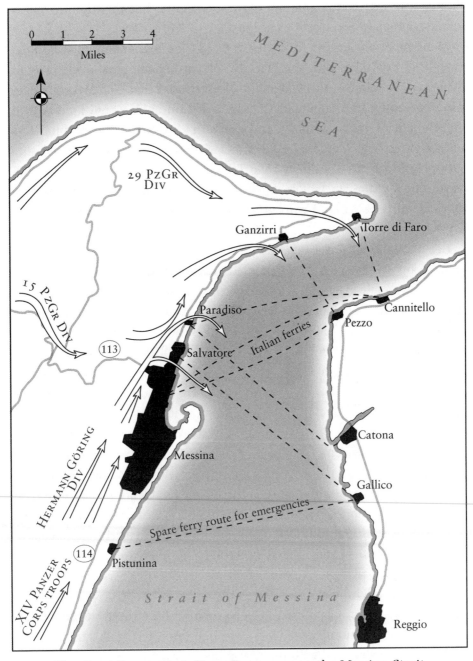

The Great Escape: Axis Ferry Routes across the Messina Strait

He planned a landing on beaches above Taormina to get behind a string of demolitions and place men and tanks within striking distance of Messina. Patton was also contemplating another seaborne lift, this time to put a whole regiment down closer to his goal.

Montgomery intended to use elite troops for his amphibious landing, supported by tanks, with the objective of cutting the coastal highway at Scaletta, 10 miles south of Messina. He proposed that No. 2 Commando, commanded by the redoubtable Lt-Col Jack Churchill, would land with a detachment of tanks, artillery and engineers, all under the command of one of Monty's El Alamein tank commanders, Brig J.C. Currie. This battle-group would block the main road to any retreating Germans and then strike out for the city to join up with the Americans. Preparations were done at short notice and with great haste, the operation set to land early on 16 August.

Gen Patton's third seaborne landing had been longer in gestation than that of his British rival, for Seventh Army's commander was planning something much bigger and more spectacular than his previous two. On 10 August, the day before the second of his 'end runs' had been launched against Brolo, Patton called Maj Gen Matthew Ridgway and Col Jim Gavin to his headquarters, along with the commander of the 52nd Troop Carrier Wing, Brig Gen Paul Williams, to be briefed on a combined amphibious/airborne operation that he was considering. Patton explained that he wanted the 509th Parachute Battalion to drop ahead of II Corps at dusk to seize the coastal road and the bridges west of Barcellona and hold until relieved by the seaborne landing of a complete regiment of infantry. None of the airborne commanders was impressed with the plans and all had deep reservations about committing airborne troops in such rugged country. Gavin pointed out that his paratroopers, with only light weapons and without sufficient anti-tank guns, would be particularly vulnerable to any counter-attack and almost certain to be overwhelmed if German armour was used against them. Brig Gen Williams was sure that his transport aircraft would suffer heavy casualties in dropping paratroops at low altitudes over a confined area known to be strongly occupied by German troops. Patton listened but remained unmoved by their arguments and decided to go ahead with the operation anyway.

Later that day he sent a message to Alexander with an outline of his plan and asked for permission to go ahead, including in his signal the phrase 'Troop Carrier Command and Paratroops have been consulted and all concur in above outline.' Alexander, true to form, immediately approved the operation and requested Tedder, as Air Operations Commander-in-Chief, to provide the necessary aircraft, explaining to Patton that he would first have to obtain 'MAC [Middle East Command, that is Tedder's] coordination'.

By 1200 hrs on 12 August Patton had heard nothing from Tedder's command regarding his proposed airborne mission and signalled Alexander asking if permission had been granted. Nothing had been heard from the Air C-in-C which required Alex to signal Tedder again asking for a prompt reply to his message of 10 August. The next day, at 1130 hrs, Tedder replied simply stating that he had sent an officer to Patton to arrange details. Alexander forwarded Tedder's reply to Patton at 1720 hrs and assumed all was now agreed, adding simply, 'Can this headquarters be of any further assistance in completing arrangements for your special operation?'

Twenty-seven minutes after Alexander had fired off this message to Patton's HQ, he received another from Tedder that changed things completely:

> Consider the Paratroop operation requested by Patton directed against the bridges west of Barcellona to be impractical as a daylight operation because of the concentration of anti-aircraft which is known to exist in that area. If an interruption of road communications through this area is desired, I believe that this should be accomplished by fighter-bomber or bomber attack with at least equal effectiveness and far greater economy of force than would result from an airborne operation. Propose therefore to lay this on to fit with Patton's plan.[37]

Tedder had unilaterally decided that he was in a better position than Patton to decide which tactics should be used during Seventh Army's advance. Patton's intentions to seize and hold the bridges to cut off the retreating enemy and also to expedite his moves on Messina would now, at the instigation of Tedder, have to be recast. The air force intended to destroy the bridges for Patton so as to cut off the enemy, leaving the Americans to remove the rubble and rebuild them again before their advance could resume. Alexander merely accepted this setback and left Patton to reconsider his next move. In the event, matters proceeded at a faster rate than had been envisaged on 10 August and Patton's intentions changed once again.

Tedder's reluctance to condone the airborne attack caused Patton's third amphibious assault to be delayed. Nonetheless, he still insisted that it go ahead with the landing of the whole of the 157th Regimental Combat Team of the 45th Division near Falcone. By the time that the operation was ready to be mounted, during the early hours of 16 August, Truscott's division had almost reached the bridges at Barcellona. To both Bradley and Truscott, the landings would serve little purpose, for German opposition was melting away at such a rate that both commanders felt that their land forces would have over-run the landing beaches before the boats arrived. Patton, not one to listen to such arguments against any of his spectacular and newsworthy events, insisted that the amphibious operation take place. He reasoned that, even though Bradley and his divisional commander might well be right, the landings would at least lift a whole regiment forward in one swift move. And go ahead it did, with Maj Gen Truscott providing two colonels on the beaches to greet the landing craft and explain that the area was already in friendly hands.[38]

Montgomery's seaborne force sailed from Augusta and Catania late on the 15th and landed at 0430 hrs the next day. The landing was unopposed but the commandos were soon in action against lorryloads of German soldiers and demolition engineers retreating along the coastal highway. But these troops were the last remnants of the German forces, for virtually all of the *Hermann Göring* Division had already passed the landing beaches and those of the scattered rearguard that remained easily evaded Brig Currie's task force. By the time that tanks and transport were ready to move against Messina, the enemy had further cut the highway in front of them in several places with obstacles and skilful demolitions. Currie ordered two troops of commandos, a half squadron of tanks, some self-propelled artillery and a party of engineers to make a dash for Messina, but by the time darkness had fallen the battlegroup was still 7 miles from the port, moving at a slow pace from crater to crater along the pock-marked highway.

To the north, along the other coastal highway, the advance guard of Truscott's 3rd Division was also closing on Messina. By late evening on the 16th, Battery B of the division's 9th Field Artillery Battalion had brought its guns onto a hill overlooking the Strait of Messina and was firing across the narrow waterway onto the Italian mainland. The 7th Infantry Regiment was even closer to the great port and at 2200 hrs, Lt Ralph Yates took a reinforced patrol from Company L down the winding hill and into a near-deserted Messina. Patton had won the race.

To Montgomery there never was a race. Certainly he was keen in the early stages of the campaign to get to Messina ahead of anyone else, because he wanted the laurels to go to his Eighth Army, but he blew his chances when he split his force south of Catania. After that the battle for control of the island became a hard, unglamorous slog and he turned his attention to the next battleground, in Italy. Eighth Army made it to Messina at 0900 hrs on the 17th when a small group of commandos led by Lt-Col Churchill arrived in the centre of the city to find the Americans there in total command.

The previous night, when news reached Patton that II Corps was at the gates of Messina, the army commander ordered a halt. Gen Bradley was told to wait until Patton himself arrived to lead a triumphal entry into the city. At 1000 hrs, a convoy of vehicles rolled down the hill and into Messina. Patton was in the lead command vehicle sporting a flag with his three general's stars glinting in the sunlight. The army commander stood erect, smartly saluting those weary and dishevelled infantry of Truscott's division that he sped past, resplendent in his best dress uniform and sporting on his chest the second Distinguished Service Cross, which had been presented to him only the day before by Eisenhower. He arrived in the piazza in the centre of a completely ruined Messina, surrounded by such damage that barely a single intact building remained, every bit the conquering hero.

Patton was greeted by joyful crowds and a festive atmosphere. A little later he spotted and was introduced to Brig Currie, who had arrived a few minutes before, accompanied by a group of tanks and commandos, to join Col Churchill's advance guard. 'We got here at ten,' the brigadier was alleged to have said as he shook Patton's hand. 'It was a jolly good race. I congratulate you.' Patton, ever suspicious of the British, thought that Currie had been sent into Messina by Montgomery to steal his victory.

It was a very congratulatory moment, for Patton's arrival in Messina marked the end of the campaign. Truscott, Keyes and Lucas were all there with the army commander, basking together in their great victory, but there was one notable absentee. Bradley had decided he would not go into the city with Patton. The corps commander was not interested in victory celebrations, or pretentious cavalcades. His snub to Patton showed a little of the contempt that had built up over the course of the campaign. Bradley did not agree with Patton's methods or with his over-the-top outbursts of anger and humiliation. Great though he was as a commander of armies, Bradley considered him a poor example as a commander of men.

CHAPTER 16

Whose Victory?

Geneneral Hube and his forces had made a complete getaway, as had the Italians. The timetable meticulously organised by Oberst Baade had worked admirably. It was flexible enough to deal with delays in getting transport into the port perimeter because of traffic jams and Allied raids, yet it had sufficient rigidity to ensure that all moves were strictly regulated and instructions were obeyed to the letter. Even on the last night of the evacuation, with Patton's artillery on the hills above the city, Baade's ferries were still ploughing back and forth across the strait.

At 0800 hrs on 16 August, Hube suggested that the ferries could be withdrawn at 0700 hrs the next day and that any stragglers would be brought back to the mainland on assault boats. Throughout the night and into the early hours the German rearguards and demolition engineers who had done such an impressive job in delaying the Allied advance took their turn on the ferries and withdrew to safety. Then came the turn of Gen Hube, who was among the last men to leave the island. True to German military tradition the resolute commander of XIV Panzer Corps remained until the end. The last ferry to leave carried a party of the 2nd Battalion *Hermann Göring* Panzer Regiment and a few engineers from the 29th Panzergrenadier Division. Then, finally, the Italian land force commander, Brig Gen Monacci, followed his engineers across after they had set mines to destroy what remained of the port installations. At 0735 hrs the next morning, the commander of 771st Engineer Battalion,

Hauptmann Paul, reported to Baade that the withdrawal was complete. Everyone who could get out, had got out.

Even on this last night of evacuation, when everyone in the Allied camp knew that the Axis forces had to be streaming back across the water opposite Messina, there was little interference from the air and none from the sea. Throughout the whole of the withdrawal period the Royal Navy and the Royal Air Force proved to be ineffective against the water traffic across the strait. Tedder was reluctant to employ his heavy strategic bombers to interfere with Axis plans and destroy the embarkation points, so it was left to the tactical bombers and fighter-bombers of Air Vice-Marshal Harry Broadhurst's Desert Air Force to try to interdict enemy movements. Because of the high concentration of anti-aircraft guns along the waterway, most of these attacks went in at night. During the day there was little to be seen in the air, and even when daylight sorties were flown, the Germans were quick to notice that they usually occurred to a strict timetable. Bombing attacks were almost never made during the hours of first light, immediately after lunchtime or in the late afternoon. Unsurprisingly the Axis forces made excellent use of these predictable intervals.

The overwhelming superiority of naval power counted for little in the narrow confines of the Strait of Messina. While warships ventured close to the southern entrance to the narrows, they rarely attempted to go much further northwards towards the ferry terminals. The only ships that did venture into the strait were a few motor torpedo boats and motor gun boats, but their light armament and vulnerability to searchlights and rapid cannon fire ensured that their attacks could only be swift hit-and-run raids. They had little material effect on the passage of the ferries, although one particular raid on the night of 11 August did disrupt the service for a few hours.

Particularly disappointing was the reluctance of Cunningham even to test the effectiveness of the Axis shore batteries guarding the straits. One would have thought that he might have tried – after all, warships had been directed into Augusta harbour on 13 July with Italian shore batteries still active. After the war it was found that the Italian heavy batteries were obsolete and their fire control primitive. The gun sites could have been located easily from the air and the weapons themselves had little protective armour. Sustained air raids by heavy bombers and a show of strength by the Royal Navy with powerful warships might have proved conclusive and the strait closed to waterborne traffic. The fact was that neither Tedder nor Cunningham attempted to produce coordinated plans to stop the Axis withdrawal. Both services were extremely reluctant to commit substantial aircraft and ships against fleeting targets that were guarded by shore batteries and flak emplacements, even though they had overwhelming power to do so. Neither seemed to appreciate that air power could unleash naval power when working in harmony or, if they did chose not to do so. The sad thing is that they never even tried to see if it was possible.

Eisenhower has also to share some of the blame – after all he was the Supreme Commander and the three commanders-in-chief were subordinate to him. There is little evidence that he had a grasp of the failure that was unfolding during the second and third weeks of August. From his headquarters in Algiers he left Alexander, Cunningham and Tedder to run the campaign according to their own agendas. One might have thought that he would have been more closely involved in the action in what was the Allies' only Mediterranean battlefield. Had he overseen events more directly they might have been played out to a successful conclusion. One of the objects of the invasion of Sicily was surely the elimination of all Axis forces engaged there to ensure they did not fight again, rather than simply the occupation of the island.

The battle for Sicily was seen as something of a victory by the Germans – one senior commander later commented that the evacuation had posed no difficulties worthy of mention and that the time at their disposal enabled them to extricate the last man and the last vehicle back to the mainland according to plan.[1] In fact, the two motorised panzergrenadier divisions ended up more mobile than they were at the start of the campaign, for they had commandeered abandoned Italian vehicles and brought them back with the troops to replenish previous shortfalls in their normal complement of transport and to replace those lost in action.

Many senior German officers were dismissive of Allied tactics and the timidity of Allied commanders. Axis forces might have lost the battle, but they had achieved one of the most successful military withdrawals in history. Hube's single corps, together with varying levels of help from the Italians, had resisted the onslaught of two Allied armies, relinquishing ground at a measured and controlled rate as part of a strategy that required the island to be given up at a time of their choosing. During the battle they managed to reinforce and resupply their forces across water that should have been dominated by the other side. They even brought supplies in over the open Mediterranean from Naples, most notably ammunition, across sea lanes that the Allied navies presumed to have under their complete control.

Most dispiriting of all for the Allies, although unknown to the men who had to do the fighting, was the successful escape of enemy formations that later in the war were to prove to be some of the very best that Germany produced. Four seasoned divisions and a corps headquarters had got away, with their command structures intact, and all were in an excellent position quickly to absorb new recruits to bring them back up to full strength. These divisions, having been allowed to extricate themselves from Sicily, had to be confronted again and again during the forthcoming long slog up the Italian peninsula. What was worse was that some of the same Allied troops who had fought them on the island had to face up to them once more. The 78th Division would meet the 1st Parachute Division again during the advance to the River Sangro and then fight a brutal battle with the German paratroopers at Cassino; Truscott's 3rd Division and the US 45th Division, along with British 5th Division, would all be confronted with Conrath's *Hermann Göring* Division around the perimeter at Anzio and the Canadians would be in action for a second time against the 15th and 29th Panzergrenadier Divisions during their bloody battles in the Liri Valley. All this was yet to be revealed, for the end of the battle brought a round of congratulations by all concerned in the Allied camp. They had, after all, chased the Germans and Italians from Sicily.

The battle was now won, even though in a real sense a greater victory had been lost and there were further disappointments at hand for the two army commanders; Gen Eisenhower was at the heart of them both. On 16 August, the Supreme Commander finalised his plans for the invasion of Italy as far as it was possible to do so considering the changing circumstances of the German withdrawal. It was bad news for Montgomery, for his Eighth Army would be given a subsidiary role to Mark Clark's Fifth Army's main event. The next day, 17 August, the very day that Patton had triumphantly entered Messina, Brig Gen Frederick Blessé, AFHQ Surgeon General, placed a report on Eisenhower's desk outlining the two slapping incidents that Patton was involved in.

Montgomery learned unexpectedly that he was to make only a simple attack across the Messina Strait onto the toe of Italy, with the objective of opening the waterway to Allied sea traffic and to act as a diversion for the landings at Salerno. In the event of the enemy withdrawing from the 'toe', Monty was told that he was to follow up with such force as could be made available and to engage as much of the enemy strength as possible in order to give assistance to Fifth Army. It was a reverse of the Sicilian campaign; Monty was to be the flank guard to the main effort put in by the Americans. Even more galling to Eighth Army's commander was the news that X Corps, now commanded by Lt-Gen Richard McCreery after Horrocks's wounding in an air raid, was to be taken from him and given to Clark. Eisenhower had given the lead to Clark even though his Fifth Army was going into battle with a number of its most senior officers yet to see action in a position of high command. For the army commander and his two corps commanders for the landings – Ernest Dawley (US VI Corps) and McCreery (British X Corps) – it was to be their first battle at the head of such formations.

Montgomery was of course most disappointed to be allocated what was a subsidiary role. He had spent a great deal of time working out how he would run the campaign in Italy, only to find that his Eighth Army was to operate on the flanks. It had been made abundantly clear to him that it was an Allied show and that his views would not be allowed to dictate the strategic aims of the campaign. The war in Italy was going to be a coalition war. Alexander would still operate as overall land commander, as far as his two headstrong subordinate army commanders would allow, and Eisenhower remained in overall charge as Allied Supreme Commander. Montgomery had, at last, been pulled into line, at least for the time being.

Patton's disappointments were more public, but they were all of his own making. After the two slapping incidents, he made no move to conceal his actions, but rather tended to gloat over them. On more than one occasion he was heard explaining how he had slapped some fight into malingering soldiers. He regarded his behaviour as doing the men something of a favour, attempting to restore their self respect. The fact remained, however, that for a superior officer to strike an enlisted man was a court-martial offence. In the week since the second incident the two assaults had become the talking point of the American camp and could no longer be ignored.

Eisenhower was shocked by the report submitted by Brig Gen Blessé, although his first reaction was to put it down to Patton's well known immoderation. He thought that Seventh Army's commander would have to be given some sort of reprimand. The Supreme Commander had, after all, just heard that Patton had entered Messina that morning as the conquering hero and had to admit that he had done a 'swell job'. Eisenhower rather hoped that the contents of the paper might be exaggerated.

Further study convinced Eisenhower that he had a 'hell of a problem' on his hands. The implications of this outrage could be catastrophic for American prestige and for Patton himself. He decided to order Blessé to go to Sicily at once to carry out a full enquiry and then sat down to pen a personal letter to Patton. He knew that, if the matter ever got back to the States, every politician would be after Patton's blood. It would mean the end of Patton as a commander and Eisenhower was extremely reluctant to let that happen. The Seventh Army's boss was now indispensable to the American war effort.

The letter that Eisenhower wrote to Patton was very strongly worded; it contained a blistering attack on the general's actions and expressed his absolute disgust with the incident. Eisenhower did not pull his punches, using such phrases as 'brutality', 'abuse of the sick' and 'uncontrollable temper in front of subordinates'. He considered Patton's conduct to be despicable. It was probably the strongest letter of censure ever written to a serving senior officer during the war. Patton was ordered to: 'Make such personal amends to individuals concerned as may be within your power'.[2]

The Supreme Commander also decided to send Maj Gen Lucas to see Patton and investigate the incidents from a soldier's point of view. Lucas was well regarded by both generals and Eisenhower was confident that he would be able investigate the matter in detail. Lucas was to see Patton and explain the Supreme Commander's deep concern about the allegations. Lucas knew about the first slapping and rather dismissed it as Patton being Patton. When he heard of the second and learned of Eisenhower's displeasure, he knew that Seventh Army's commander was in real trouble. Lucas arrived in Sicily on 20 August and Patton was there at the airport to meet him.

Lucas spoke with Patton as a friend and gave him some kindly advice. He suggested that Patton should apologise to the soldiers he had slapped and to the doctors and nurses who were present at the time. He also recommended that he apologise to all personnel in every division in his army and, finally, to promise never to repeat the act. By this public act of contrition, he might get Eisenhower to forego court-martial proceedings and allow him to stay in the Mediterranean theatre.

Patton could do nothing but humble himself and comply. The next day he arranged for Private Bennett to visit him to hear his formal apology. Bennett held no animosity towards his army commander and the meeting ended with the two men shaking hands. A later report on the matter found that Bennett's demeanour improved after the encounter and that his morale was considerably raised by Patton's action. A similar meeting was arranged with the other victim, Private Kuhl, two days later.

On 22 August it was the turn of the doctors and nurses. These were summoned to Patton's headquarters in Palermo to hear of his change of heart. He told them that his impulsive actions were driven by a sincere belief that men could be shocked back to reality and told them of a close friend of his who had committed suicide in the Great War. Patton said that his comrade might well have been saved if someone had tried to snap him out of the depressed mental condition that was troubling him at the time. He believed that men suffering from the fear of battle could be directed away from their inner doubts if they were given something else to hate. The medical staff were all less than impressed by Patton's new-found compassion; most of them believed that his remorse was driven more by the situation he found himself in than a sudden appreciation of the distress caused by shell shock. Col Currier, the commander of the second hospital, later wrote that Patton's remarks sounded like no apology at all; rather they were an attempt to justify his actions.

The doctors and nurses were right of course. Patton still believed that he was basically correct in tackling shirkers and malingerers, although he did understand that his methods were a little too direct and much too forceful. He continued in private to insist that his motives were proper and stressed that 'skulking' could not be permitted to exist in a disciplined army.

Back in Algiers, Eisenhower was agonising over what to do about Patton's behaviour. He believed that Patton's performance during the Sicilian campaign was quite brilliant. He had driven Seventh Army forward through extremely hostile terrain and particularly tenacious enemy resistance, never giving the Axis forces a moment's respite. Patton was without doubt the best combat commander that America had. Eisenhower was loath to lose him and decided that the best course of action was to try to suppress the story as well as he was able and to do nothing more than call for reports from a variety of sources and then file the matter away.

There was, however, the matter of the press, for just after Eisenhower had received the report of the incidents from Brig Gen Blessé, three correspondents came to see him and asked what he was going to do about Patton's behaviour. Untainted by military protocol, they were blunt with the Supreme Commander; they wanted Patton dismissed. One of them thought that all of the men in Seventh Army loathed their commander and would gladly shoot him, while another was of the opinion that Patton had temporarily gone mad.

Eisenhower persuaded the reporters that America's best interests were satisfied by retaining a commander who was absolutely vital to the war effort. In his opinion Patton's unquestionable ability had to be preserved for the great battles still to come. Eisenhower explained that he had given the general a severe reprimand, ordered him to apologise to everyone concerned for his actions and demanded that there never be a repetition of his behaviour. Eisenhower went on to say that they must do what they thought was best and that there would be no censorship from his office if they wished to send the story back to the States. They must use their own judgement as to how America might be best served by the outcome of the incident. After such an impassioned plea, the three correspondents all agreed to drop the story out of respect for Eisenhower.

In Sicily Patton did the rounds of his army with his own unique and rather veiled apology. His speech, often full of earthy language and profanities, referred to certain incidents that had better be forgotten and his tendency sometimes to criticise individuals harshly. Of course the men knew that this doubletalk obliquely referred to the slapping incidents. The reception Patton received from individual formations varied from complete indifference to rousing cheers. The men he was addressing were fighting men who had little time or sympathy for senior commanders. At this point in the war the Patton 'cult' had not reached its peak and the time-honoured scepticism that all enlisted men have towards their top brass meant that they didn't really give a damn. Some thought that perhaps the cowards really did deserve to get their faces slapped; perhaps a few more of the shirkers should be dealt with in that way. In any case, generals did what they wanted to do anyhow with little regard to the men who had to die for them. At some formations, Patton's arrival was stage-managed and the troops were roused to cheer their conquering general when he arrived – the reception given by the men of 9th Infantry Division was so noisy and prolonged that Patton never did get to make his speech and he left with tears in his eyes.

So Patton was let off the hook. The bombast who only weeks before was quick to order that shell-shocked victims should face court martial for cowardice in the face of the enemy had escaped facing his own court martial for what some people regarded as his own act of bullying and cowardice against two young men unable by military discipline to defend themselves against his assault. The striking of a subordinate by an officer, in this case a very senior officer, is a particularly spiteful crime, for the victim is obliged to stand to attention and take the punishment. The fact that a gun was pulled and waved at the head of one of the victims makes the actions seem beyond comprehension. The only course of redress for the unfortunate is for the code of military law to be invoked on his behalf, but no one in authority was prepared to do this. What was worse was that Patton's behaviour was not just a single outburst of anger, but a pattern of conduct, for he repeated his offence and then showed little remorse for his actions until his career was threatened.

Bradley had a chance to do something about it when the original report from 94th Evacuation Hospital landed on his desk. He did nothing but chose to sit on the evidence, lamely claiming he could not go over Patton's head to Eisenhower and forwarding the report to Patton himself would accomplish nothing. At least if he had forwarded the report through normal channels he would have done something. Bradley's inaction was rather disingenuous, for after the war he claimed that, if it had been up to him, he would have relieved Patton instantly and had nothing more to do with him.[3] Eisenhower likewise chose initially to do nothing and would have completely buried the story if it had not been for the three correspondents and Brig Gen Blessé. Even Eisenhower's letter of censure to Patton was a personal one and therefore was not put on Patton's official record. Neither the corps commander nor the Supreme Commander felt that the victims of the outbursts should have had some reparation for the assaults inflicted upon them.

The whole slapping affair was successfully covered up until a particularly unsavoury reporter, Drew Pearson, who was not party to the gentlemen's agreement and was well noted for his muck-raking approach to scandal, got wind of the story four months later. Pearson broadcast a sensationalised account of the incident to the great American public in his weekly radio slot. The nation was astonished by the outrage and a storm of criticism of Patton's behaviour swept America. Calls went out for Patton to be dismissed, but Gen Marshall in Washington and Gen Eisenhower in Algiers both refused to bow to this public pressure, with Eisenhower claiming that he still felt that his decision was sound.[4] Others, quite substantial in number, backed Patton, for in the intervening four months since the incidents, his reputation as a military commander had grown considerably through the publication of numerous books and articles on the Sicilian campaign. For a while the affair rumbled on, but like all news stories, it eventually faded away to be replaced in the public's mind by other events in the Mediterranean and Pacific theatres. The affair did, however, cause Eisenhower to reassess Patton's capability for further advancement and he later wrote to Marshall stating emphatically: 'In no event will I ever advance Patton beyond army command.'[5]

Details of the Patton incident eventually made it to Germany. Here the news was greeted with astonishment. In the German Army an individual found malingering or showing signs of cowardice was often taken out and shot on the spot. Even in Sicily, threats of summary punishment for a number of transgressions had been issued by the high command on several occasions: Gen Conrath's published order of 2 August warning that anyone not exercising the most rigid discipline in the forthcoming evacuation would be shot and Gen Hube's exhortation to club or shoot anyone showing signs of panic or indiscipline, are two notable examples.[6]

The overall outcome of the Sicilian campaign was an enhancement of Gen George Patton's reputation as a combat commander. The standing of 'old blood and guts' had been improved by US Seventh Army's drive on Messina and the swift capture of Palermo. His personal fame grew as more and more elaborate stories were written by the press about everything from his ivory-handled pistols to his meticulous attention to the state of dress of his fighting men. The Germans had also begun to take note of this American general and by the end of the war had singled him out as being the best that the Western Allies had. The personal misfortune that he brought upon himself because of the slapping incidents was soon forgotten. Patton was to err again later in the war and made Eisenhower almost mad enough to sack him, but the glory he won with his armoured thrusts in north-west Europe ensured that the legend of Patton lived on after his premature death in a road accident in 1946. Unsurprisingly, in Britain Patton's achievements are tainted by his extraordinary personal behaviour and the time wasted chasing a hollow victory at Palermo.

Montgomery's lasting fame was already secure in the minds of the British public long before the invasion of Sicily. He was the hero of El Alamein and could do no wrong in their eyes. It was inevitable that he would be given the main role in Britain's struggle against the Nazis and so it was no surprise when he was appointed to lead the ground forces in the Allied invasion of France in June 1944. His actions during the planning and execution of the campaign in Sicily, however, soured relationships with the Americans. Most of their commanders, including Eisenhower, thought that he was an over-rated general, cautious, uninspired and only able to attack when he was sure of success. This opinion still holds true among American historians today. In Britain Montgomery remains the country's greatest general of the war with a huge reputation; however, more and more are coming to realise this may be a little undeserved.

Alexander's showing during the whole campaign left much to be desired. At no time did he stamp his authority on the shape or execution of 'Husky'. The planning stages were coalition warfare at its worst, with Alexander completely at the mercy of Montgomery's continual changes, accepting them almost without question as though they were inspired by the fount of all military knowledge. Once the landings had been successful, Alexander showed scant regard for American interests and once more succumbed to the dictates of Montgomery. A successful conclusion to the battle was thrown away when he allowed Eighth Army to take Highway 124 from US Seventh Army. With this one move he handed over the initiative to the enemy and prolonged the campaign. British XIII and XXX Corps were not up to the demanding role that Montgomery had unceremoniously seized for them and the campaign was reduced to a slow battle of attrition through the mountainous heartland of the island. Great generalship did not win the battle of Sicily for the Allies; poor generalship actually let a great victory slip from their grasp.

Notes

Chapter 1: The Two Generals *(pages 1–9)*

1. Horrocks, Lt-Gen Sir Brian, *A Full Life*, London, Collins, 1960, p. 144. This anecdote might be apocryphal, for one of Monty's other corps commanders, Lt-Gen Oliver Leese, claimed that he asked Patton for his appreciation of Montgomery's lecture, receiving more or less the same reply as stated by Horrocks. (See also Ryder, Rowland, *Oliver Leese*, London, Hamish Hamilton, 1987, p. 124.)
2. Brooks, Stephen (ed.), *Montgomery and the Eighth Army*, London, Army Records Society, 1991, p. 136.
3. Essame, H., *Patton the Commander*, London, Batsford, 1974, p. 5.
4. Montgomery, Field Marshal the Viscount, *Memoirs*, London, Collins, 1958, p. 17.
5. *Ibid.*, p. 30.

Chapter 2: Planning the Invasion *(pages 11–36)*

1. Morgan, Ted, *FDR: A Biography*, London, Grafton Books, 1986, p. 652.
2. National Archives, WO 214/18.
3. Brooks, *Montgomery and Eighth Army*, p. 228.
4. *Ibid.*, p. 230.
5. *Ibid.*, p. 151.
6. Chalmers, Rear Admiral W.S., *Full Cycle*, London, Hodder & Stoughton, 1959, p. 162.
7. Nicholson, Lt-Col G.W.L., *The Canadians in Italy 1943–1945*, Canada, Minister of National Defence, 1956, p. 15.
8. Hamilton, Nigel, *Monty Master of the Battlefield*, London, Hamish Hamilton, 1983, p. 248.

9. Molony, Brig C.J.C., *The Mediterranean and Middle East*, Vol. V, London, HMSO, 1973, p. 22.
10. Howard, Michael, *Grand Strategy*, Vol. IV, London, HMSO, 1970, p. 369.
11. Pack, S.W.C., *Cunningham The Commander*, London, Batsford, 1974, p. 254.
12. Ryder, Rowland, *Oliver Leese*, p. 134.
13. Blumenson, Martin, *The Patton Papers 1940–1945*, Boston, Houghton Mifflin, 1974, p. 235.
14. *Ibid.*, p. 236.
15. *Ibid.*, p. 236.
16. Jackson, W.G.F., *Alexander of Tunis as Military Commander*, London, Batsford, 1971, p. 215.
17. Molony, *The Mediterranean and Middle East*, Vol. V, p. 23.
18. Blumenson, Martin, *The Patton Papers 1940–1945*, p. 237.
19. Brooks, *Montgomery and Eighth Army*, p. 122.
20. This was later changed in his published memoirs to Montgomery going to look for Bedell Smith and tracking him down to the lavatory.
21. Cunningham of Hyndhope, Admiral of the Fleet Viscount, *A Sailor's Odyssey*, London, Hutchinson, 1951, p. 538.
22. *Ibid.*, p. 537.
23. Brooks, *Montgomery and Eighth Army*, p. 223.
24. *Ibid.*, p. 196.
25. Hamilton, Nigel, *Monty Master of the Battlefield*, p. 266.
26. *Ibid.*, p. 267.
27. Brooks, *Montgomery and Eighth Army*, p. 236.
28. Molony, *The Mediterranean and Middle East*, Vol. V, p. 24.

Chapter 3: Final Plans *(pages 37–45)*

1. Blumenson, *The Patton Papers*, p. 241.
2. Garland, M., & Smythe, A., *Sicily and the Surrender of Italy*, Washington, Center of Military History, 1965, p. 66.
3. A later study on the effects of mass bombing on concrete shelters and gun emplacements on Pantelleria provided a great deal of useful information. The lessons learned were put to good use in later operations in north-west Europe, most notably against similar heavily fortified positions along the Normandy coast.

Chapter 4: Preparations *(pages 47–59)*

1. Dover, Maj Vernon, *The Sky Generals*, London, Cassell, 1981, p. 72.
2. *Ibid.*, p. 68.
3. Chatterton, George, *The Wings of Pegasus*, London, Macdonald, 1962, p. 42.
4. *Ibid.*, p. 42.
5. Mrazek, James E., *The Glider War*, London, Robert Hale, 1975, p. 82.
6. Blumenson, *The Patton Papers*, p. 281.
7. Durnford-Slater, Brig. J., *Commando*, London, William Kimber, 1953, p. 106.

Chapter 5: The Defenders (*pages 61–70*)

1. Molony, *The Mediterranean and Middle East*, Vol. V, p. 38.
2. *Ibid.*, p. 39.
3. Kesselring, Field Marshal Albrecht, *Memoirs*, London, William Kimber, 1953, p. 159.
4. Weinberg, Gerhard, Heiber, Helmut and Glantz, David (eds.), *Hitler and his Generals: Military Conferences 1942–1945*, New York, Enigma Books, 2003, p. 135.
5. Molony, *The Mediterranean and Middle East*, Vol. V, p. 41.
6. *Ibid.*, p. 41.
7. von Senger und Etterlin, General Frido, *Neither Fear Nor Hope*, London, Macdonald, 1960, p. 127.
8. *Ibid.*, p. 127.
9. *Ibid.*, p. 129.
10. Kesselring, *Memoirs*, p. 160.
11. *Ibid.*, p. 162.
12. *Ibid.*, p. 161.
13. *Ibid.*, p. 162.

Chapter 6: Invasion: The Airborne Landings (*pages 71–8*)

1. Chatterton, *The Wings of Pegasus*, p. 74.
2. *Ibid.*, p. 84.
3. Gavin, James, *On To Berlin*, London, Leo Cooper, 1979, p. 19.
4. Garland, M., & Smythe, A., *Sicily and the Surrender of Italy*, p. 117.
5. Gavin, *On To Berlin*, p. 22.
6. *Ibid.*, p. 24.
7. *Ibid.*, p. 26.
8. Garland & Smythe, *Sicily and the Surrender of Italy*, p. 119.

Chapter 7: Invasion: The British Landings (*pages 79–98*)

1. Durnford-Slater, Brig. J., *Commando*, p. 113.
2. Marrinan, Patrick, *Colonel Paddy: A Biography of Lt Col R. Blair Mayne*, The Ulster Press, no date, p. 110.
3. Molony, *The Mediterranean and Middle East*, Vol. V, p. 62.
4. *Ibid.*, p. 61.
5. Salmond, J.B., *The History of the 51st Highland Division 1939–1945*, Edinburgh, William Blackwood, 1953, p. 105.
6. *Ibid.*, p. 105.
7. Gilchrist, Maj R.T., *Malta Strikes Back. The Story of 231 Infantry Brigade*, Aldershot, Gale & Polden, 1945, p. 43.
8. Clay, Maj Ewart W., *The Path of the 50th*, Aldershot, Gale & Polden, 1950, p. 157.
9. National Archives, WO 169/8494.
10. Mrazek, *The Glider War*, p. 97.

11. *Ibid.*, p. 98.

Chapter 8: Invasion: The American Landings *(pages 99–108)*

1. Garland & Smythe, *Sicily and the Surrender of Italy*, p. 131.
2. Truscott, Lt Gen L.K., *Command Missions*, New York, E.P. Dutton & Co., 1954, p. 214.
3. Darby, William O., *Darby's Rangers: We Led the Way*, Novato CA, Presidio Press, 1993, p. 88.
4. Garland & Smythe, *Sicily and the Surrender of Italy*, p. 144.

Chapter 9: The Second Day – 11 July *(pages 109–26)*

1. Aris, George, *The Fifth British Division 1939 to 1945*, London, 5th Division Benevolent Fund, 1959, p. 119.
2. Bradley, Omar N., *A Soldier's Story*, New York, Henry Holt, 1951, p. 130.
3. Hamilton, Nigel, *Monty Master of the Battlefield 1942–1944*, London, Hamish Hamilton, 1983, p. 298.
4. Darby, *Darby's Rangers*, p. 90.
5. Essame, *Patton the Commander*, p. 94.
6. Gavin, *On To Berlin*, p. 30.
7. *Ibid.*, p. 33.
8. Kuhn, Volkmar, *German Paratroops in World War II*, London, Ian Allan, 1974, p. 182.
9. National Archives, WO 214/22.
10. *Ibid.*
11. Blumenson, *The Patton Papers*, p. 283.
12. National Archives, WO 214/22.
13. *Ibid.*
14. Whiting, Charles, *Slaughter Over Sicily*, London, Leo Cooper, 1992, p. 131.
15. National Archives, WO 214/22.

Chapter 10: The Third Day – 12 July *(pages 127–43)*

1. Blumenson, *The Patton Papers*, p. 283.
2. Marrinan, *Colonel Paddy*, p. 120.
3. Kesselring, *Memoirs*, p. 163.
4. Molony, *The Mediterranean and Middle East*, Vol. V, p. 91.
5. Kesselring, *Memoirs*, p. 164.
6. National Archives, WO 214/18.
7. *Ibid.*
8. Hamilton, *Monty Master of the Battlefield*, p. 305.
9. Kesselring, *Memoirs*, p. 163.
10. Blumenson, *The Patton Papers*, p. 288.
11. Bradley, *A Soldier's Story*, p. 135.

Chapter 11: Primosole Bridge and the Commando Landings (*pp. 145–59*)

1. Durnford-Slater, *Commando*, p. 116.
2. Mrazek, *The Glider War*, p. 98.
3. Hamilton, *Monty Master of the Battlefield*, p. 302.
4. St George Saunders, Hilary, *The Green Beret*, London, Michael Joseph, 1949, p. 161.
5. Durnford-Slater, *Commando*, p. 123.
6. *Ibid.*, p. 125.
7. James, Julian, *A Fierce Quality: A Biography of Brig Alastair Pearson*, London, Leo Cooper, 1989, p. 76.
8. Kent, Ron, *First In! Parachute Pathfinder Company*, London, Batsford, 1979, p. 51.
9. Frost, Maj-Gen John, *A Drop Too Many*, London, Cassell, 1980, p. 182.

Chapter 12: The Campaign after 13 July (*pages 161–72*)

1. Blumenson, *The Patton Papers*, p. 287.
2. Hamilton, *Monty Master of the Battlefield*, p. 305.
3. Molony, *The Mediterranean and Middle East*, Vol. V, p. 98.
4. *Ibid.*, p. 98.
5. Frost, *A Drop Too Many*, p. 184.
6. *Ibid.*, p. 185.
7. Clay, *The Path of the 50th*, p. 190.
8. *Ibid.*, p. 195.
9. Nicholson, Lt-Col G.W.L., *The Canadians in Italy 1943–1945*, p. 92.
10. Molony, *The Mediterranean and Middle East*, Vol. V, p. 107.

Chapter 13: Missed Opportunities (*pages 173–88*)

1. Molony, *The Mediterranean and Middle East*, Vol. V, p. 108.
2. Blumenson, *The Patton Papers*, p. 290.
3. Huebner was removed from Alexander's headquarters and replaced by Lyman Lemnitzer soon after this meeting on 24 July. It appears Alexander requested the move and Eisenhower's deputy Bedell Smith approved it. Patton wrote in his diary that he believed Huebner was transferred out of the British-dominated headquarters because he stood up for American interests. 'It is a sad commentary', Patton wrote, 'that a man must suffer from being American.' He believed that the incident hurt the entente between the two countries. Huebner himself was quickly taken up by Patton and took over the command of US 1st Infantry Division from Maj Gen Allen. He continued to prosper and later led US V Corps during the campaign in north-west Europe.
4. Blumenson, *The Patton Papers*, p. 290.
5. Molony, *The Mediterranean and Middle East*, Vol. V, p. 110.
6. *Ibid.*, p. 111.
7. Gavin, *On To Berlin*, p. 45.
8. Blumenson, *The Patton Papers*, p. 294.

9. Bradley, *A Soldier's Story*, p. 142.

10. Blumenson, *The Patton Papers*, p. 288.

11. Irving, David, *The War Between The Generals*, London, Allen Lane, 1981, p. 96.

12. *Ibid.*, p. 96.

13. Ryder, Rowland, *Oliver Leese*, p. 140.

14. Hamilton, *Monty Master of the Battlefield*, p. 343.

15. Bradley, *A Soldier's Story*, p. 143.

16. Molony, *The Mediterranean and Middle East*, Vol. V, p. 120.

17. National Archives, WO 214/21.

18. Molony, *The Mediterranean and Middle East*, Vol. V, p. 115.

Chapter 14: The Fall of Mussolini *(pages 189–94)*

1. Hinsley, F. H. *British Intelligence in the Second World War*, Vol. III Part 1, London, HMSO, 1984, p. 101.

2. Irving, David, *Hitler's War*, London, Focal Point, 2001, p. 606.

3. Howard, *Grand Strategy*, Vol. IV, p. 471.

4. Irving, *Hitler's Wars*, p. 608.

5. Mussolini was later held in captivity in a hotel 6,000 feet up on the Grand Sasso massif in the Italian Alps. Student's men tracked him down and ordered a commando raid by special troops under Otto Skorzeny to rescue the Italian dictator. The group landed at night, swooping silently down by glider and coming to rest within a few yards of the hotel. Skorzeny and his nine men quickly overcame the *Carabinieri* guard without a shot being fired, then persuaded the remainder of the 250 Italians on the site to surrender. Mussolini was flown off the mountain in a light Storch aircraft, crouching between the knees of Skorzeny and the pilot. The Duce was then moved to Rome and later Hitler's headquarters.

Chapter 15: Breaking the German Line *(pages 195–244)*

1. Ford, Ken, *D-Day Commando*, Stroud, Sutton Publishing, 2003, p. 10.

2. Unpublished diary of Maj Derek de Stacpoole in the author's collection.

3. National Archives, WO 214/21.

4. During the invasion of Sicily Montgomery had used only veteran Eighth Army formations which he had under his command in North Africa. Canadian 1st Division did not, of course, have this pedigree, but it had been forced on Montgomery through political necessity.

5. Ford, Ken, *Battleaxe Division*, Stroud, Sutton Publishing, 1999, p. 60.

6. Bradley, *A Soldier's Story*, p. 58.

7. Blumenson, *The Patton Papers*, p. 312.

8. *Ibid.*, p. 306.

9. *Ibid.*, p. 309.

10. Ford, *Battleaxe Division*, p. 64.

11. Blumenson, *The Patton Papers*, p. 307.

12. Farago, Ladislas, *Patton: Ordeal and Triumph*, London, Arthur Barker, 1966, p. 197.
13. Descriptions of this incident are take from Farago, *Patton*, p. 194, and Blumenson, *The Patton Papers*, p. 330.
14. Bradley, *A Soldier's Story*, p. 152.
15. National Archives, CAB 106/855.
16. National Archives, WO 214/22.
17. *Ibid.*
18. *Ibid.*
19. Ford, Ken, *Cassino: The Four Battles*, Marlborough, Crowood Press, 2001, p. 51.
20. Molony, *The Mediterranean and Middle East*, Vol. V, p. 165.
21. *Ibid.*, p. 165.
22. National Archives, WO 214/22.
23. Molony, *The Mediterranean and Middle East*, Vol. V, p. 167.
24. Bradley, *A Soldier's Story*, p. 156.
25. D'Este, Carlo, *Bitter Victory: The Battle for Sicily 1943*, London, Collins, 1988, p. 475.
26. Blumenson, *The Patton Papers*, p. 331.
27. Bradley, *A Soldier's Story*, p. 160.
28. Truscott, *Command Missions*, p. 235.
29. Blumenson, *The Patton Papers*, p. 319.
30. Truscott, *Command Missions*, p. 240.
31. Bradley, *A Soldier's Story*, p. 161.
32. Ford, *Battleaxe Division*, p. 74.
33. Molony, *The Mediterranean and Middle East*, Vol. V, p. 178.
34. National Archives, WO 214/22.
35. Molony, *The Mediterranean and Middle East*, Vol. V, p. 166.
36. *Ibid.*, p. 180.
37. National Archives, CAB 106/368.
38. Truscott, *Command Missions*, p. 243.

Chapter 16: Whose Victory? *(pages 245–55)*

1. D'Este, *Bitter Victory*, p. 516.
2. Eisenhower letter to Patton quoted in D'Este, *Bitter Victory*, p. 488 and Blumenson, *The Patton Papers*, p. 329.
3. D'Este, *Bitter Victory*, p. 491.
4. Garland & Smythe, *Sicily and the Surrender of Italy*, p. 431.
5. *Ibid.*
6. National Archives, CAB 44/285.

Bibliography

Anon., *Airborne Forces*, The Air Ministry, 1951

Alexander of Tunis, Field Marshal The Earl, *The Alexander Memoirs, 1940–1945*, London, Cassell, 1962

Aris, George, *The Fifth British Division 1939 to 1945*, London, 5th Division Benevolent Fund, 1959

Belchem, Maj-Gen David, All *in the Day's March*, London, Collins, 1978

Blumenson, Martin, *Patton The Man Behind The Legend 1885–1945*, London, Jonathan Cape, 1986

———, *The Patton Papers 1940–1945*, Boston, Houghton Mifflin, 1974

Bradley, Omar N., *A Soldier's Story*, New York, Henry Holt, 1951

Brooks, Stephen (ed.), *Montgomery and the Eighth Army*, London, Army Records Society, 1991

Chalmers, Rear Admiral W.S., *Full Cycle: The Biography of Admiral Sir Bertram Home Ramsay*, London, Hodder & Stoughton, 1959

Chatterton, George, *The Wings of Pegasus*, London, Macdonald, 1962

Churchill, Winston S., *The Second World War*, Vol. V, *Closing The Ring*, London, Cassell, 1952

Cunningham of Hyndhope, Admiral of the Fleet Viscount, *A Sailor's Odyssey*, London, Hutchinson, 1951

Clay, Maj Ewart W., *The Path of the 50th*, Aldershot, Gale & Polden, 1950

Darby, William O., *Darby's Rangers: We Led the Way*, USA, Presidio Press, 1993

De Guingand, Maj-Gen Sir Francis, *Operation Victory*, London, Hodder & Stoughton, 1947

D'Este, Carlo, *Bitter Victory: The Battle for Sicily 1943*, London, Collins, 1988

Dover, Maj Vernon, *The Sky Generals*, London, Cassell, 1981

Durnford-Slater, Brig J., *Commando*, London, William Kimber, 1953

Edwards, Roger, *German Airborne Troops*, London, Macdonald and Jane's, 1974

Eisenhower, Dwight D., *Crusade in Europe*, New York, Doubleday, 1948

Ellis, John, *Brute Force*, London, Andre Deutsch, 1990

Essame, H., *Patton The Commander*, London, Batsford, 1974

Farago, Ladislas, *Patton: Ordeal and Triumph*, London, Arthur Barker, 1966

Ford, Ken, *Battleaxe Division*, Stroud, Sutton Publishing, 1999

———, *D-Day Commando*, Stroud, Sutton Publishing, 2003

———, *Cassino: The Four Battles*, Marlborough, Crowood Press, 2001

Fowler, Will, *SAS Behind Enemy Lines*, London, Collins, 1987

Frost, Maj-Gen John, *A Drop Too Many*, London, Cassell, 1980

Garland, M., & Smythe, A., *Sicily and the Surrender of Italy*, Washington, Center of Military History, 1965

Gavin, James M., *On To Berlin*, London, Leo Cooper, 1979

Gelb, Norman, *Ike and Monty, Generals at War*, London, Constable, 1994

Gilchrist, Maj R.T., *Malta Strikes Back. The Story of 231 Infantry Brigade*, Aldershot, Gale & Polden, 1945

Hamilton, Nigel, *Monty Master of the Battlefield 1942–1944*, London, Hamish Hamilton, 1983

Hamilton, Stephen D., *50th Royal Tank Regiment The Complete History*, Cambridge, The Lutterworth Press, 1996

Hinsley, F.H., *British Intelligence in the Second World War*, Vol. III Part 1, London, HMSO, 1984

Horrocks, Lt-Gen Sir Brian, *A Full Life*, London, Collins, 1960

Howard, Michael, *Grand Strategy*, Vol. IV, *August 1942–September 1943*, London, HMSO, 1970

Irving, David, *Hitler's War*, London, Focal Point, 2001

———, *The War Between The Generals*, London, Allen Lane, 1981

Jackson, W.G.F., *Alexander of Tunis as Military Commander*, London, Batsford, 1971

James, Julian, *A Fierce Quality: A Biography of Brig Alastair Pearson*, London, Leo Cooper, 1989

Kent, Ron, *First In! Parachute Pathfinder Company*, London, Batsford, 1979

Kesselring, Field Marshal Albrecht, *Memoirs*, London, William Kimber, 1953

Kuhn, Volkmar, *German Paratroops in World War II*, London, Ian Allan, 1974

Ladd, James, *Commandos and Rangers of World War II*, London, Macdonald & Jane's, 1978

Lewin, Ronald, *Ultra Goes to War*, London, Hutchinson, 1978

Lloyd, Alan, *The Gliders*, London, Leo Cooper, 1982

Lucas, James, *Storming Eagles: German Airborne Forces in World War Two*, London, Arms and Armour Press, 1988

Macmillan, Harold, *Blast of War 1939–1945*, London, Macmillan, 1967

Marrinan, Patrick, *Colonel Paddy: A Biography of Lt Col R. Blair Mayne*, The Ulster Press, no date

Mitcham, Samuel W., *Hitler's Legions*, London, Leo Cooper, 1985

Molony, Brig C.J.C., *The Mediterranean and Middle East*, Vol. V, London, HMSO, 1973

Montgomery, Field Marshal the Viscount, *Memoirs*, London, Collins, 1958

Morgan, Ted, *FDR: A Biography*, London, Grafton Books, 1986

Mrazek, James E., *The Glider War*, London, Robert Hale, 1975

Nicholson, Lt-Col G.W.L., *The Canadians in Italy, 1943–1945*, Canada, Minister of National Defence, 1956

Neillands, Robin, *The Raiders. The Army Commandos 1940–46*, London, Weidenfeld & Nicolson, 1989

Pack, S.W.C., *Cunningham The Commander*, London, Batsford, 1974

Patton, George S. Jr., *War As I Knew It*, New York, Houghton Mifflin Co., 1947

Richardson, Gen Sir Charles, *Flashback: A Soldier's Story*, London, William Kimber, 1985

Ryder, Rowland, *Oliver Leese*, London, Hamish Hamilton, 1987

Salmond, J.B., *The History of the 51st Highland Division 1939–1945*, Edinburgh, William Blackwood, 1953

St George Saunders, Hilary, *The Green Beret*, London, Michael Joseph, 1949

von Senger und Etterlin, General Frido, *Neither Fear Nor Hope*, London, Macdonald, 1960

Synge, Capt. W.A., *The Story of the Green Howards*, Richmond, The Green Howards Regiment, 1952

Taylor, John M., *General Maxwell Taylor: The Sword and the Pen*, USA, Doubleday, 1989

Truscott, Lt Gen L.K., *Command Missions*, USA, E.P. Dutton & Co., 1954

Weinberg, Gerhard, Heiber, Helmut and Glantz, David (eds.), *Hitler and His Generals: Military Conferences 1942–1945*, New York, Enigma Books, 2003

Whiting, Charles, *Slaughter Over Sicily*, London, Leo Cooper, 1992

Index